The Law for AI in Healthcare

This book presents a timely overview of how artificial intelligence (AI) is transforming modern healthcare. Combining legal, ethical and practical viewpoints, it explores the impact of AI on patients, clinicians, healthcare organisations and regulators in the European Union, the United Kingdom and the United States.

It delves into the fundamentals of clinical AI systems, explaining how they function and make decisions. It also addresses practical concerns such as safety, fairness, transparency and patient trust. Drawing on real-world examples, such as AI-assisted diagnosis, clinical decision-support tools and machine-learning programmes in hospitals, this book highlights the challenges of aligning law and policy with rapid technological advancements. Key topics explored include bias in medical algorithms, accountability for automation errors and the importance of patient autonomy and data rights for digitally enabled care.

The book will appeal to students, policymakers, practitioners and anyone looking to understand the future law of AI in healthcare.

Man Teng Iong is Assistant Professor at Faculty of Law, the University of Macau, specializing in health law, tort and contract law, and AI regulation. He holds a PhD in private law and publishes extensively on medical and legal topics.

The Law for AI in Healthcare

Man Teng Iong

Routledge
Taylor & Francis Group
LONDON AND NEW YORK

This book is published with financial support from the University of Macau (SRG2024-00038-FLL).

First published 2026
by Routledge
4 Park Square, Milton Park, Abingdon, Oxon OX14 4RN

and by Routledge
605 Third Avenue, New York, NY 10158

Routledge is an imprint of the Taylor & Francis Group, an informa business

British Library Cataloguing in Publication Data
A catalogue record for this book is available from the British Library

ISBN: 978-1-041-14066-5 (hbk)
ISBN: 978-1-041-32963-3 (pbk)
ISBN: 978-1-003-78538-5 (ebk)

DOI: 10.4324/ 9781003785385

Typeset in Times New Roman
by Deanta Global Publishing Services, Chennai, India

To my children Meng Hin Iong and Seng Hong Iong, and to my wife Iao Man Hong, without whom this book would have been completed earlier

Contents

List of Tables *ix*
List of Abbreviations *x*

Part I
Foundations (Comparative, Concise, Consistent) **1**

1 Introduction: Why AI in Healthcare Needs Law and Ethics? 3

2 AI in Healthcare: Concepts and Use Cases 11

3 Regulatory Landscapes: EU, UK and US 29

4 Ethical Principles to Governance Tools 45

Part II
Core Legal Risk Domains (Patient-Centered Sequence) **59**

5 Data Governance and Privacy in AI-Enabled Care 61

6 Patient Autonomy and Informed Consent in AI Supported Care 78

7 Bias, Fairness and Algorithmic Accountability in Clinical AI 98

8 Liability, Safety and Oversight for AI in Healthcare 114

Part III
Case Studies & Horizons **131**

9 Frontier Applications: Generative AI and Extended Reality in Clinical Care 133

10 Future Directions and Closing Synthesis 146

Index *155*

Tables

5.1 Privacy Impact Matrix 76
5.2 Clinician's Checklist 77
6.1 Summary of the Model of Communication between Ancient Greece and 19th century 81

Abbreviations

AAMI	Association for the Advancement of Medical Instrumentation
AD	Advance Directive
AI	artificial intelligence
AMA	American Medical Association
API	application programming interface
AR	augmented reality
CAG	Confidentiality Advisory Group
CDS	clinical decision support
CE	Conformité Européenne (European Conformity)
CEN	European Committee for Standardization
CENELEC	European Committee for Electrotechnical Standardization
CT	computed tomography
DPA	Data Protection Act
DPIA	Data Protection Impact Assessment
DPO	Data Protection Officer
EDPB	European Data Protection Board
EHRC	Equality and Human Rights Commission
EMA	European Medicines Agency
EU	European Union
FDA	Food and Drug Administration
FTC	Federal Trade Commission
GDPR	General Data Protection Regulation
GMLP	Good Machine Learning Practice
HHS	Health and Human Services
HIPAA	Health Insurance Portability and Accountability Act
ICO	Information Commissioner's Office
IEC	International Electrotechnical Commission
IEEE	Institute of Electrical and Electronics Engineers
IG	Information Governance
IMDRF	International Medical Device Regulators Forum
IRB	Institutional Review Board
ISO	International Organization for Standardization
LGBTQ+	Lesbian, Gay, Bisexual, Transgender, Queer, and Questioning, and all other sexual orientations and gender identities not listed

MDCG	Medical Device Coordination Group
MDR	Medical Devices Regulations
MHRA	Medicines and Healthcare products Regulatory Agency
ML	Machine Learning
MRI	magnetic resonance imaging
NICE	National Institute for Health and Care Excellence
NHS	National Health Service
NHSX	National Health Service X (NHS England as host)
OCR	Office for Civil Rights
ONC	US Department of Health and Human Services' Office of the National Coordinator for Health Information Technology
PCCP	Predetermined Change Control Plan
PHI	personal health information
PMA	Pre-Market Approval
PMS	Post-Market Surveillance
PMSR	Post-Market Surveillance Report
PSUR	Periodic Safety Update Report
QMS	Quality Management System
RCTs	randomised controlled trials
TPO	treatment, payment, or healthcare operations
UK	United Kingdom
UNESCO	United Nations Educational, Scientific and Cultural Organization
US	United States
VR	virtual reality
XR	extended reality

Part I

Foundations (Comparative, Concise, Consistent)

1 Introduction

Why AI in Healthcare Needs Law and Ethics

Abstract

Artificial intelligence (AI) is heavily embedded in the realm of healthcare, and has vast potential to establish a more efficient route for diagnoses and clinical treatments in healthcare, as well as to enhance patient outcomes. At the same time, AI systems raise unique issues of ethics and law, like threats to patient privacy, algorithmic bias, opacity of decision-making and uncertainty of responsibility in the case of harm caused. This introductory chapter argues that law and ethics are not just marginal to healthcare AI but are fundamental modes of governance that will determine the limits on whether such technologies can be adopted in a manner that will be safe and trustworthy. Rather than offering either a technical overview of the applications of AI or a detailed regulatory analysis, the chapter seeks to lay out a uniting thematic argument: the integration of AI into healthcare alters the traditional understandings associated with professional judgment, patient autonomy and responsibility as well as generating a demand for robust legal and ethical guardrails. Using an illustrative example of AI-assisted clinical triage as a means of understanding the implications of failures in the domains of transparency, oversight and validation, this chapter shows how failures in these areas can directly translate to patient harm. It further discusses the interactions between ethical values (such as beneficence, non-maleficence, autonomy and justice) on the one hand and legal tools (such as data protection, medical device regulations and liability regimes) on the other hand for building trust in AI-enabled health systems. By placing these issues in the broader movements of European Union, United Kingdom and United States governance approaches, the chapter lays the conceptual groundwork for the more granular discussions of data governance, consent, fairness, liability and institutional oversight of AI-driven healthcare in the rest of the book.

AI is changing healthcare at an incredible pace from more accurate diagnosis to personalising treatment. In fields like medical imaging and predictive analytics, for example, AI systems are in a position to crawl through tremendous modes of data to look out for medical patterns or signs of disease beyond human capacity. These innovations promise huge benefits – faster diagnosis, better care and potential improvement for the patient. However, the same qualities of AI that make it so powerful raise some of the most troubling ethical and legal questions. AI

DOI: 10.4324/9781003785385-2

algorithms use data to learn and make their autonomous or semi-autonomous decisions that can have life-and-death implications for medical decision-making, with no direct involvement from a human. This reality envisions us to pose and critically evaluate this question: how do we make such systems safe, fair and accountable? Robust legal and ethical governance is not a choice but instead a top priority to ensure the integration of AI's application in healthcare in a way that protects the patient and ensures public trust. In this introductory chapter, I report the compelling case for legal and ethical oversight of healthcare AI as the foundation for its adoption in a way that is safe and trustworthy.

I. The Dual Promise and Peril of AI in Healthcare

AI's promise to improve medicine is accompanied by a need to be able to control the associated risks. On the one hand, AI-powered tools can be used to enhance clinical decision-making – a good example of this is their ability to analyse radiographs or lab results faster or more accurately than a clinician in some cases.[1] On the other hand, these tools can go wrong in unforeseeable ways, or even make existing problems in healthcare worse if left unchecked. Patient privacy is an area of great concern. Effective AI solutions require large amounts of health data to be used to train algorithms – which contains personal sensitive information. Without proper governance, such data could be used in violation of patient confidentiality, or for nefarious purposes. Data protection legislation like the European Union's General Data Protection Regulation (GDPR) and the United States' Health Insurance Portability and Accountability Act (HIPAA) are strict laws regarding how medical data is handled and AI systems must comply with these laws to allow the data of patients to remain safe.[2] Data security and obtaining consent for data use by AI's data-hungry operations is an ethical and legal imperative, failure to which could undermine public trust and thus violate the fundamental rights of patients.

Another major issue is algorithmic bias and fairness. AI systems in healthcare may inadvertently reproduce or even exacerbate healthcare disparity with regard to treatment outcome.[3] If an AI tool is trained with historical or unrepresentative data, then it may work poorly for some populations – for example, an under-diagnosis of diseases in some minority populations, because they were underrepresented in the training data. Studies have brought to light some egregious examples: one commercial health algorithm relied on cost of care as a proxy for need, which caused far fewer Black patients to be flagged for extra care than White patients who were just as sick, because of historical deficiencies in access to healthcare for people of

1 Thomas Davenport and Ravi Kalakota, 'The Potential for Artificial Intelligence in Healthcare' (2019) 6(2) Future Healthcare Journal 94–98. See also Robert Kaczmarczyk et al., 'Evaluating Multimodal AI in Medical Diagnostics' (2024) 7(1) npj Digital Medicine 205.

2 Tuan Pham, 'Ethical and Legal Considerations in Healthcare AI: Innovation and Policy for Safe and Fair Use' (2025) 12(5) Royal Society Open Science 241873.

3 ibid.

color.[4] Such cases are an example of how bias in AI can mean inequitable care, at odds with another key principle of medical ethics – justice. Addressing the biases necessitates careful oversight in the selection of the dataset, model design and performance auditing. Indeed, many AI models are "black boxes" where the decision-making process is opaque even to the individuals who created them.[5] This opacity makes it hard to see why an AI is making a mistake or to correct its behaviour, making it essential to have measures in place for carefully overseeing and ensuring accountability in the development and deployment of AI technologies.[6] Ethical principles of fairness and equity require that AI tools are made and controlled to meet the needs of all groups of patients effectively, instead of reinforcing inequalities.

Perhaps the thorniest problem is accountability. When an AI informs or automates a clinical decision, who is to blame when something goes wrong? Consider a scenario where the AI-based diagnostic system does not flag a life-threatening condition, or on the other hand, a false alarm is generated by the system thereby causing unnecessary invasive procedures. In traditional care, the duty of care of a treating physician and his or her potential liability for negligence are well established.[7] AI complicates this picture. If, for example, a machine learning program misdiagnosed a patient, responsibility might be, more or less, shared between the people who wrote the software code, the hospital that implemented the system and the clinicians using it. Current malpractice and product liability legislation is being challenged by these circumstances, as it is unclear whether an AI should be considered like a medical device, a service or an extension of the clinical team.[8] Legal scholars point out that healthcare AI has not been tested in court to any significant extent,[9] but the lack of precedent of clear liability patterns means there isn't much certainty for providers or patients when it comes to liability. With no clear-cut rules, there is a risk that patients suffering due to faulty AI will have a hard time getting redress, or on the other hand that too many fears of liability will stifle beneficial innovation. There needs to be a balanced approach – one that offers the avenues to compensate patients when AI does harm, while also bringing clear obligations for the developers and users. As the European Commission has observed, it is important to create a strong framework for victims to be able

4 Irene Dankwa-Mullan, 'Health Equity and Ethical Considerations in Using Artificial Intelligence in Public Health and Medicine' (2024) 21 Preventing Chronic Disease 240245.

5 ibid.

6 ibid.

7 Ibrahim Habli, Tom Lawton and Zoe Porter, 'Artificial Intelligence in Health Care: Accountability and Safety' (2020) 98(4) Bull World Health Organ 251–256.

8 Nadia de la Houssaye et al., 'Healthcare AI in the United States – Navigating Regulatory Evolution, Market Dynamics, and Emerging Challenges in an Era of Rapid Innovation' (2025) 15 National Law Review 275.

9 W Nicholson Price II, Sara Gerke and I. Glenn Cohen, 'Liability for Use of Artificial Intelligence in Medicine' in Barry Solaiman and I. Glenn Cohen (eds), *Research Handbook on Health, AI and the Law* (Edward Elgar 2024) 150–166.

to seek compensation for the harm caused by the use of defective AI systems in healthcare.[10] In short, accountability and law are of the utmost importance if we are to get clinicians and patients to believe in the use of AI tools that make important health decisions.

II. Why Law and Ethics Are Essential Guardrails

Given these challenges, the law and ethics are in play as key guardrails to the adoption of AI in medicine. They address complementary issues in addressing the central question – how can we embrace innovation in healthcare without compromising patient safety, rights and societal values? Ethical guidelines express general principles of moral good practice – such as beneficence (furthering patient well-being), non-maleficence (avoiding causing harm), autonomy (respecting patients' right to make informed decisions) and justice (ensuring fairness in care). These principles form a compass to guide the design and use of AI for compliance with the principles of duty of care and compassion that are at the centre of medicine.[11] For example, an ethics-based approach to AI would call for transparency (so that clinicians can make sense of an AI's suggestion and patients can be informed when AI is involved in their care) and human oversight (so that automated recommendations do not go unchecked).[12] Such measures serve to preserve the primacy of human judgement and consent in healthcare even as we benefit from cutting-edge algorithms in healthcare. In practice, ethics committees in hospitals and professional guidelines are starting to grapple with questions such as: do doctors need to reveal their assistance by AI to patients? Or, how could AI tools be leveraged to benefit patients' specific interests?[13]

Law, meanwhile, puts some of these "high level principles" into tangible and enforceable requirements and incentives. Regulation can require the implementation of baseline safeguards – for example, forcing AI systems to be thoroughly tested and validated before they are ever deployed in the world, much like pharmaceutical or medical devices have to be proven safe and effective. In the United States, the Food and Drug Administration (FDA) has already approved or cleared hundreds of medical devices that are enabled by AI, which is the speed with which

10 European Commission, 'Artificial Intelligence in Healthcare' <https://health.ec.europa.eu/ehealth-digital-health-and-care/artificial-intelligence-healthcare_en> accessed 23 August 2025.

11 ibid.

12 World Health Organization, *Ethics and Governance of Artificial Intelligence for Health* (WHO Guidance, 28 June 2021) 23–30 <https://www.ictworks.org/wp-content/uploads/2021/10/who-ethics-artificial-intelligence-healt.pdf> accessed 1 October 2025.

13 For instance, see AMA, *Augmented Intelligence in Health Care* (*AMA Policy Report*, 2018) <https://www.ama-assn.org/system/files/2019-01/ai-2018-report.pdf> accessed 14 December 2025; AMA, *Code of Medical Ethics Opinion 1.1.1 (Patient-Physician Relationships)* <https://code-medical-ethics.ama-assn.org/ethics-opinions/patient-physician-relationships> accessed 14 December 2025; NHS England, *A Code of Conduct for Data-Driven Health and Care Technology* (*NHS*, 2021) <https://www.gov.uk/government/publications/code-of-conduct-for-data-driven-health-and-care-technology> accessed 14 December 2025.

the technology has spread into US clinics.[14] However, researchers have found that the information given at the time of approval is often not enough to fully determine the performance of these devices in a variety of patient populations.[15] This finding shows the need for continued regulatory oversight and post-market monitoring: laws and regulations should ensure that AI tools are continually evaluated in the real world and then re-calibrated as necessary to ensure the safety and effectiveness of such tools.[16] Policymakers are realising that current legislation relating to health would need to be updated in order to keep up with the complexities posed by AI. They have the difficult task of balancing the aim of protecting patients and accountability without unduly stifling innovation.[17] Good governance of AI, therefore, must be a matter of finding the right balance – encouraging beneficial use of AI in healthcare (so that society can reap the rewards of innovation) whilst ensuring firm boundaries against unacceptable risks.

Crucially, a legal and ethical framework contributes also to trust. Healthcare is based fundamentally on trust: patients trust clinicians with their intimately held information and even their lives; clinicians trust that the tools and treatments they employ are reliable and in the patient's best interest. If AI systems are to be accepted, patients and providers alike will need to be reasonably certain that the technologies have been vetted for safety, have respect for the rights of patients and that they have mechanisms in place to prevent, or deal with, any failures.[18] Scandals or accidents involving unregulated AI could set back public confidence terribly. Conversely, proving the AI tools to work within a robust oversight framework – that there are standards, audits and accountability – can improve the acceptance of AI in care. In that sense, law and ethics are enablers of innovation: they create the conditions for sustainable, socially acceptable progress. A 2021 study found, for instance, that a commonly used AI sepsis prediction model, which was used in many different hospitals, was much less accurate than publicised – it failed to spot about two-thirds (67%) of cases of sepsis and often resulted in false alarms.[19] This type of result not only puts patients at risk, but also makes clinicians less confident in AI. If clinicians are aware that an algorithm has undergone independent testing, and they know aspects of its limitations and the fact that they remain in control of the final decision-making, then they are going to be more willing to trust and responsibly use AI assistance. Law and ethics help establish this trust through validation, transparency and human oversight as a prerequisite for integrating AI.

14 Daniel Windecker et al., 'Generalizability of FDA-Approved AI-Enabled Medical Devices for Clinical Use' (2025) 8(4) JAMA Network Open e258052.

15 ibid.

16 ibid.

17 Pham (n 2).

18 European Commission (n 10).

19 Andrew Wong, Erkin Otles and John P. Donnelly, 'External Validation of a Widely Implemented Proprietary Sepsis Prediction Model in Hospitalized Patients' (2021) 181(8) JAMA Internal Medicine 1065–1070.

III. An Illustrative Case: AI Triage and the Need for Oversight

To provide some context as to why these governance measures are important, consider an AI-based system of triage implemented in an emergency room. Imagine that the AI has been tasked with analysing the symptoms and vital signs of incoming patients in order to prioritise who requires immediate attention. Such a system could be immensely helpful in a busy hospital – potentially lifesaving if it flags up quickly a patient with sepsis or a stroke that has perhaps been missed in the crowded queue. But without adequate legal and ethical checks, this same system could be extremely dangerous. For example, what if the AI's training data was flawed with holes? Perhaps it has learned from a dataset that doesn't have enough examples of how certain illnesses manifest in women or in minority ethnic groups. The outcome could be an algorithm that routinely under-triages those patients, putting them in danger and falsely giving staff themselves a pat-on-the-back sense that the tool is objective. If the hospital decided to deploy this AI without auditing it for bias or testing it to make sure it worked as well in cases of diversity, it could systematically harm vulnerable groups – a clear failure on ethical grounds and a potential legal nightmare. Indeed, this scenario is not hypothetical: such problems have been demonstrated by real-world tools for AI. In one case, an algorithm that is widely used to guide care management decisions was shown to heavily underestimate the needs of Black patients in comparison with White patients with the same medical profiles.[20] In another, the aforementioned sepsis alert system (developed by a major vendor) provided a false sense of security with its failure to cover most of the patients who really needed urgent treatment.[21] These examples highlight the fact that the errors or biases of AI translate directly into harm to the patient if left unchecked. They make tangible, for example, the need for ethical scrutiny (e.g. asking if the AI was developed fairly and tested for unintentional bias) and legal oversight (e.g. that it must have a regulatory approval process, and performance standards set and that liability is put in place in case the tool fails). A well-constructed governance regime could have required the triage AI to be trained using inclusive data, and evaluation by independent parties before it was deployed, as well as ongoing evaluation after its deployment. Additionally, the clinicians would have to have guidelines on how to use the AI's recommendations – for example, to treat them as decision support, not gospel, preserving a human safety net over the machine's suggestions.

IV. Towards Trustworthy AI in Health Systems

Across leading jurisdictions, there is overall increased consensus that AI in healthcare must be "trustworthy" – i.e. lawful, ethical and robust in practice. The European Union has made a bold regulatory step with their AI Act which considers medical

20 Dankwa-Mullan (n 4).
21 Wong, Otles and Donnelly (n 19).

AI systems as "high-risk" and enforces strict requirements.[22] Under this new law, any AI used for diagnosis, treatment or other clinical purposes will have to undergo thorough risk assessment and mitigation efforts, ensure quality (non-biased) data training, provide transparent information to users and ensure capable human oversight provided by healthcare professionals.[23] The above-mentioned ethical principles are operationalised in many ways by these legal obligations, which in effect thereby hardwire fairness, transparency and accountability into the AI systems that will be introduced into Europe's hospitals. In the United Kingdom, regulators and policymakers are also working to step up the oversight. In 2025, the United Kingdom's Medicines and Healthcare products Regulatory Agency (MHRA) commissioned a national commission on the regulation of AI in healthcare with the aim of recommending a new regulatory framework that is appropriate for the unique problems of the AI.[24] By pulling together experts in the areas of AI, medicine and law, this work recognises that current regulations for medical devices need to be updated and a coordinated approach is needed to ensure that AI is introduced into the NHS in a safe way. Meanwhile, in the United States, although there is no single overarching AI legislation, authorities are sat on a combination of sectoral rules and guidelines. The FDA continues to refine its approach to AI-enabled medical devices, both to encourage innovation (through fast track approvals) and to puzzle out how to require continued algorithmic monitoring and the management of adaptive AI that is able to change after it is deployed. In fact, there are already more than a thousand healthcare tools based on AI that have already been approved by the FDA, most of them in areas such as radiology.[25] This exponential growth in the United States market imposes renewed urgency on developing sound oversight measures – from pre-market evaluation standards to post-market surveillance and clarity in the malpractice and product liability doctrines – to ensure that these measures truly benefit patients. Each of these regional approaches takes a different form, but the common thread running through them all is driven by a similar understanding that the promise of AI can be lost if the avoidable harms, in addition to public mistrust, are allowed to take over.

In summary, there is a fundamental and pressing need for law and ethics in healthcare AI. This chapter has argued that what is required to harness the potential of AI in a responsible manner is effective governance. By considering the benefits of AI and the disadvantages of AI – privacy violation, biased outcomes, lack of

22 Article 6(2) and Annex III of the EU AI Act.

23 European Commission (n 10).

24 MHRA, 'Summary Minutes: First Meeting of National Commission into the Regulation of AI in Healthcare (15 October 2025)' (*MHRA*, 15 October 2025) <https://assets.publishing.service.gov.uk/media/69257c789fd433badebc30fe/Summary_minutes_first_meeting_of_National_Commission.pdf> accessed 14 December 2025.

25 Hannah Murphy, 'Less than 30% of FDA-authorized Radiology AI Devices have Undergone Clinical Testing' (*Radiology Business*, 12 November 2025) <https://radiologybusiness.com/topics/artificial-intelligence/less-30-fda-authorized-radiology-ai-devices-have-undergone-clinical-testing> accessed 14 December 2025.

transparency, responsibility gap, etc. – it becomes evident that technology alone cannot guarantee "good" healthcare. It must be subject to human values and regulated by institutions. Legal rules and ethical norms are in place to ensure that innovation in the field of medicine is human-centred, consistent with the fiduciary obligations of providers of care and the rights of the patient. Understanding this balance is of such importance to an interdisciplinary audience composed of clinicians, legal scholars, policymakers and informed citizens. We are at this crossroads where we have the opportunity for health systems to embrace AI at scale, and how we choose to design oversight will define whether this transformation is a positive one to produce a trusted care system, or if it is dangerous to produce a new risk. The later chapters will build from this base, taking a deeper look into the details of particular areas including data governance, patient consent, fairness with algorithms and liability. Each topic will bring to light the ability of law and ethics to provide answers to the more nuanced challenges that AI presents in that context – from ensuring the protection of patient privacy to ensuring its explainability and redress mechanisms when things go wrong. By the end of this book, the hope is that the readers will have a better sense of not only how AI in healthcare can be governed, but why such governance is indispensable. The unifying theme, introduced here, is that if we want AI to really work in service of humanity in the clinic, it should exist in a construct of accountability, transparency and ethical integrity. Only then can we utilise the vast power of AI safely and trustfully in promoting human health.

2 AI in Healthcare

Concepts and Use Cases

Abstract

This chapter discusses the concepts and clinical practice of AI in healthcare, such as diagnostics, CDS and surgical robotics. It describes the fundamental technology behind machine learning, deep learning and natural language processing and investigates the implementation of AI to analyse medical images, forecast patient risks, aid in planning treatment and enhance surgical accuracy. The United States, United Kingdom and European Union have a similar understanding of the high-risk nature of AI in clinical settings, but different regulatory strategies: the European Union uses strict *ex ante* models (MDR, AI Act), the United States uses flexibility and statutory carve-outs, and the United Kingdom uses principle-based direction. The chapter emphasises the ongoing issues of black box opacity, bias, narrow generalisability and lack of clear liability, but also states that clinicians are legally and ethically required to use their independent judgement. In my opinion, regulators should keep innovation and patient protection in balance, enhancing evidence requirements, human oversight and clarifying accountability. The chapter, therefore, forms the premise of the further discussions of liability, data protection and ethical governance in AI-powered healthcare.

I. Introduction

The utilisation of AI has been changing the field of clinical medicine. No longer a promise of the future, AI-powered tools are already helping clinicians diagnose diseases, make recommendations and even carry out parts of surgery. In this chapter, I examine the core concepts of AI in healthcare and survey key clinical applications – focusing on diagnostics, clinical decision support (CDS) systems and surgical robotics – with a comparative lens on the European Union, United Kingdom and United States. These use cases demonstrate the valuable opportunity of AI to enhance patient care and the medico-legal issues that are involved. It is a fact that AI can improve accuracy and efficiency, but it also poses risks of error, bias, ambiguity in accountability, etc.[1] This chapter will provide a critical overview, which will be objective

1 European Parliament: Directorate-General for Parliamentary Research Services and others, 'Artificial Intelligence in Healthcare – Applications, Risks, and Ethical and Societal Impacts' (*Publica-*

DOI: 10.4324/9781003785385-3

and will form a background to the more detailed legal discussion in later chapters. In such a way, I will include my own critical remarks, including the necessity to strike an adaptive balance between innovation and patient safety by regulators, to identify where the current frameworks are weak. This chapter will start by briefly explaining some of the AI concepts that are relevant to the discussion and then look at each of the major application areas one by one comparing the way the European Union, United Kingdom and United States are responding to these developments.

II. Fundamental AI Concepts in Medical Applications

A. The Concepts of AI, Machine Learning and Natural Language Processing

AI is the more general term to describe computer systems that have been programmed to perform tasks that would otherwise be performed by human intelligence, such as learning, reasoning, or decision-making.[2] Machine learning techniques are a major driver of modern AI, in which algorithms are not explicitly programmed, but instead learn to perform their tasks by being trained on large datasets. Deep learning is a prominent branch of machine learning which consists of multi-layered neural networks to recognise complex patterns (e.g. detecting features in medical images). This technology has demonstrated a high degree of precision in particular tasks: a meta-analysis has shown that some deep learning models can perform as well as expert clinicians in diagnostic tasks.[3] Most reported successes are however limited: studies tend to evaluate algorithms on isolated data sets or retrospectively, and few prospective trials have been conducted to test performance in real clinical environments.[4] In practice AI systems can be black boxes, arriving at correct answers without offering human-interpretable reasoning, which makes trust and accountability more difficult. The black box problem has given rise to demands for explainable AI, especially in healthcare where the reasoning behind a recommendation is ethically and legally pertinent.[5]

The other major area is natural language processing that enables AI to comprehend and generate human language. In healthcare, natural language processing algorithms can be used to analyse unstructured clinical documents (such as notes by doctors

tions Office of the EU, 25 July 2022) 15–29 <https://data.europa.eu/doi/10.2861/568473> accessed 23 August 2025. See also Francesco De Micco and others, 'Robotics and AI into Healthcare from the Perspective of European Regulation: Who Is Responsible for Medical Malpractice?' (2024) 11 Frontiers in Medicine 2.

2 De Micco and others (n 1) 1–2.

3 Xiaoxuan Liu and others, 'A Comparison of Deep Learning Performance against Health-Care Professionals in Detecting Diseases from Medical Imaging: A Systematic Review and Meta-Analysis' (2019) 1 The Lancet Digital Health e271.

4 ibid.

5 Ruth Beckers and Pascale Van Hoydonck, 'Impact of the Regulatory Framework on Medical Device Software Manufacturers: Are the Guidance Documents Supporting the Practical Implementation? Comment on "Clinical Decision Support and New Regulatory Frameworks for Medical Devices: Are We Ready for It? – A Viewpoint Paper"' (2023) 12 International Journal of Health Policy and Management 2.

or medical literature) to derive useful information, or even chat with patients using chatbots. Recent generative AI models – e.g. large language models like ChatGPT – have shown the ability to produce fluent medical advice or draft clinical documentation. These tools hold promise as virtual assistants (for instance, helping summarise medical records or answer clinicians' queries), but they also present new concerns. Early research indicates that although these models can seem knowledgeable, they can generate inaccurate or nonsensical medical advice and thus must be carefully monitored by humans.[6] As a result, regulators stress that these AI models must be used as decision-*support* rather than decision-*makers* in themselves.[7]

B. "Learning" Versus Fixed Algorithms

Traditional medical software was deterministic and rule-based (e.g. an early CDS system would check drug interactions using a list of encoded rules). In comparison, a lot of current AI systems learn continuously based on new data or modify their behaviour through complex statistical models. Such flexibility is promising – a diagnostic AI can learn more and get better with every patient case it sees – even though it also produces regulatory problems. With an AI model that evolves over time (a self-learning or adaptive algorithm), it is hard to ensure continuous safety and effectiveness.[8] For instance, the US FDA normally approves medical software based on a defined algorithm; significant post-approval changes typically require new review. A self-updating AI might therefore become unstable and might learn undesirable behaviours. Both the FDA and European regulators are struggling with how to permit positive AI evolution and still have oversight.[9] The FDA has proposed a system of Predetermined Change Control Plans (PCCPs) to permit safe, controlled updates to AI software,[10] whereas the European Union's new AI Act likewise imposes ongoing risk management for adaptive AI in high-risk uses.[11] In my view, it is critical to develop strong lifecycle monitoring mechanisms of learning algorithms; otherwise, the current regulatory approvals may become irrelevant as AI systems drift away in their originally validated performance.

6 De Micco and others (n 1) 2.

7 US Food & Drug Administration, 'Clinical Decision Support Software Frequently Asked Questions (FAQs)' (20 December 2024) <https://www.fda.gov/medical-devices/software-medical-device-samd/clinical-decision-support-software-frequently-asked-questions-faqs> accessed 23 August 2025.

8 Claudia Mello-Thoms and Carlos AB Mello, 'Clinical Applications of Artificial Intelligence in Radiology' (2023) 96 The British Journal of Radiology 2.

9 Beckers and Hoydonck (n 5) 3.

10 US Food and Drug Administration, 'Predetermined Change Control Plans for Machine Learning-Enabled Medical Devices: Guiding Principles' (October 2023) <https://www.fda.gov/medical-devices/software-medical-device-samd/predetermined-change-control-plans-machine-learning-enabled-medical-devices-guiding-principles> accessed 23 August 2025.

11 Directorate-General for Health and Food Safety, 'Interplay between the Medical Devices Regulation & In Vitro Diagnostic Medical Devices Regulation and the Artificial Intelligence Act (June 2025)' 2 <https://health.ec.europa.eu/document/download/b78a17d7-e3cd-4943-851d-e02a2f22bbb4_en?filename=mdcg_2025-6_en.pdf> accessed 23 August 2025.

With these ideas in place, we will discuss the key clinical areas in which AI is being implemented. For each – diagnostics, decision support and surgery – I will describe how AI is used, note the benefits and risks identified in the literature, and compare how the European Union, United Kingdom and United States are addressing the technology through law and policy. The analysis shows that there is a significant overlap (e.g. all three jurisdictions consider many AI tools to be medical devices that are regulated in terms of safety) but also significant differences that reflect different regulatory philosophies.

III. AI in Diagnostics

Possibly, the most developed and common application of AI in healthcare is in diagnostics. In this case, AI systems assist in the diagnosis of diseases or conditions, which is typically accomplished by interpreting clinical data like medical images, laboratory results or vital signs. The archetypical one is AI in medical imaging, algorithms that process radiological scans (X-rays, CTs, MRIs) or digital pathology slides to detect abnormalities. It has been shown in many studies that deep learning models can perform as well as or better than human experts in certain image-recognition tasks, such as lung nodule detection on chest CT or diabetic retinal disease screening.[12] As an example, an AI system in mammography was demonstrated to detect early indicators of breast cancer with the same degree of accuracy as experienced radiologists.[13] In the same vein, in the area of pathology, AI has demonstrated expert-level performance in the detection of metastatic cancer in lymph node tissue images.[14] These tools demonstrate significant potential: they operate tirelessly and consistently and can flag subtle findings that a rushed clinician might overlook. Moreover, AI diagnostics could expand access to care in regions with shortages of specialists – e.g. an automated system could screen retinal photographs for diabetic retinopathy in clinics without ophthalmologists.[15]

A. Real-World Adoption and Evidence

In spite of thousands of research papers, the actual penetration of AI diagnostics in the real world is rather low to date. Clinicians are both optimistic and sceptical according to surveys. A 2020 survey of the American College of Radiology found

12 Bejnordi Babak Ehteshami and others, 'Diagnostic Assessment of Deep Learning Algorithms for Detection of Lymph Node Metastases in Women with Breast Cancer' (2017) 318 JAMA 2199. Kaustav Bera and others, 'Artificial Intelligence in Digital Pathology – New Tools for Diagnosis and Precision Oncology' (2019) 16 Nature Reviews Clinical Oncology 703.

13 European Commission, 'Artificial Intelligence in Healthcare' <https://health.ec.europa.eu/ehealth-digital-health-and-care/artificial-intelligence-healthcare_en> accessed 23 August 2025.

14 European Parliament: Directorate-General for Parliamentary Research Services and others (n 1) 6.

15 Elise Reuter and Jasmine Ye Han, 'The Number of AI Medical Devices Has Spiked in the Past Decade' (*MedTech Dive*, 9 October 2024) <https://www.medtechdive.com/news/fda-ai-medical-devices-growth/728975/> accessed 23 August 2025.

that only about one-third of radiologists were already using any AI in practice, and among non-users, the majority saw no obvious benefit to justify the cost.[16] European radiologists also reported a similar reluctance, with many believing that the current AI tools actually added workload (through workflow integration problems) as opposed to reducing it.[17] Deep under the hood, many AI models have had problems with generalisability – they work well on data in the environment where they were trained but fail when transferred to a different hospital or different imaging equipment. As an example, an AI pneumonia detector that was very accurate on scans at two US hospitals performed poorly on a third hospital dataset.[18] In the same line, a retinal disease AI mistook variation between imaging machines as pathological variation: when the system was presented with scans of a machine type not included in its training set, the error rate jumped from 5.5% to 46%.[19] These failures point to the risk of black box models. Regulators and researchers are increasingly demanding the need to have strong external validation of AI diagnostics, preferably prospective trials in real clinical practice, prior to their broad use.[20] I am in full agreement with this focus. From my perspective, the current regulatory approval processes (especially in the United States) have been too lax and allowed the approval of dozens of AI algorithms on the basis of post-factum studies or small-scale evaluations. Strict evidence requirements akin to those in pharmaceutical trials may be needed to actually demonstrate that an AI diagnostic is safer and leads to improved patient outcomes across a range of populations.

B. Regulatory Classification (European Union/United Kingdom vs. United States)

The classification and the licensing of AI diagnostic tools also differ across jurisdictions. Most AI diagnostic systems in the European Union are classified as medical devices, in particular as software used in the field of medicine under the EU Medical Devices Regulations, or MDR (MDR 2017/745).[21] The MDR, which fully came into force in 2021, made the requirements on software much stricter. In its

16 Bibb Allen and others, '2020 ACR Data Science Institute Artificial Intelligence Survey' (2021) 18 Journal of the American College of Radiology 1153.
17 Christoph D. Becker and others, 'Current Practical Experience with Artificial Intelligence in Clinical Radiology: A Survey of the European Society of Radiology' (2022) 13 Insights into Imaging 107.
18 John R. Zech and others, 'Variable Generalization Performance of a Deep Learning Model to Detect Pneumonia in Chest Radiographs: A Cross-Sectional Study' (2018) 15 PLOS Medicine e1002683.
19 Jeffrey De Fauw and others, 'Clinically Applicable Deep Learning for Diagnosis and Referral in Retinal Disease' (2018) 24 Nature Medicine 1342.
20 See, for instance, Bibb Allen and others, 'Evaluation and Real-World Performance Monitoring of Artificial Intelligence Models in Clinical Practice: Try It, Buy It, Check It' (2021) 18 Journal of the American College of Radiology 1489; Manisha Bahl, 'Artificial Intelligence in Clinical Practice: Implementation Considerations and Barriers' (2022) 4 Journal of Breast Imaging 632; Alice C. Yu, Bahram Mohajer and John Eng, 'External Validation of Deep Learning Algorithms for Radiologic Diagnosis: A Systematic Review' (2022) 4(3) Radiology. Artificial Intelligence e210064.
21 Directorate-General for Health and Food Safety (n 11) 2.

Rule 11, software that presents information to be used for diagnostic or therapeutic purposes is typically classified at least as Class IIa (or higher risk), requiring the oversight of a notified body. Indeed, the MDR classification is so strict that even relatively low-risk diagnostic software (e.g. an application that advises clinical management in a non-severe condition) is usually Class IIa by default.[22] This is a high baseline due to the precautionary approach of the European Union. Besides, the European Union has since 2024 implemented the AI Act, a horizontal regulation that categorises AI systems according to risk. The use of AI in diagnosis is explicitly considered *high-risk*, and therefore must meet a variety of requirements, such as risk management, quality data, transparency to users and human oversight.[23] The requirements of the AI Act are parallel to the MDR.[24] The EU regulators have made it clear that compliance measures should be simplified (manufacturers can use MDR technical documentation to satisfy many of the AI Act requirements), but effectively an AI diagnostic device in Europe now must pass two regulatory gates.[25]

The United Kingdom, no longer a part of the European Union, is pursuing a different path but is at the moment very close. The UK Medical Devices Regulations 2002 (as amended) continue to reflect the EU framework (they adopted the older EU regulations and are in the process of updating to MDR-like regulations). The MHRA in the United Kingdom has announced the *Medical Devices (Post-Market Surveillance Requirements) (Amendment) (Great Britain) Regulations 2024*[26] that came into effect from 16 June 2025 to both enhance access to innovative devices (including AI) and maintain safety. UK law continues to treat diagnostic AI as medical devices requiring approval (Post-Market Surveillance) and the United Kingdom allows reliance on approvals from trusted foreign regulators to speed up availability.[27] The United Kingdom has not adopted an AI Act, but instead focused on a principles-based, sector-specific approach to AI governance. In the United Kingdom, the health sector is regulated by policies (including the NHS Code of Conduct for AI) that focus on safety, transparency and accountability, yet there is no single law on AI. I would add that this difference between EU hard law and UK softer governance may influence the speed at which AI diagnostics reach the market and clarity of responsibility. The EU regime is more legally certain but more burdensome to comply with, and the UK regime may be more agile but leave

22 Beckers and Hoydonck (n 5) 2.

23 European Commission (n 13).

24 Directorate-General for Health and Food Safety (n 11) 2.

25 ibid.

26 The Medical Devices (Post-Market Surveillance Requirements) (Amendment) (Great Britain) Regulations 2024, 2024 No. 1368 <https://www.legislation.gov.uk/uksi/2024/1368/made> accessed 24 August 2025.

27 azmed, 'MHRA AI Imaging Reforms 2025' (*azmed*, 23 July 2025) <https://www.azmed.co/news-post/mhra-2025-ai-radiology-regulations> accessed 24 August 2025. See also Al-Faruque Ferdous, 'MHRA to Move Forward with Medical Device Reliance Plans' (*RAPS*, 22 July 2025) <https://www.raps.org/news-and-articles/news-articles/2025/7/mhra-to-move-forward-with-medical-device-reliance> accessed 24 August 2025.

more grey areas. It is yet to be seen which will be more beneficial to innovation and patient safety in the long term.

In the United States, AI is not subject to a specific medical device regulation; AI diagnostic tools are regulated by the FDA under existing medical device pathways. Most AI-based diagnostics are moderate-risk devices (approximately Class II) and are subject to the 510(k) premarket notification process (substantial equivalence to an existing device).[28] Certain new AI devices have necessitated *De Novo* classification requests (a pathway of low-to-moderate risk devices with no predicate). As of 2024, the FDA had cleared or approved almost 1,000 AI-enabled medical devices, with the largest number in the radiology area.[29] The growth has been striking – only a handful of AI devices were cleared in 2015, but over 200 were cleared in 2023 alone.[30] This is a sign of the progress in AI and the FDA trying to promote positive innovation. Some commentators note that FDA clearance is usually based on relatively limited validation. As an example, a recent study observed that only 16% of radiology AI products approved by the FDA had been tested in a multi-reader, multi-centre study, and many had no published peer-reviewed clinical evidence of performance.[31] Unlike the European Union, the United States does not presently mandate that the training data used to train an AI tool must be of a certain quality or representativeness, other than the general expectations of safety and effectiveness. Nor does the FDA require post-market performance monitoring specific to AI (although general device surveillance is required). To its credit, the FDA has acknowledged these deficiencies and has published an *Artificial Intelligence and Machine Learning Software as a Medical Device Action Plan* that will provide future guidance on transparency and good machine learning practices.[32] However, in my view, the US regulatory regime has been more lenient and relied on market forces and *ex post* measures (such as tort liability) to deal with risks that in the European Union are regulated *ex ante* through strict approval procedures. The consequences of this contrast will be observed as we discuss each use case.

C. Liability and Standards of Care

The important legal concern about diagnostic AI is the effects on professional liability and standard of care. What happens to the doctor who uses the diagnosis

28 Reuter and Han (n 15); Rohan Singh and others, 'How AI Is Used in FDA-Authorized Medical Devices: A Taxonomy across 1,016 Authorizations' (2025) 8 npj Digital Medicine 388.

29 Reuter and Han (n 15).

30 ibid.

31 Mello-Thoms and Mello (n 8).

32 US Food and Drug Administration, 'Artificial Intelligence in Software as a Medical Device' (25 March 2025) <https://www.fda.gov/medical-devices/software-medical-device-samd/artificial-intelligence-software-medical-device> accessed 25 August 2025. Regarding the Action Plan, see US Food and Drug Administration, 'Artificial Intelligence and Machine Learning Software as a Medical Device Action Plan' <https://www.fda.gov/media/145022/download?attachment> accessed 25 August 2025.

recommendation of AI, and the recommendation proves to be inaccurate? Currently, there is no special framework of immunity or shifted liability of AI in any of the three jurisdictions. The doctor making the treatment decision is still accountable for the diagnostic decision, whether or not it is influenced by AI. In the United Kingdom and United States, the use of AI by a doctor would be assessed through the prism of negligence – e.g. was it reasonable to trust the AI and did the doctor act negligently in failing to check the error made by the AI? There is no case law that is squarely on point, but it can be analogised to other decision-support tools. As an example, the UK guidance recommends that doctors who adopt assistive technologies should be aware of their limitations and should not abdicate their clinical judgment; a violation may constitute negligence.[33] In the United States, no malpractice suit involving an AI diagnosis has been reported,[34] although precedent would apply similar reasoning to those involving tele-radiology or automated alert systems.[35] In the meantime, patients who were harmed by a malicious AI may also possibly sue the producer, based on product liability laws.[36] The European Union is in fact making a step in this direction: a new Product Liability Directive update was proposed to expressly cover standalone software/AI and even an AI Liability Directive to facilitate the burden of proof to patients in fault-based claims.[37] These were proposals as of 2025; the AI Liability Directive in particular has been subject

33 See, for instance, General Medical Council, *Good Medical Practice* (2024) paras 1–3, 7, 23–27; Department of Health and Social Care (England), *Code of Conduct for Data-Driven Health and Care Technologies* (v2.0, 2019) Principles 1, 2, 5, 6 and 9; Academy of Medical Royal Colleges, *Artificial Intelligence in Healthcare* (2019) 6–8, 16–18; British Medical Association, *AI in Healthcare and Medical Practice: BMA Position and Policy* (2020) 5–7; NHS England, *DCB0129* (2018); NHS England, *DCB0160* (2018); NICE, *Evidence Standards Framework for Digital Health Technologies* (updated 2022) sections on clinical effectiveness and "intended purpose". For case law, see, for instance, *Bolam v. Friern Hospital Management Committee* [1957] 1 WLR 582 (CA); *Bolitho v. City and Hackney Health Authority* [1998] AC 232 (HL); *Montgomery v. Lanarkshire Health Board* [2015] UKSC 11 [2015] AC 1430.

34 W Nicholson Price II, Sara Gerke and I. Glenn Cohen, 'Potential Liability for Physicians Using Artificial Intelligence' (2019) 322(18) JAMA 1765–1766; I. Glenn Cohen, 'Informed Consent and Medical Artificial Intelligence: What to Tell the Patient?' (2020) 108 Georgetown Law Journal 1425–1469, 1432–1435.

35 Diane Hoffmann and Virginia Rowthorn, 'Legal Impediments to the Diffusion of Telemedicine' (2011) 14(1) Journal of Health Care Law and Policy 2; Sharona Hoffman and Andy Podgurski, 'Big Bad Data: Law, Public Health, and Biomedical Databases' (2013) 41(S1) The Journal of Law, Medicine & Ethics 56–60.

36 Restatement (Third) of Torts: Products Liability § 1 and § 19 (1998). About the case law, see, for instance, *Medtronic, Inc v. Lohr* 518 US 470 (1996); *Riegel v. Medtronic, Inc* 552 US 312 (2008); *Buckman Co v. Plaintiffs' Legal Committee* 531 US 341 (2001).

37 Lena Niehoff, 'New Product Liability Risks for AI Products' (*Taylor Wessing*, 6 March 2025) <https://www.taylorwessing.com/en/synapse/2025/ai-in-life-sciences/new-product-liability-risks-for-ai-products> accessed 26 August 2025; Barbora Dlabolová, 'The Issue of Liability in the Use of AI in Healthcare' (*ARROWS, law firm. Legal services quickly and globally*, 19 April 2024) <https://www.arws.cz/news-at-arrows/the-issue-of-liability-in-the-use-of-ai-in-healthcare> accessed 26 August 2025.

to debate and was recently withdrawn in its original form.[38] In the United States, there is one notable case, *Taylor v. Intuitive Surgical, Inc.*,[39] a patient injured during robot-assisted surgery (also discussed below) sued the device manufacturer on the basis of failure to warn about the risks; the Washington State Supreme Court found that the manufacturer had a duty to warn only the learned intermediary (the surgeon) and not the patient or hospital.[40] By analogy, an AI software developer may have a duty to warn doctors about the limitations of the tool (e.g. types of cases the tool is less accurate in). In the event that such warnings are insufficient, the manufacturer may be liable to the patient in the event of injury under failure-to-warn theories. This is a complicated interplay of medical negligence and product liability in AI diagnosis, and I will discuss it in subsequent chapters. The main thing now is that the introduction of AI does not eliminate the necessity of human supervision. In the European Union, United Kingdom and United States, doctors are morally and legally obliged to exercise independent judgment and to approach AI outputs as informative rather than definitive. It is a common refrain to say that the doctor will be in the loop. I would argue that this principle is critical to patient safety, but it does bring up the question of whether, given that AI can become more accurate than humans in certain tasks, the standard of care might require doctors to make use of AI assistance. We are already seeing foreshadowing of this: failure to use a broadly accepted diagnostic AI in the future could in itself be considered negligent should it result in a missed diagnosis that the AI would have caught. Law will have to adapt in both directions – ensuring AI is safe to use, and also ensuring it is used when safe and beneficial.

IV. AI in Clinical Decision Support

Besides diagnosis, AI is increasingly being applied within CDS systems that can help doctors in making treatment decisions, managing patient care, or predicting their future health events. These include AI-based risk prediction models (such as predicting which patients in hospital are at high risk of sepsis, cardiac arrest or readmission) and recommendation engines that offer personalised treatment options based on a patient. Its ability to integrate large quantities of data, which may include electronic health records, clinical guidelines, genomics and real-time vital signs, can give doctors insights (e.g. "there is a 90% predicted chance of complications in discharging this patient"). In the NHS in the United Kingdom, AI has been tested to assist with triage: one system reviews emergency department waiting lists to prioritise patients on the basis of risk, and another (the Babylon Health chatbot)

38 Katrin Helle and Bethany J. Hills, 'White & Case LLP International Law Firm, Global Law Practice' (*White & Case LLP*, 22 July 2025) <https://www.whitecase.com/insight-alert/new-eu-responsibility-and-liability-landscape-smart-medical-devices-global-context> accessed 26 August 2025.

39 *Taylor v. Intuitive Surgical, Inc.* 184 Wn. 2d 1033, 379 P. 3d 957 (2016).

40 About this case law, see <https://caselaw.findlaw.com/court/wa-court-of-appeals/1707123.html#:~:text=%C2%B6%2028%20Taylor%20argues%20that,We%20disagree> accessed 26 August 2025.

provided primary care patients with initial medical advice and triage suggestions.[41] In the United States, a famous example was the Watson for Oncology, an AI that attempted to propose cancer treatment plans, but ultimately failed to achieve doctor adoption because of accuracy and transparency problems.[42] A more successful tool has been more specific ones, e.g. an AI that keeps track of the vital signs and lab results of hospital patients to alert of impending sepsis hours before clinicians might detect it.[43] These cases are lifesaving when treated in time. Decision support AIs are also applied in prescribing (alerting dangerous drug interactions or advising on optimal doses), surgery planning (predicting high-risk patients and requiring extra attention) and even in the public health sector (AI-based early warning systems of disease outbreaks or resource requirements).[44]

A. Benefits and Challenges

The potential of AI in decision support is that it can minimise human error and variation in clinical decision-making. Human clinicians may be susceptible to cognitive overload, biases or heuristic shortcuts, especially where time is a consideration.[45] Through data crunching and pattern following, AI could see what humans can't. As an example, a decision support algorithm could avoid such oversights as a contraindicated medication or detect a minor correlation that reflects a rare diagnosis. Research indicates that in certain situations, when AI suggestions are used along with physician judgement, outcomes can be improved – one meta-analysis found that, in approximately 60% of cases, junior doctors performed better when they had the assistance of AI, and they overruled the AI in other cases, indicating a complementary relationship.[46] Nevertheless, CDS AI also has the same issue as the black

41 Oliver Large and others, 'Preparing the NHS for the AI Era: Why Smarter Triage and Navigation Mean Better Health Care' (*Tony Blair Institute*, 18 March 2025) <https://institute.global/insights/public-services/preparing-the-nhs-for-the-ai-era-why-smarter-triage-and-navigation-mean-better-health-care> accessed 26 August 2025; Department of Health and Social Care and The Rt Hon Wes Streeting MP, 'AI Doctors' Assistant to Speed up Appointments a "Gamechanger"' (*Gov.uk*, 27 April 2025) <https://www.gov.uk/government/news/ai-doctors-assistant-to-speed-up-appointments-a-gamechanger> accessed 26 August 2025.

42 Sara Gerke, Timo Minssen and Glenn Cohen, 'Ethical and Legal Challenges of Artificial Intelligence-Driven Healthcare' in Adam Bohr and Kaveh Memarzadeh (eds), *Artificial Intelligence in Healthcare* (Elsevier 2020) 295–336; Jo Cavallo, 'Confronting the Criticisms Facing Watson for Oncology' (*The ASCO Post*, 10 September 2019) <https://ascopost.com/issues/september-10-2019/confronting-the-criticisms-facing-watson-for-oncology> accessed 26 August 2025; Casey Ross and Ike Swetlitz, 'IBM Pitched Watson as a Revolution in Cancer Care. It's Nowhere Close' (*STAT*, 5 September 2017) <https://www.statnews.com/2017/09/05/watson-ibm-cancer/> accessed 26 August 2025; Henrico Dolfing, 'Case Study 20: The $4 Billion AI Failure of IBM Watson for Oncology' (*Henrico Dolfing*, 7 December 2024) <https://www.henricodolfing.com/2024/12/case-study-ibm-watson-for-oncology-failure.html> accessed 26 August 2025.

43 European Commission (n 13).

44 ibid.

45 European Parliament: Directorate-General for Parliamentary Research Services and others (n 1) 7.

46 Mello-Thoms and Mello (n 8) 2.

box: most of them employ sophisticated models (such as neural networks) that cannot justify a particular recommendation. This can be a problem in cases where, e.g. an AI suggests that a patient is ready to be discharged or that a standard treatment should be overridden – clinicians are rightly hesitant to trust a machine without understanding why. Such a right (not to be subject to purely automated decisions without explanation) is even entrenched in the EU GDPR, reflecting a very strong policy against inscrutable AI in sensitive decisions. In healthcare, although the scope of Article 22 is questionable, the spirit is that patients and providers have a right to know the rationale behind critical choices.[47] In addition, the use of AI decision aids may lead to new sources of error: e.g. using biased or flawed training data may perpetuate and even increase inequities. A striking illustration was provided by an algorithm that US health insurers used to assign high-risk patients more careful management of their needs, which turned out to underestimate the risk of Black patients because it relied on health spending as a proxy measure of health needs, and historically less money was spent on Black patients with the same conditions.[48] These implicit biases may give way to discriminatory results (in this case, reduced referrals of Black patients to high-risk care programs).[49] This has led to demands of algorithmic fairness and auditing requirements, which the EU AI Act now explicitly demands of high-risk AI: providers are to assess and mitigate bias in training data and performance.[50]

B. Comparative Regulatory Approaches: The US Carve-Out

A major regulatory difference can be seen in the decision support software. In the United States, there is a special statutory carve-out of some CDS software: the 21st Century Cures Act of 2016 amended the FDA jurisdiction by excluding some decision support tools from the definition of a regulated medical device. In particular, the software that satisfies the four conditions of section 520(o)(1)(E) – (1) the software is not intended to process images or signals of a patient; (2) the software is intended to display or analyse medical information already supplied by a healthcare professional; (3) the software is intended to support or give recommendations to a doctor about prevention, diagnosis or treatment; and (4) the software is designed so that the doctor can independently review the basis of the recommendations – is not a medical device under the FDA law.[51] In simpler terms, in case the decision support

47 Vera Lúcia Raposo, 'The Fifty Shades of Black: About Black Box AI and Explainability in Healthcare' (2025) 33(1) Medical Law Review fwaf005; see also Elias Aidun, 'Implications of Utilizing AI in Healthcare Settings' (*University of Cincinnati Law Review Blog*, 9 January 2025) <https://uclawreview.org/2025/01/09/implications-of-utilizing-ai-in-healthcare-settings/> accessed 26 August 2025.

48 European Parliament: Directorate-General for Parliamentary Research Services and others (n 1) 20–21.

49 ibid.

50 Directorate-General for Health and Food Safety (n 11) 2.

51 US Food & Drug Administration (n 7).

software merely assists a physician by sorting out patient information and providing recommendations, and most importantly in case the software exposes its rationale (so that a physician can verify it), the FDA will not treat it as a device. The justification is to prevent the excessive regulation of software that only offers directions and leaves the choice to human beings. In 2022, the FDA issued guidance that provides further clarity on this: software that cross-references the symptoms of a patient with clinical guidelines to suggest possible diagnoses and references the medical literature supporting those suggestions would be considered non-device CDS and not require FDA clearance.[52] Conversely, where the software processes raw patient data (such as imaging or lab results) or where it obscures its logic (a so-called black box recommendation), the FDA will regulate it as a device.[53] This implies that some AI tools that would be regulated under the European framework can currently be used in the United States without any FDA oversight, e.g. certain symptom-checker apps or risk calculators made available to physicians, so long as they disclose their rationale, are essentially unregulated as a device. This is both good and bad in terms of safety. It promotes innovation and access to useful software (decreasing regulatory burdens), but it is also up to clinicians to figure out which tools are good and which are bad.

In Europe, on the other hand, there is no carve-out. According to the EU MDR, any software which offers diagnostic or therapeutic advice to a professional is a medical device unless it conducts purely administrative or operational procedures.[54] The idea of a transparent algorithm being exempt is not accepted; even an explicable drug-interaction checker remains a regulated device when applied to patient care.[55] The EU guidance on software qualification (MDCG 2019–11) makes this explicit, and it was a concern raised by industry that the European Union did not offer a lighter touch on low-risk CDS.[56] Two jurisdictions may therefore regulate the same software differently: a hypothetical app that gives suggestions of possible diagnoses based on input symptoms and explains its rationale may be freely sold in the United States (no FDA clearance), but in the European Union it would probably require Conformité Européenne (European Conformity, or CE) marking and conformity assessment as at least Class IIa.

The United Kingdom, after Brexit, is now in the same position as the European Union in practice – the United Kingdom has not implemented the US Cures Act exemption. The majority of CDS software is still regulated by the MHRA as a device provided it has a medical purpose. The United Kingdom is, however, monitoring these developments; as seen in its 2023 policy paper on AI regulation, it

52 Beckers and Hoydonck (n 5) 2.

53 ibid.

54 ibid.

55 ibid.

56 ibid. Regarding the MDCG 2019-11, see Directorate-General for Health and Food Safety, 'Update MDCG 2019-11 rev.1 – Qualification and classification of software – Regulation (EU) 2017/745 and Regulation (EU) 2017/746 (June 2025)' (17 June 2025) <https://health.ec.europa.eu/document/download/b45335c5-1679-4c71-a91c-fc7a4d37f12b_en?filename=mdcg_2019_11_en.pdf> accessed 26 September 2025.

considered the possibility of the regulators considering factors such as transparency and risk to determine the level of strictness with which AI should be regulated.[57] It is conceivable that the United Kingdom will be more flexible (e.g. through sandbox trials of low-risk AI tools) given that it intends to have a pro-innovation regulatory regime. Until then, it is safe to assume that any AI offering clinical advice in the United Kingdom needs to be approved in the same way as in the European Union.

C. Practical Governance and Guidelines

In addition to hard law, the three regions have been formulating guidelines on safe and effective AI in CDS. The United Kingdom's National Institute for Health and Care Excellence (NICE) has published an Evidence Standards Framework on digital health technologies that provides a clear path of what evidence (effectiveness, economic impact, etc.) an AI or digital tool should have before NHS adoption.[58] This involves a demonstration of clinical validity and (where appropriate) that it does not exacerbate health inequalities. The NHSX (now part of NHS England) also published principles of AI, which include the need to be transparent about algorithms and mitigate bias;[59] these concerns also relate to decision support AIs, which may inadvertently encode biases embedded in healthcare data. The European Union, in addition to legally binding rules, has also invested in ethics guidelines (the High-Level Expert Group on AI Ethics Guidelines) which, although general, focus on concepts such as transparency, non-discrimination and human oversight in healthcare AI.[60] The EU AI Act also demands that the users (clinicians) are duly informed of the intended use and limitations of an AI system.[61] In the United States, medical associations like the American Medical Association (AMA) have published policy statements that AI decision tools must be transparent, evidence-based and aid, but not replace, physician decision-making.[62]

57 Department for Science, Innovation and Technology (UK Government), 'A Pro-Innovation Approach to AI Regulation' (*GOV.UK*, 29 March 2023) Part 2: The current regulatory environment <https://www.gov.uk/government/publications/ai-regulation-a-pro-innovation-approach/white-paper> accessed 26 August 2025.

58 National Institute for Health and Care Excellence, *Evidence Standards Framework for Digital Health Technologies* (March 2019), Section A (effectiveness) and Section B (economic impact) <https://www.nice.org.uk/Media/Default/About/what-we-do/our-programmes/evidence-standards-framework/digital-evidence-standards-framework.pdf> accessed 27 August 2025.

59 Indra Joshi and Jessica Morley, *Artificial Intelligence: How to Get it Right. Putting Policy into Practice for Safe Data-Driven Innovation in Health and Care* (*NHSX*, 2019) <https://law.queensu.ca/sites/lawwww/files/files/Research/MachineMD/NHSX_AI_report.pdf> accessed 27 August 2025.

60 European Commission High-Level Expert Group on Artificial Intelligence, *Ethics Guidelines for Trustworthy AI* (April 2019) <https://ec.europa.eu/newsroom/dae/document.cfm?doc_id=60419> accessed 27 August 2025.

61 European Commission (n 13).

62 American Medical Association, 'Augmented Intelligence in Medicine' (*American Medical Association*, 7 August 2025) <https://www.ama-assn.org/practice-management/digital-health/augmented-intelligence-medicine> accessed 27 August 2025.

On a legal scholarship side, one of the emerging issues is how AI will impact the quality of care in treatment decisions. What would happen in the event that an AI recommends a specific clinical path and a physician diverges? Would that be used as evidence that a physician fell below the standard of care? On the other hand, when the AI causes damage to the patient, and the doctor acts in accordance with it, does it protect the doctor? There are no definite answers to these questions. In negligence law, the customary practice often forms the basis of the standard of care, which in the future may include the use of AI. It will probably be fact-specific. I would argue that at this time, AI is an aid, and clinicians should use their discretion to decide when to trust or disregard it. However, as AI demonstrates itself (in certain areas it will become provably better than unaided human judgement), the legal expectations will change. In a decade, it is easy to envisage a malpractice action where an emergency physician is found guilty of negligence because he or she did not use an available AI risk score that would have detected the condition of a patient earlier. It will be important that jurisdictions remain vigilant to make sure that medico-legal standards encourage best practices, which may likely mean a well-tuned collaboration of human and AI.

V. AI in Surgical Robotics

Robotic systems have been employed in surgery for decades, and this is mainly as aids to surgeons to do minimally invasive surgery. A well-known example is the *da Vinci* Surgical System, a robotic system that allows a surgeon to control instruments inside the patient with a high degree of precision, through a console. The traditional surgical robots such as *da Vinci* are basically advanced tele-manipulators – they do not make independent decisions but rather execute the instructions of the surgeon (albeit filtered to remove tremor and scaled to provide fine motion). However, surgical robotics is developing in the direction of greater autonomy and the use of AI. We are seeing the emergence of preliminary versions of AI-aided surgical assistance: systems that can, e.g. automatically stitch tissue or autonomously steer to a specific anatomical destination under the guidance of a surgeon. Some orthopaedic robots already allow pre-planned bone cuts to be performed with high precision, using preoperative 3D models and AI planning.[63] In 2017, an autonomous robotic dental implant surgery was reported where the robot inserted implants without direct human control (though under monitoring) – an example of how far the technology can go.[64] A similarly cited milestone is the *Lindbergh Operation* in 2001, during which surgeons in New York remotely operated on a patient in France using a robotic system; with 5G networks, the possibility of regu-

63 De Micco and others (n 1) 2.

64 Alice Yan, 'Chinese Robot Dentist is First to Fit Implants in Patient's Mouth without Any Human Involvement' (*South China Morning Post*, 21 September 2017) <https://www.scmp.com/news/china/article/2112197/chinese-robot-dentist-first-fit-implants-patients-mouth-without-any-human> accessed 26 September 2025.

lar telesurgery over long distances is increasing.[65] Such processes can be facilitated by compensating latency, instructing instrument positioning, or even automating routine subtasks. In the near future, we might have semi-autonomous robots that perform simple surgical tasks (stapling, suturing) so that the human surgeon can concentrate on the complex decision-making. The European Union even has a term "embodied AI", which is essentially AI in the physical world, and there is no more dramatic application of that than a robot assistant in an operating theatre.[66]

A. Safety and Efficacy

The claimed advantages of surgical robotics are increased precision, smaller incisions and, therefore, faster recovery and human error reduction (a robot does not get tired or shaky).[67] In fact, robot-assisted microsurgery has also been able to perform such tasks as the suturing of minute blood vessels that would be very challenging to perform with the use of hands alone. Nonetheless, there are risks that are created by robots. They are complicated devices that are subject to technical failure (program bugs or mechanical failure), and their proper utilisation requires long surgeon training. It has been shown that robotic surgery has a learning curve wherein the incidence of complications can go up during early adoption. Examples of malpractice suits include such high-profile cases as internal injuries or burns due to improperly used robotic equipment. One of the most interesting cases is the case of *Taylor v. Intuitive Surgical, Inc.* discussed above: a patient experienced severe adverse events allegedly caused by a surgeon who was inexperienced with the *da Vinci* robot and the unsuitable anatomy of the patient (morbid obesity).[68] Although the final legal decision exonerated the manufacturer based on the learned intermediary doctrine (i.e. the surgeon was primarily responsible for how to use the machine properly), the case serves to show that when AI/robots are involved, the fault may not be solely on the human operator or the machine, but a combination of both. It also points out a genuine concern: in the case of an errant robot or AI during an operation that leads to injury, patients will not be able to easily prove liability: was it a surgeon error? A bug in a software? A failure of a component? These difficulties in ascribing fault have prompted scholars (and EU policymakers) to think about whether new liability regimes are required when it comes to autonomous systems.[69]

B. Regulation of Surgical Robots

Each of the three jurisdictions currently regulates surgical robots as medical devices. In the European Union, the surgical robot systems correspond to Class

65 De Micco and others (n 1) 2.
66 ibid.
67 ibid.
68 *Taylor v. Intuitive Surgical, Inc* (n 39).
69 De Micco and others (n 1) 2.

IIb or Class III medical instruments under the MDR, as they are invasive and can have a severe effect on patients. They demand detailed conformity analyses, and manufacturers must assure compliance with critical requirements (including safety of hardware and software, reliability and so on). In a case where the robot contains AI capabilities (e.g. an algorithm that automatically optimises the movements), it would also fall under the EU AI Act as a high-risk AI system used in the medical field.[70] Another interesting debate in the EU context has been whether highly autonomous robots might require a legal category of electronic personhood, where advanced autonomous robots would have some form of legal personality to ensure accountability (such as a fund to compensate victims).[71] This concept is controversial and has not been reflected in legislation; the European Commission specifically abandoned this approach in favour of revising existing legislation (such as product liability). Therefore, currently, a surgical robot is simply a product (albeit a complicated one), and any liability is assigned between humans (surgeons, hospitals, manufacturers) under traditional rules. The European Union has revised its Product Liability Directive[72] since 2024 to extend to software and AI: the proposed reform simplifies patients suing the makers of AI-driven devices by not requiring that the patient identify the exact defect and creating presumptions of causality in some instances. Under the new EU regime, a court could presume a defect in the case that the manufacturer did not comply with certain safety requirements or that the output of the robot was clearly erroneous.

The United Kingdom, at least, still enforces its Consumer Protection Act 1987 (which adopted the older EU product liability regulation) on robots – that a patient must demonstrate a defect, and that the defect was the cause of the injury. No UK case on the liability of surgical robots' product has been reported so far, but the same arguments as in *Taylor v. Intuitive Surgical, Inc.* would be expected if one arose. The medical device regulatory reforms proposed by the United Kingdom will probably contain particular software and AI information, following or at least mirroring the European Union on topics such as continuous learning algorithms and transparency, though the specifics are yet to be determined.

Surgical robots in the United States are controlled by FDA device approvals (e.g. *da Vinci* has FDA approval in many procedures). After entering the market, injuries that could have been caused by a robot are normally left to state tort law to be determined. The legal system in the United States has taken hundreds of suits over robotic surgery (some of them were aggregated through multi-district litigation about a decade ago). These have brought about concerns as to whether manufacturers provided adequate training and warnings. The general approach of US courts to robots has been similar to how they approach any other surgical tool: the manufacturer is obliged to disclose the risks it is aware of or ought to be aware of,

70 Directorate-General for Health and Food Safety (n 11) 2.

71 De Micco and others (n 1) 3.

72 Directive (EU) 2024/2853 of the European Parliament and of the Council <https://eur-lex.europa.eu/eli/dir/2024/2853/oj/eng> accessed 27 August 2025.

and the surgeon/hospitals are obliged to use the equipment correctly. In a different case, the Washington Supreme Court ruled that a manufacturer had a duty to warn both the hospital and the surgeon when the hospital is the purchaser and the device contains risks that are not apparent to the hospital (this was, in fact, the *Taylor* case on remand following the prior appeal ruling, the state supreme court in 2017 ruled the manufacturer had a duty to warn the hospital, building upon the result of the trial).[73] That is quite a break with the typical learned intermediary doctrine and indicates that courts can make changes in the situation of complex medical AI/robots when there are multiple actors involved in safety. Briefly, US surgical AI liability is developing with litigation, and the European Union is proceeding with codification of some claimant-friendly regulations in expectation of AI problems. I think both ways have their advantages: litigation is capable of flexible, fact-finding justice, and it can be slow and unpredictable; statutory reform is capable of clarity and consistency, but it risks being either too broad or soon obsolete due to technology.

C. Autonomy and the Future

One of the futuristic problems is the way the law will treat fully autonomous surgical AI. Currently, there is no surgery that is completed by an AI robot without human intervention. But studies are on the way to that possibility, at least for constrained tasks. When a patient is able to give consent to an autonomous robotic surgery within one day, who will legally perform the surgery? Only licensed practitioners may practise medicine; would the autonomous robot have to have some sort of a licence, or would the supervising physician be considered the operator? It has been argued that certain degrees of autonomy in robots may require a paradigm shift, possibly to treat highly autonomous AI in the same way as pharmaceutical agents (the product carries the risk through strict liability, and the role of the physician is primarily to select and supervise).[74] Philosophical debates also exist regarding whether to provide AI systems with a legal status to bear liability, which is still in theory. I uphold the view that in the foreseeable future, surgical AI will be supportive, a human surgeon will always be in the loop and the treatment will ultimately depend on the human surgeon. In the European Union, United Kingdom and United States, regulatory authorities all place importance on human oversight of high-risk AI. As an illustration, the EU AI Act will mandate that high-risk AI (such as the control software on a surgical robot) is designed in such a way that human users can understand and intervene when needed.[75] The FDA has also emphasised the notion of "human in the loop" when discussing autonomous AI in

73 *Taylor v. Intuitive Surgical, Inc* (n 39).
74 De Micco and others (n 1) 2.
75 Directorate-General for Health and Food Safety (n 11) 16.

healthcare.[76] In such a way, one probable approach to law is that an autonomous surgical system would not be permitted to run without a competent surgeon overseeing and available to assume control – similar to how autonomous vehicles under testing on roads often require a safety driver. When a robot has caused an injury even after precautions have been taken, liability may be divided between the manufacturer (over any flaws in design), the surgeon (over insufficient supervision) and perhaps the hospital (over insufficient training or maintenance). The social issue is how to find the right balance between innovation and accountability: making liability too high on the side of manufacturers will discourage innovation; making no obvious recourse available to patients will undermine societal trust in medical AI. The European Union's inclination towards strict liability for certain AI uses, and the United Kingdom's likely openness to adaptive regulation, will be fascinating to observe as surgical AI advances.

VI. Conclusion

AI in healthcare has been revealing significant potential in the fields of diagnostics, CDS and surgical robotics, but it is still caught up in safety, accountability and legal ambiguities. Comparative analysis of the European Union, United Kingdom and United States uncovers not only common principles, including the consideration of AI as high-risk in the case of an effect on clinical outcomes and the emphasis on human oversight, but also different regulatory philosophies, with the European Union implementing strict *ex ante* demands, the United States offering permissive routes and the United Kingdom taking a principles-based intermediate course. The lesson is, in my opinion, that only by actively building trust into law and policy can AI live up to its promise: by insisting on strong evidence of efficacy, by enforcing transparency wherever possible and by making liability clear, so that patients are not harmed but innovation is not stifled.

76 US Food and Drug Administration, 'Total Product Lifecycle Considerations for Generative AI – Enabled Devices' (20–21 November 2024) 18 <https://www.fda.gov/media/182871/download> accessed 28 August 2025.

3 Regulatory Landscapes

European Union, United Kingdom and United States

Abstract

This chapter offers a comparative analysis of the extent to which the European Union, United Kingdom and United States regulate AI in healthcare, and more precisely, AI for medical devices, CDS systems and adaptive algorithms. It studies classification for drugs, pre-market approval regimes, post-market surveillance, transparency requirements, liability regimes, etc. The European Union bases its perspectives on the fields of AI and digital services on a precautionary rights-based approach: the MDRI and the AI Act foresee *ex ante* conformity obligations and lifecycle obligations. The United Kingdom has a hybrid, principle-based approach with foundations from law derived from the European Union but in the process of reform as MHRA, for example in the form of the post-market surveillance changes in 2025. Using a digital business model approach that is agile and innovative, the United States has leveraged FDA clearance processes, post-market monitoring conditions and emerging technologies such as PCCPs. Responsibilities differ: the European Union and United Kingdom fault the strict product liability and physician, while the United States has further restrictions through the pre-emption doctrines. The chapter brings out convergence with respect to regulatory objectives but divergence with respect to legal technique and provides critical insight into the equilibrium between innovation, safety and accountability in AI-enabled healthcare from global governance models.

I. Introduction

AI has been employed more in the healthcare field for everything from initial sepsis alerts to autonomous image analysis. Regulators in various jurisdictions are trying to ensure that these systems are safe and effective, while at the same time not suppressing innovation. Their legal strategies are quite different. The European Union has taken a preventive approach in its legislation, such as in the MDR[1] and AI Act

1 Regulation (EU) 2017/745 of the European Parliament and of the Council of 5 April 2017 on medical devices (Medical Devices Regulation).

DOI: 10.4324/9781003785385-4

2024.[2] In the United States, on the other hand, there is no "AI law"; regulation is based on the FDA's medical device scheme and general tort law, with a statutory carve-out for certain CDS software from regulation.[3] The United Kingdom, inheriting rules on medical devices from the European Union, is working on its own post-Brexit strategy grounded in high-level principles, agility and flexibility rather than a long new list of new rules – wanting to become "a home of responsible innovation" in the field of medical AI, while respecting safety.[4] This chapter makes a comparative analysis of the regulation of AI in healthcare in each jurisdiction, referring to the points of: (1) the classification and pre-market approval, (2) the post-market control (including the adaptiveness of AI systems), (3) the transparency of AI systems; and (4) the liability for harm caused by AI.

II. Classification and Pre-market Requirements

The first step would be to identify which AI systems are subject to the provisions of the medical device laws and how they would be categorised for risk. The European Union cast a wide net – under the MDR any software intended for medical purposes (diagnosis, treatment, monitoring, etc.) is considered a medical device and must be compliant with medical device regulations.[5] But according to this broad definition, most AI tools used in clinical care are regulated. The EU AI Act strengthens this by that healthcare AI is predominantly classified as "high-risk" AI systems which must comply with a number of requirements before being used.[6] The United Kingdom is in line with the European Union, using its MHRA to implement the criteria for the MDR and offering no general exceptions for software.[7] US law, on the other hand, explicitly exempts certain decision-support AI from FDA: it's not a medical device if, under the 21st Century Cures Act 2016, CDSS is limited to only generating options that the physician can then independently review and decide based on the reasoning.[8] In effect, the United States draws a distinction between AI that is "more transparently advisory" (and thus potentially exempt from FDA regulation) and AI that diagnoses or treats patients directly (and is always subject to regulation).

2 Regulation (EU) 2024/1689 (EU AI Act), entering into force 1 August 2024 (most provisions applicable from 2026).

3 21st Century Cures Act 2016 (US), §3060 (amending 21 U.S.C. §360j(o)): excluding certain CDS software from the FDA's device definition; see also FDA, *Clinical Decision Support Software: Guidance for Industry and Food and Drug Administration Staff* (September 2022), which narrows the exemption by clarifying when decision-support tools are subject to FDA oversight.

4 MHRA (UK), *Software and AI as a Medical Device Change Programme – Roadmap* (14 June 2023) (setting out plans to ensure the United Kingdom is "recognised globally as a home of responsible innovation for medical device software").

5 Medical Devices Regulation (n 1).

6 Article 6(2) and Annex III of the EU AI Act.

7 MHRA (n 4).

8 21st Century Cures Act 2016 (US) (n 3).

Once it's understood that an AI-based product is a regulated device, the next question becomes what its risk class is, and what the level of pre-market review is or should be. The Classification in the European Union's MDR is based on risk (Class I – lowest risk, to Class III – highest risk). For example, most standalone software programmes with diagnostic or therapeutic intents are classified by MDR Rule 11 up to at least Class IIa (moderate risk) and are thus subject to the needs for an independent conformity assessment by a notified body prior to entering the market.[9] Typically, an AI diagnostic system in the European Union is not self-certified by the manufacturer; instead, it has to be CE marked after demonstrating appropriate safety and performance qualifications based on, for example, clinical validation data validated by a third-party analyst.

EU regulators have recently increased pre-market requirements. The European Union's MDR has led to increased classification and evidence requirements for software: under MDR Annex VIII (Rule 11) most forms of diagnostic or decision support AI software are up classified to at least Class IIa/IIb, unless they are low-risk non-diagnostic software.[10] This means that the majority of AI-driven medical software in Europe has been upgraded to a "high-risk" classification, leading to a need for Notified Body review, an MDR-compliant quality management system (QMS) and a robust clinical performance validation process prior to CE marking and deployment. Furthermore, the EU AI Act contains additional *ex ante* obligations for high-risk AI systems – such as stringent risk management, transparency and data governance measures, technical documentation and post-market monitoring – as well as an obligation to carry out an independent conformity assessment before any high-risk AI could be put into service.[11]

The US FDA also operates under a risk-based regulatory framework (Class I/II/III) but does not have a software-specific rule like the MDR does. In fact, many AI devices in the United States fall into the moderate risk group (roughly analogous to EU class II) and are reviewed by a pre-market notification [510(k) clearance] which would only require demonstration that the new AI is as safe and effective as a predicate device.[12] Novel AI devices without any predicate device may get classified through De Novo (FDA), creating a new class I/II device category for

9 Medical Devices Regulation (n 1), Annex VIII, rule 11 (classification rule for software); see e.g. Ruth Beckers and Pascale Van Hoydonck, 'Impact of the Regulatory Framework on Medical Device Software Manufacturers: Are the Guidance Documents Supporting the Practical Implementation?; Comment on "Clinical Decision Support and New Regulatory Frameworks for Medical Devices: Are We Ready for It? – A Viewpoint Paper"' (2023) 12(1) International Journal of Health Policy and Management 1–4 (noting up-classification of most software under MDR).

10 Siwen Zhang and others, 'A Decade of Review in Global Regulation and Research of Artificial Intelligence Medical Devices (2015–2025)' (2025) 12 Frontiers in Medicine 1630408, 3–4.

11 ibid 4.

12 Elise Reuter and Jasmine Ye Han, 'The Number of AI Medical Devices Has Spiked in the Past Decade' *MedTech Dive* (9 October 2024) <https://www.medtechdive.com/news/fda-ai-medical-devices-growth/728975/> accessed 23 August 2025; Rohan Singh and others, 'How AI Is Used in FDA-Authorized Medical Devices: A Taxonomy across 1,016 Authorizations' (2025) 8 npj Digital Medicine 388.

moderate-risk innovations, and only the highest-risk AI systems (e.g. AI systems making autonomous treatment decisions) are treated as Class III devices requiring full pre-market approval (PMA).[13] So far, not many AI-based products are Class III – in the United States to date, only about 0.4% of FDA-approved AI/machine learning (ML) medical devices have been cleared under the stricter PMA process (a handful of devices per year), the remainder (over 95%) have been cleared under the less stringent 510(k) medical device clearance process.[14] Developers tend to build these AI tools to assist clinicians (not replace them outright), so their potential use is on a moderate-risk scale. As a result, most in-market AI medical products in the United States have been approved through 510(k) filings for substantial equivalence with an earlier FDA-approved medical product, with just a few approved through trial (Full PMA) review – testimony to the FDA's more flexible, incremental approach in AI oversight.[15]

A real-world example can show the differences in classification and approval. The "Epic Sepsis Model", a machine-learning-based alert system for early sepsis detection, was widely deployed in US hospitals without FDA review, on the basis that it met the criteria for non-device CDS (offering risk scores that the doctor could interpret themselves). In practice, the tool did not work well: one study found that it only identified 33% of actual sepsis cases while raising many false positives, which should raise serious concerns for patient safety.[16] This case revealed a gap in the US regime – an AI tool posing high risk to patients reached them without at least some pre-market scrutiny because of the statutory exemption. By comparison, in the European Union such a system of AI would be patently regulated. Sepsis alert algorithms influencing clinical decisions meet the MDR's definition of a medical device – under Rule 11 it would likely fall under class IIa or IIb (missing sepsis can be life threatening). Before deployment the manufacturer would have been obliged to provide a CE mark, to prove that the system met the relevant performance standards (sensitivity and specificity, for example, from validation studies) and that any remaining critical requirements were met and assessed by a notified body. In a nutshell, the European Union approach is more up-front with regard to classification and pre-market review, while the US approach – while onerous for some new devices – has left some software products unregulated, relying on post-market mechanisms for detecting problems. Indeed, in response to the collapse of the SEPSIS model(s), the FDA has in fact published guidance in 2022 limiting the decision support exemption, defining that hardware or software tools for aiding decisions that are opaque to the treating clinician cannot be accepted for marketing

13 Mateo Aboy, Cristina Crespo and Ariel Stern, 'Beyond the 510(k): The Regulation of Novel Moderate-risk Medical Devices, Intellectual Property Considerations and Innovation Incentives in the FDA's De Novo Pathway' (2024) 7 npj Digital Medicine 29.

14 Geeta Joshi and others, 'FDA-Approved Artificial Intelligence and Machine Learning (AI/ML)-Enabled Medical Devices: An Updated Landscape' (2024) 13(3) Electronics 498.

15 Zhang and others (10) 3.

16 Andrew Wong et al., 'External Validation of a Widely Implemented Proprietary Sepsis Prediction Model' (2021) 181(8) JAMA Internal Medicine 1065.

as a medical device.[17] The European Union, for its part, considers such tools to be high risk in the AI Act to ensure that they are subject to comprehensive requirements to be imposed before and during their deployment.[18]

III. Post-Market Oversight and Adaptivity

Regulation does not stop once an AI system is put into a consumer's hands – governance of any form is essential, particularly as most AI algorithms have the ability to learn over time and be updated through software. While traditional medical device regulations took a fixed product for granted, AI's plasticity (evolving as a result of new information or program updates) is disruptive to these traditional models. The European Union, United States and United Kingdom, respectively, are all grappling with what should be done to track how AI performs in real-world use and how to control changes of the software or its continuous learning.

Under the MDR, the European Union has a well-established and operational post-market surveillance and vigilance system. Manufacturers of medical devices are required to have plans for proactively collecting and analysing performance data from the real world and notifying the regulators about serious medical incidents or any safety corrective actions within tight timelines.[19] This means that if an AI diagnostic tool is named as a contributing factor to an adverse event (i.e. missing an existing condition that it was supposed to reveal), the incident must be reported and investigated, and corrections (in the form of software updates or warnings) must be disseminated. Informational safety update reports must be sent for more dangerous devices, which may include information that an AI's performance is drifting or degrading over time. Furthermore, the new AI Act imposes additional requirements for high-risk AI systems: providers of such AI must have active monitoring of compliance and new risks, keep automatic logs of how the AI operates in order to facilitate traceability and report any serious incidents involving AI to authorities.[20] In other words, EU law has introduced continuous risk management for AI throughout its lifecycle. However, with regard to changes to the AI itself, the European Union still takes a cautious approach. Under MDR rules, a substantial modification to a medical software (for example, a significant update to the algorithm or an increase in the use in clinical practice) is understood as creating a new device – requiring a new conformity assessment and regulatory approval (unless the change is minor).[21] This static approach guarantees control of changes but can be sufficiently slow for facilitating positive change. If an AI producer in Europe wants to make a significant

17 FDA (n 3).

18 Article 6 and Annex I (listing Regulation 2017/745 on medical devices), and Annex III, point 5(d) (emergency call and patient triage AI classified as high-risk) of the EU AI Act.

19 Medical Devices Regulation (n 1), Articles 83–90 (post-market surveillance and vigilance obligations on manufacturers and Member States).

20 Articles 9, 61–65 of the EU AI Act (obligations for providers of high-risk AI systems to conduct post-market monitoring, log data and report serious incidents).

21 Medical Devices Regulation (n 1), Article 120(3).

improvement to its algorithm, it must strictly manage software changes and often must return to a notified body for the first time. The EU system in its present form does not allow for incorporating continuous learning algorithms self-renewable in real time; any such adaptive behaviour would risk being run in virtue of altered certified terms of use. European regulators know about this stifling rigidity and have already disscused about guidance or standards around "minor" vs "significant" change, but the default position (until 2025) is to regard change control as stringent.[22] The AI Act also implies future options for flexibility (e.g. regulatory sandboxes for AI innovation),[23] but those measures are at the early stages of conception. Thus, in an EU hospital, an AI tool must be used according to its approval – if it is re-trained on new data locally or is otherwise adapting to change performance, the change seems to need to be validated and approved as if it were a new product, to maintain safety.

The US FDA has been more flexible in adapting its regulatory approach to AI given its iterative nature. Traditionally, any post-market modification to a device that can impact the safety or effectiveness of the product affects the FDA's review process, necessitating a new submission to the agency [510(k) or PMA].[24] This rule was not functional for AI systems that are retrained regularly or enhanced through software updates. In response, the FDA proposed a new framework in 2019[25] and, after several years of pilots and consultation, in 2024 issued final guidance on PCCPs for AI/ML-based devices.[26] Under this approach, a manufacturer may submit in its initial application to the FDA a detailed plan for anticipated algorithm changes and how they will be developed, validated and controlled. If the FDA approves the device and the change control plan, the company is then free to implement the specified changes at a later date without having to submit a new application each time. For instance, a cardiac monitoring AI might be cleared with a PCCP that pre-authorises updates to the algorithm's sensitivity with the receipt of new training data (provided that specific performance thresholds and validation scheduled at the time of origination are satisfied). This helps the AI evolve within set boundaries – the manufacturer merely informs the FDA of the changes according to the plan approved by the FDA, instead of going through a full review for

22 Directorate-General for Health and Food Safety (European Commission), *MDCG 2020-3 Rev.1: Guidance on Significant Changes under Article 120 MDR* (European Commission, May 2023), 2 <https://health.ec.europa.eu/document/download/800e8e87-d4eb-4cc5-b5ad-07a9146d7c90_en?filename=mdcg_2020-3_en_1.pdf> accessed 17 September 2025.

23 Article 57 and Recitals 138–140 of the EU AI Act (for sandbox framework).

24 21 Code of Federal Regulations §807.81(a)(3) (FDA regulation requiring a new submission for significant changes to a cleared device).

25 FDA, Proposed Regulatory Framework for Modifications to Artificial Intelligence/Machine Learning (AI/ML)-Based Software as a Medical Device (SaMD) – Discussion Paper and Request for Feedback (*FDA*, 2019) <https://www.fda.gov/files/medical%20devices/published/US-FDA-Artificial-Intelligence-and-Machine-Learning-Discussion-Paper.pdf> accessed 17 September 2025.

26 FDA, *Marketing Submission Recommendations for a Predetermined Change Control Plan for AI/ML-Enabled Device Software Functions: Guidance for Industry and Food and Drug Administration Staff* (*FDA*, 4 December 2024, updated on 18 August 2025) (outlining how manufacturers can obtain FDA pre-approval for future algorithm changes).

each tweak. The PCCP paradigm is an important step in a "total product life cycle" oversight paradigm, in which the FDA's primary goal is to promote continuous improvements while still ensuring validation of changes. In addition, clearances and approvals for AI devices often come with post-market study commitments or requirements to follow up with real-world performance and report back (particularly for new AI).[27] The FDA is also working with other organisations, including the International Medical Device Regulators Forum, the regulators in Canada and the United Kingdom on international principles for applying AI changes.[28] It should be noted, however, that AI tools which completely bypass FDA regulation (due to the above-mentioned exemption for certain decision support software) are not subject to these FDA post-market controls at all – their oversight lies with healthcare system vigilance or liability in the event that something goes wrong.[29] Overall, the United States is headed towards more nimble regulatory oversight for regulated AI, where safety is assured in a managed evolution of algorithms, rather than "freezing" an algorithmic application design at the time of approval. This is illustrated with reference to the FDA's willingness to allow AI devices approved to self-update according to an implementation plan that the FDA and FDA-approved investigator agree on, which is not currently available under EU regulations.

In the United Kingdom, post-market regulation has been redesigned to strike an innovative and safe balance. The UK MDR 2002 was amended by *The Medical Devices (Post-Market Surveillance Requirements) (Amendment) (Great Britain) Regulations 2024* for implementation on 16 June 2025, introducing a new PMS Part 4A.[30] This legislation provided for strengthened and risk proportionate post-

27 Daniel Windecker and others, 'Generalizability of FDA-Approved AI-Enabled Medical Devices for Clinical Use' (2025) 8(4) JAMA Network Open e258052; see also Kyrie' Chandler and Beth K. Toberman, 'FDA Releases Draft Guidance on AI-Enabled Medical Devices' (*GreenbergTraurig*, 31 January 2025) <https://www.gtlaw.com/en/insights/2025/1/fda-releases-draft-guidance-on-ai-enabled-medical-devices> accessed 18 September 2025; Daniel Weinstein, Rachel L. Sher and Nicholas W. Bath Jr., 'The FDA and the Future of AI Oversight' (*manatt*, 27 February 2024) <https://www.manatt.com/insights/newsletters/health-highlights/the-fda-and-the-future-of-ai-oversite> accessed 18 September 2025.

28 Elizabeth Smith, 'Five Major Principles for Predetermined Change Control Plans Regarding Machine Learning-Enabled Devices' (*MEDIcept*, 30 October 2023) <https://www.medicept.com/five-major-principles-for-predetermined-change-control-plans-regarding-machine-learning-enabled-devices/> accessed 18 September 2025; 'Artificial Intelligence/Machine Learning-Enabled' (*International Medical Device Regulators Forum*, 2025) <https://www.imdrf.org/working-groups/artificial-intelligencemachine-learning-enabled> accessed 18 September 2025.

29 Douglas McNair and W. Nicholson Price II, 'Health Care Artificial Intelligence: Law, Regulation, and Policy' in Michael Matheny and others (eds), *Artificial Intelligence in Health Care: The Hope, the Hype, the Problem, the Peril* (National Academy of Medicine 2022) 197–234, 202; see also Katie Adams and Maya Sandalow, *Oversight Beyond the FDA: Understanding the Regulation of Health AI Tools* (Bipartisan Policy Center June 2025) 4; Erin Schumaker, 'Artificial Intelligence Assurance Labs are Coming, HHS Chief AI Officer Says' (*POLITICOPRO*, 18 September 2024) <https://subscriber.politicopro.com/article/2024/09/artificial-intelligence-assurance-labs-are-coming-hhs-chief-ai-officer-says-00179815> accessed 18 September 2025.

30 The Medical Devices (Post-Market Surveillance Requirements) (Amendment) (Great Britain) Regulations 2024 No. 1368 <https://www.legislation.gov.uk/uksi/2024/1368/contents/made> accessed 19 September 2025.

market surveillance (PMS) obligations, to bring Great Britain's requirements into line with international standards (similar to the MDR framework in the European Union) but adapted to the UK context.[31] Manufacturers are now required to have extensive PMS plans, continuously collect and analyse real-world data on device performance throughout the life of the product, report adverse incidents timeously and submit safety reports [post-market surveillance reports (PMSRs) or periodic safety update reports (PSURs) depending on the device class] to the MHRA at intervals.[32] By enhancing vigilance and traceability (to effectively detect and control safety issues) without placing undue burdens on re-approval, the United Kingdom intends to ensure that patients are kept safe while at the same time contributing to an environment which facilitates the introduction of the most innovative healthcare products, including those with AI.[33] Importantly, this regulatory change ties in with the ongoing "Software and AI as a Medical Device" change programme by the MHRA (including the affectively named "Project Ship of Theseus" on AI Adaptivity).[34] Through this programme, the regulator is investigating what guidance there could be as to whether an evolving algorithm for an AI device might be considered a new device that requires approval, i.e. whether certain algorithm updates should be allowed without the need for full re-approval if stringent rules are in place to ensure that steps to maintain the safety and effectiveness of the algorithm are strictly applied through a system of PMS.[35] In conclusion, the post-market model in the United Kingdom is trending towards an effective middle ground – keeping a rigorous regulatory regime and patient protection in place, but applying adaptable monitoring technologies and processes to allow fast access to transformative medical technologies (like AI) without compromising safety.[36]

IV. Transparency Requirements

Trust is emerging as a key requirement in healthcare when it comes to AI algorithms. Clinicians and patients should have an understanding, to at least a basic level, of what an AI is doing and what its limitations are. The European Union has gone furthest with respect to mandating transparency. The AI Act expressly

31 Chris Occleshaw, 'UK Post-Market Surveillance Rules for Medical Devices Take Effect' (*sedgwick*, 6 August 2025) <https://www.sedgwick.com/blog/uk-post-market-surveillance-rules-for-medical-devices-take-effect/> accessed 18 September 2025.

32 ibid.

33 Medicines and Healthcare products Regulatory Agency, 'Regulatory Roadmap Points the Way Ahead for New Measures to Support Safe Access to Medical Technology Including AI and Diagnostics' (*GOV.UK*, 9 January 2024) <https://www.gov.uk/government/news/regulatory-roadmap-points-the-way-ahead-for-new-measures-to-support-safe-access-to-medical-technology-including-ai-and-diagnostics> accessed 18 September 2025.

34 Huw Beverley-Smith, Paige Lauren Izquierdo and Charlotte Perowne, 'AI Regulation in the U.K. – New Government Approach (Updated)' (*JDSUPRA*, 2 December 2022) <https://www.jdsupra.com/legalnews/ai-regulation-in-the-u-k-new-government-9963645> accessed 18 September 2025.

35 ibid.

36 Medicines and Healthcare products Regulatory Agency (n 33).

mandates high-risk AI systems to be designed and documented in a manner that can be understood by the user, who can use the system's output appropriately.[37] In a medical context, this means that an AI tool must come with information to enable a doctor to know how to apply its recommendations – for example, information about the intended purpose of the AI, performance measures (accuracy rates, known failure modes) and any circumstances in which the AI might not provide accurate recommendations. This is consistent with current EU medical devices regulations which require manufacturers to give comprehensive instructions for use. For an AI medical device, the documentation is supposed to describe the role of the algorithm (for example "a decision support tool for identifying signs of diabetic retinopathy in retinal images"), the level of accuracy achieved by the algorithm in the validation and warnings about known issues such as patient groups where AI is less validated. While the European Union does not require companies to disclose their source code and proprietary algorithms, it does require them to be functionally transparent – that is, the logic and performance of the system must not be a black box to users.[38] In Europe too, technical standards are being developed for AI explainability to facilitate such compliance with legal requirements.

Although we do not have statutory transparency requirements for AI in healthcare in the United Kingdom as of 2025, the United Kingdom overwhelmingly supports the idea in policy. The UK government's guidance on AI and the NHS Code of Conduct for digital health technology emphasises the importance of AI systems being transparent, with regard to their purpose, performance, etc.[39] Efforts are being made such as the MHRA's *Project "Glass Box"*, which is looking towards developing ways to improve algorithmic explainability to regulators and clinicians.[40] In the future, it may be that the United Kingdom includes transparency requirements as part of the guidance or even product clearance requirements (for example, the MHRA may require that an AI model be accompanied by confidence scores or explanations for the outputs the model has generated). For now, the principles-based approach is the one the United Kingdom will take: a reliance on having manufacturers be open about the workings and limitations of their AI, with no concrete legal mandate for it.

37 Article 15(1) of the EU AI Act (requiring that high-risk AI systems be designed and developed with *appropriate transparency* so that users can interpret and use the AI output); see also Georgios Pavlidis, 'Unlocking the Black Box: Analysing the EU Artificial Intelligence Act's Framework for Explainability in AI' (2024) 16(1) Law, Innovation & Technology 293–308 (discussing the Act's transparency requirements).

38 Article 15(1) of the EU AI Act.

39 Department of Health & Social Care, 'A Guide to Good Practice for Digital and Data-driven Health Technologies' (*GOV.UK*, September 2018, updated 19 January 2021), Principles 7 <https://www.gov.uk/government/publications/code-of-conduct-for-data-driven-health-and-care-technology/initial-code-of-conduct-for-data-driven-health-and-care-technology> accessed 18 September 2025.

40 Alison McAdams, Hamza Drabu and Darryn Hale, 'MHRA Publishes Medical Software and AI Roadmap for Way Ahead' (*DAC BEACHCROFT*, 27 October 2022) <https://www.dacbeachcroft.com/en/What-we-think/MHRA-publishes-medical-software-and-AI-roadmap-for-way-ahead> accessed 18 September 2025.

In the United States, there is no general legal requirement for the explainability of AI for healthcare. In fact, the FDA is not focused on understanding the decision-making process of AI while reviewing AI devices but on performance and safety. For an AI device, this will include labelling for intended use, context of use, performance data from trials (such as sensitivity/specificity) and many warnings such as "Not evaluated in paediatric populations" to advise the human user of the potential dangers inherent in using that tool.[41] But the FDA does not push for disclosure on how the algorithm makes decisions internally. Interestingly, the 2016 law in the United States exempting certain CDSS in effect built in a transparency principle: in order to be eligible for the exemption by the US FDA, the software must permit the physician to see the basis of its recommendations.[42] In other words, it is impossible to freely market a completely opaque AI as an unregulated product – if the clinician cannot independently question the reason for each recommendation or patient choice, the product should be subject to FDA regulation. This provision creates an incentive for AI developers (who want to avoid FDA regulation) to include some explainability, or rationale, with their outputs. In practical terms, however, a lot of AI models (such as deep learning networks) are still complex, and the FDA has had to clarify with guidance that if the logic doesn't "make sense" then the exemption is invalid.[43] Beyond regulation, transparency in the United States is also indirectly encouraged by liability and professional norms: doctors may not be willing to use AI they do not understand because they know that if something goes wrong they could be held responsible for relying on it.[44] Realising that ethical expectations for transparency in AI's use are implied and probably will become law in many cases, many hospitals also have policies to inform patients that AI is being used in their care.[45]

In a nutshell, the European Union takes the lead on formal transparency requirements (making it a matter of fundamental rights and safety), the United Kingdom promotes transparency through soft law and is testing modalities for

41 Brandon J. Nelson and others, 'An FDA Guide on Indications for Use and Device Reporting of Artificial Intelligence-Enabled Devices: Significance for Pediatric Use' (2023) 20(8) Journal of the American College of Radiology 738–741; Risa M. Wolf and others, 'Autonomous Artificial Intelligence Increases Screening and Follow-up for Diabetic Retinopathy in Youth: The ACCESS Randomized Control Trial' (2024) 15 Nature Communications 421.

42 21st Century Cures Act 2016 (US) (n 3), §3060; FDA (n 3).

43 Lisa M. Dwyer and others, 'FDA's Final Clinical Decision Support Guidance: The Good News and the (Really) Bad News' (*King & Spalding*, 12 October 2022) <https://www.kslaw.com/news-and-insights/fdas-final-clinical-decision-support-guidance-the-good-news-and-the-really-bad-news> accessed 18 September 2025.

44 Lauren Xiong and Timothy Chow, 'Cloud on the Horizon: Why Medical Negligence Needs to Take a New Approach to AI Driven Medical Decisions' (2025) 14 The Oxford University Undergraduate Law Journal 272–273.

45 Joe W. Bowers, 'AI Is Reshaping Black Healthcare: Promise, Peril, and the Push for Improved Results in California' (*The San Diego Voice & Viewpoint*, 28 April 2025) <https://sdvoice.info/ai-is-reshaping-black-healthcare-promise-peril-and-the-push-for-improved-results-in-california/> accessed 19 September 2025 (mentioning that a recently proposed law, Assembly Bill (AB) 3030, would require healthcare providers to inform patients about the use of AI in their care, and this trend reflects an ethical commitment to transparency with patients)

operationalising it and the United States relies on a combination of specific conditions (for unregulated tools) and market forces for promoting transparency. They all acknowledge that it's problematic to have full "black box" opacity in healthcare, but also that it's technically difficult to get to true AI explainability, at least for complex AI. A likely point of convergence is at least contextual transparency – for example, giving users a confidence score or key factors behind an AI's output (such as indicating what parts of an image had an impact on an AI's diagnosis). Indeed, the current provisions of the EU AI Act concerning transparency would force developers in that direction, as the Act mandates that the AI outputs developed by companies be explainable to the users.[46]

V. Liability for AI-Driven Harm

A final and critical aspect of regulation concerns how the legal system exercises allocation of responsibility in cases where an AI in healthcare causes harm. These include product liability (manufacturers being held liable for producing defective products) and professional liability (negligence by healthcare providers). Here, underlying legal systems differ: product liability regimes in the European Union and United Kingdom used to be alike historically, while the United States has some unique features such as federal pre-emption and the interaction of malpractice law.

A. European Union: Updated Product Liability Framework for AI in Medical Devices

In the European Union, a patient injured by an AI-based medical device (or anything else) can sue the manufacturer under strict product liability laws. These rules were for a long time based on the Product Liability Directive 85/374/EEC, but that directive from 1985 was repealed and replaced by a modern Directive (EU) 2024/2853.[47] The new directive – which will have to be transposed into national legislation by the end of 2026 – broadens the definition of "product" to include clearly intangible digital elements, including software and AI systems.[48] The liability is strict,[49] i.e. it does not require the patient to establish that the care he received was negligent, but only that it was defective (i.e. not as safe as the public is entitled to expect to be safe) and that defect caused the injury.[50] Compliance with any regulatory specifications (for instance, a CE mark) does not guarantee

46 Article 15(1) of the EU AI Act; Pavlidis (n 37).

47 Directive (EU) 2024/2853 of the European Parliament and of the Council of 23 October 2024 on liability for defective products and repealing Council Directive 85/374/EEC.

48 ibid Preamble (13).

49 ibid Preamble (9).

50 Richard A. Matthews and others, 'ByteSize: The New EU Product Liability Directive and its Application to AI, Software and Connected Products' (*Eversheds Sutherland*, 4 July 2024) <https://www.eversheds-sutherland.com/en/czech-republic/insights/bytesize-the-new-eu-product-liability> accessed 19 September 2025.

protection for the manufacturer – a device can meet all the approval criteria yet be found defective if the product fails to perform in a safe way in practice. However, evidence of regulatory compliance may be taken by the court as one consideration when it determines defectiveness.

Accompanying this overhaul, the European Union also considered introspecting a proper AI Liability Directive, to be responsible for the fault-based claims. The European Commission's proposal (in 2022) intended to create measures that lightened the burden on injured parties – for example, rebuttable "presumption of causality" in some cases (putting the burden of proof onto the AI vendor for AI that is likely to have caused injury) and powers for courts to add disclosure requirements for high-risk AI systems.[51] The goal was to assist patients in addressing the challenge of overcoming negligence in the context of complex AI-driven harm scenarios. As of 2025 this proposal hasn't been signed into law: the Commission withdrew the proposal because of a lack of consensus from EU lawmakers.[52] Therefore, at least for now, victims of AI causes of medical injuries in Europe can only rely on the existing strict liability structure or classical negligence law, without the specific presumptions envisioned by the AI-specific proposal.

B. United Kingdom: Consumer Protection Act and Medical Negligence in the AI Era

The United Kingdom, for its part, still reflects the European Union's general approach. The United Kingdom's Consumer Protection Act 1987 – which implemented the old EU directive – is still in force and gives an option to sue under strict liability against manufacturers for defective products.[53] Just like in the EU system, a UK patient only needs to demonstrate that the product in question was defective and caused harm, not necessarily that the manufacturer was negligent. Meanwhile, the law of medical negligence in the United Kingdom holds clinicians to a test of reasonable care (the Bolam test – their actions are judged relative to what a responsible body of medical opinion would do). Currently, there is no AI-specific liability legislation in the United Kingdom. It is watching evolution at the EU level, as the Law Commission has started an examination of whether the United Kingdom regime would need to be updated to make provision for new forms of technology such as AI.[54] In an AI-related injury case nowadays, the UK courts would likely exercise a degree of familiar legal principles: if a patient experiences

51 Proposal for a DIRECTIVE OF THE EUROPEAN PARLIAMENT AND OF THE COUNCIL on adapting non-contractual civil liability rules to artificial intelligence (AI Liability Directive) COM/2022/496 final, 2022/0303 (COD).

52 European Commission, '2025 Commission Work Programme and Annexes' (11 February 2025), Annex IV No. 32 <https://commission.europa.eu/publications/2025-commission-work-programme-and-annexes_en> accessed 19 September 2025.

53 Andrew Austin and others, 'UK Product Liability Reform – New Redress Rules for AI Systems?' (*Freshfields*, 5 August 2025) <https://riskandcompliance.freshfields.com/post/102kz0x/uk-product-liability-reform-new-redress-rules-for-ai-systems> accessed 19 September 2025.

54 ibid.

harm as a result of a faulty product developed with an AI algorithm (for instance, a faulty algorithm for diagnosis in a medical device), the manufacturer could be held strictly liable for such damage under the Consumer Protection Act 1987; if the harm is caused by a clinician's misuse or misinterpretation of an AI tool, the claim would be brought under the concept of clinical negligence based on fault.

Another issue that's arising is that of standard of care as AI tools become more prevalent: could one be considered negligent for not using an established AI for diagnosis or treatment? Some commentators argue that in future, if doctors do not employ a diagnostic aid that is available and highly reliable, they may be found to be in breach of their duty of care by not meeting the evolving standard.[55] Even though this idea hasn't been tested by any court yet, it is widely discussed about in legal literature as a potential liability twist. This prospect puts pressure on regulators to ensure trustworthy AI tools are available and vetted, so that doctors can use them with confidence (and not to be faulted either for using or not using AI).

On the whole, like the situation in the European Union, the UK framework puts the burden of ensuring the safety of AI-powered medical products onto manufacturers (given the background of strict liability) but also holds doctors accountable for its use. A clinician cannot simply blame "the machine" if they are acting in an unreasonable way or ignoring standard medical practice when using an AI tool.

C. United States: Product Liability with Pre-Emption, and the Role of Clinicians

The US system of product liability similarly enables patients to sue product manufacturers based on strict liability or negligence if an AI device is defective. However, the FDA approval process is intertwined with these lawsuits by means of the doctrine of federal pre-emption. Under the US Federal Food, Drug and Cosmetic Act, if the FDA has set specific requirements upon a device (particularly Class III devices, which went through PMA), state tort law cannot place conflicting or additional requirements on the device.[56] The US Supreme Court ruling in *Riegel vs. Medtronic (2008)* ruled that a patient's state law claim that a device was unsafe or incorrectly labelled is pre-empted if the device received FDA PMA approval because the lawsuit would be imposing requirements beyond what the FDA approved for the device.[57] In mundane terms, if an AI were deemed Class III, and it received FDA PMA approval, the manufacturer would be quite shielded from being sued for design defects or warning defects; injured patients in such

55 Frank Griffin, 'Artificial Intelligence and Liability in Health Care' (2021) 31 Health Matrix: Journal of Law-Medicine 65–106, 97–100.

56 For primary US authority, see Federal Food, Drug, and Cosmetic Act, 21 USC § 360k(a); *Riegel v. Medtronic, Inc* 552 US 312 (2008); *Medtronic, Inc v. Lohr* 518 US 470 (1996); *Buckman Co v. Plaintiffs' Legal Committee* 531 US 341 (2001). For explanatory secondary source, see Mindy Duffourc and Sara Gerke, 'Decoding US Tort Liability in Healthcare's Black-Box AI Era: Lessons from the European Union' (2023) 27(1) Stanford Technology Law Review 1–70.

57 *Riegel v. Medtronic, Inc.*, 552 U.S. 312 (2008) (holding that FDA PMA approval preempts state law claims challenging the safety or labelling of that medical device).

cases may have very limited recourse (they may only be able to sue on grounds that parallel the FDA requirements, for example, if the manufacturer had failed to report known issues to FDA). So far, most AI devices in the United States have not been Class III/PMA, so this pre-emption shield has not been test driven widely in the AI environment. But it remains an important difference: an EU or UK patient could always sue a manufacturer for a faulty AI, but in the United States a patient might be barred due to the fact that the AI was given the highest measure of FDA approval. For the many AI tools that have been cleared through 510(k) (which imposes more general requirements), pre-emption does not apply in quite the same broad way, so those manufacturers do face product liability exposure. US device makers also often use the learned intermediary doctrine as a defence against failure-to-warn claims. This doctrine states that a medical product manufacturer has met its duty of warning patients if it gives adequate warnings to the prescribing or supervising physician, who then acts as an "informed intermediary" between the medical product and the patient.[58] In the AI context, if the company was clear about facts that the AI has certain limitations (such as, "This tool can miss certain rare conditions, use clinical judgment"), the company can argue that it is not liable for the injury to a patient because the doctor was properly informed and responsible for a final decision. Courts generally accept this doctrine but there are exceptions – e.g. if the manufacturer knows the product will be used without the physician intermediary; or the "intermediary" is actually the hospital purchasing the AI system. In one notable case, *Taylor v. Intuitive Surgical (2017)*, a state supreme court determined that the surgical robot manufacturer owed a duty to the hospital (as opposed to the surgeons) to provide direct notice and training on use and risk, given that the hospital's decision-making was the key factor in its adoption of the technology.[59] Applied to AI, this means that companies should ensure providing healthcare institutions with AI risks and correct usage in addition to providing information to individual doctors.

US patients have the right to sue clinicians for medical malpractice if AI makes a mistake, and this includes accidental errors, negligence and incorrect diagnoses, among others. One of the most important questions is whether or not employing or relying upon the AI is consistent with the standard of care. Early commentary suggests that doctors do not get to blindly defer to AI – if an AI recommends a wrong diagnosis, it wouldn't be a legal excuse for misdiagnosis if a good doctor would have noticed the mistake.[60] On the other hand, ignoring a correct AI warning could amount to negligence if the majority of one's peers would heed a warning. As with Europe, these scenarios are still emerging, but the existence of AI can't remove clinicians of their duty of care. In the United States, the dynamic

58 *Taylor v. Intuitive Surgical, Inc.*, 389 P.3d 517 (Wash. 2017) (applying learned intermediary doctrine and finding manufacturer had duty to warn hospital about device risks).

59 ibid.

60 Michelle M. Mello and Neel Guha, 'Understanding Liability Risk from Using Health Care Artificial Intelligence Tools' (2024) 390(3) New England Journal of Medicine 271–278. See also *Sampson v. HeartWise Health Systems Corp* 386 So 3d 411 (Ala 2023).

is somewhat different because of litigation patterns: patients arguably might be more prone to suing doctors (who tend to have malpractice insurance) especially if it is difficult or impossible to sue the manufacturer due to pre-emption or other factors making it very hard to prove a defect. This could result in a scenario where US clinicians are more exposed to liability than manufacturers, in comparison with the EU/UK environment. Such fears might also influence adoption – fear of liability might make some US doctors reluctant about using AI or, conversely, over-reliant on it in their defence.

Lawmakers in all jurisdictions are aware that liability rules must achieve a delicate equilibrium between accountability and innovation: the hope is that AI developers are sufficiently motivated to build safe systems and that the clinicians using AI are being prudent. Ultimately, no legal system is placing blame on the AI itself – blame remains on the humans and companies behind the AI. The emerging consensus is one of shared liability: the manufacturers shafted for faulty AI design or implementation of AI tools, then the medical professionals for the proper use of the tool in practice.

VI. Conclusion

While the European Union, United Kingdom and United States have all acknowledged the significance of AI for the healthcare industry, they have taken different regulatory approaches. The European Union's system is an example of a precautionary, comprehensive approach: wide area of regulation, stringent checks before the market and detailed rules (through instruments such as the MDR and AI Act), to minimise risks before and during deployment. The US approach is more innovation-friendly and pragmatic: it calls for existing laws to be adjusted, and where those laws do not suffice, guidance to be used to fill gaps in the law – generally ensuring that AI products can get to market faster under flexible standards, adjusting course with post-market monitoring and accountability if necessary. The United Kingdom is making an attempt to balance in a hybrid fashion: keeping tough baseline protections (and in many cases these are European Union aligned) but adding more flexibility in terms of guidance and iteration over time to encourage responsible innovation. There is convergence on the issues but divergence on regulatory approaches, primarily in the three key areas of classification, adaptivity and transparency as well as liability.

In particular, all three jurisdictions are learning from each other: the European Union has its eyes on the FDA's moves on adaptive AI, the United States and United Kingdom are cognizant of the trust and transparency that more *ex ante* regulation can establish and international alignment is growing (in the form of harmonisation efforts and forums). As AI in healthcare continues to change, these regulatory landscapes will change as well. From a comparative point of view, it seems probable that no approach – be it that of the European Union with its stricter regime or that of the United States with its emphasis on innovation – can claim a monopoly on safety or innovation: the framework of the former will tend to prevent some harm at the expense of speed and flexibility while the latter will encourage innovation at the expense of a competent level of oversight. The ongoing experiment in the United Kingdom could adopt a middle path. Ultimately, regulators from all jurisdictions face a common problem – how to safeguard patients and provide a positive incentive for AI development – and constant dialogue and dynamic policy will be needed. By nesting the strengths of each approach, future AI health governance may shift towards even more cohesion among the public to protect the future of this transformative technology as it advances the state of healthcare and maintains legal and ethical standards.

4 Ethical Principles to Governance Tools

Abstract

This chapter considers how fundamental principles such as transparency, accountability, human oversight and fairness are applied as governance tools in clinical healthcare concerning AI. It includes an understanding of how transparency requirements are operationalised as measures of documentation, labelling and explainability of decision support systems to fight opacity. Accountability is built into conformity evaluations, incident reporting and liability frameworks that ensure developers, institutions and clinicians are accountable for the outcomes of their AI. Human oversight is protected by mandates in the form of regulatory requirements for human-in-the-loop or human-in-command structures, training of clinicians and safeguards against automation; this is the case since we consider human supervision to be an ethical imperative of professional judgement and patient autonomy protection. Fairness is, on the other hand, implemented via criteria for representative data, bias tests for algorithms, checking performance in subgroups and post-market procedures to examine whether there are any discriminatory effects, combining the aspects of equality and non-discrimination as compliance criteria. Drawing on innovations in the EU AI Act, and FDA guidance in the United States and Office for Civil Rights with regard to discrimination and the NHS in the United Kingdom, the chapter illustrates how ethical values underpin legal frameworks. It suggests that although issues will still need to be solved regarding how to balance these principles with innovation, creating these principles within binding obligations is essential to establish trustworthy AI in healthcare.

I. Introduction

AI in clinical care holds great promise, but it also raises fundamental ethical requirements that law and policy must address. Four fundamental values – transparency, accountability, human oversight and fairness – have been identified as pillars for building trustworthy AI in healthcare. These values have achieved broad acceptance in code and policy and are being turned into specific management practices by the authorities. Of note, requirements for the development and implementation of clinical AI systems (e.g. documentation requirements, conformity assessment processes, risk-based classification, human-in-the-loop requirements, liability rules)

DOI: 10.4324/9781003785385-5

are being implemented in the European Union, the United Kingdom and the United States. This chapter considers how each of the ethical principles influences such legal governance tools, and focuses on AI in diagnostics and decision support in healthcare. Following on from previous chapters, which explored AI applications and regulatory contexts, it provides a critical look at some of the more specific mechanisms that are meant to guarantee moral AI practices.

II. Transparency

To mitigate clinical AI's "black box" problem, it's critical to increase transparency, which can help to build the trust of practitioners and patients. Transparency is about providing stakeholders with enough information to understand how an AI system works, what it can and cannot do and why it made a particular decision.[1] In terms of healthcare, this tenet has been translated into various instruments for governance. For instance, AI developers are usually governed by documentation requirements: according to the EU AI Act 2024, providers of high-risk AI systems are required to prepare technical documentation outlining the design of their model, types of data used to train the model, performance metrics and risk management procedures employed.[2] Such documentation makes it easier to both review the AI in light of the regulations and to provide "meaningful public scrutiny" of how the AI is built and used.[3] It also supports medical device regulations for transparency in technical files and instructions for use.

Transparency is further ensured and enforced through *information duties* to users. In clinical contexts, this means that AI tools need to be accompanied by appropriate labelling information and by user manuals, describing the intended use of the product, basic and relevant clinical characteristics, socially and ethically acceptable use and the potential limitations. EU law now requires high-risk AI systems to be accompanied by clear instructions and information for clinicians so that they can understand the system's logic and how it should be used.[4] Disclosure is also a prominent regulatory issue in the United States. The FDA, along with international counterparts, has set forth guidelines on *Transparency of Machine*

1 World Health Organization, *Ethics and Governance of Artificial Intelligence for Health* (WHO Guidance, 28 June 2021) 26–27 <https://www.ictworks.org/wp-content/uploads/2021/10/who-ethics-artificial-intelligence-healt.pdf> accessed 1 October 2025. See also FDA, Health Canada and MHRA, 'Transparency of Machine Learning-Enabled Medical Devices: Guiding Principles' (13 June 2024) <https://www.fda.gov/media/179269/download?attachment> accessed 1 October 2025.

2 Bernd Schmidt, 'Transparency Obligations in Data and Digital Law – First Steps Towards Compliance with the AI Act, Data Act, and Co.' (*Planit Legal*, 16 June 2025) <https://planit.legal/en/transparency-obligations-in-data-and-digital-law-first-steps-towards-compliance-with-the-ai-act-data-act-and-co/> accessed 1 October 2025. Regarding the documentation obligations of the EU AI Act, see Articles 11, 13 and 50 of the EU AI Act.

3 World Health Organization (n 1) 26–27.

4 Kicky Gerhilde van Leeuwen, Leon Doorn and Erik Gelderblom, 'The AI Act: Responsibilities and Obligations for Healthcare Professionals and Organizations' (29 May 2025) Diagnostic and Interventional Radiology (Advance online publication). DOI: 10.4274/dir.2025.252851.

Learning-Enabled Medical Devices, emphasising the need for all information that impacts risks and outcomes to be communicated to those using or affected by the AI (clinicians, patients, etc.).[5] This means having clarity about how the AI is intended to be used, how it was trained (source of training data) and understanding how its outputs are to be interpreted. Indeed, transparency at all stages of an AI's lifecycle is considered to be a crucial factor for safety: it ensures that knowledge that might affect risk and patient outcomes is shared with everyone who works with the device.[6]

The second tool is the *algorithmic explainability requirements*. While it may be the case that complex machine learning models are difficult to interpret, governance requirements can require at least interpretability for a model's output – or for explanations appropriate to the expertise of the intended end user.[7] For example, if there's a diagnosis that would have been suggested by the supporting AI model, the system could show the user which of the data's features or factors were most important in leading to that diagnosis. The United Kingdom's NHS guidance says systems must be "explicable" to people who use them, and beyond that there is a risk to trust in not being able to explain why a system has made a decision.[8] Under the principle of interpretability, clinicians should be able to get a reason for an AI recommendation, and patients have the right to be informed about when they are under AI care. Several jurisdictions are considering making patient notification a predicate for AI substantially influential in clinical decision-making. The EU AI Act doesn't require patient-facing disclosure for most medical AI (because there's a human professional in the loop), but it does demand that health professionals (the users of the AI tool) are appropriately informed about the tool's functioning and limitations so they in turn can make meaningful disclosures to patients.[9]

This procedure increases transparency as well as the opportunity for critical comment. As the technology in use may be proprietary, extensive documentation and explanation can place a heavy burden on developers, and could leak proprietary information. Furthermore, transparency runs counter to what actually occurs in practice: many state-of-the-art diagnostic algorithms (i.e. deep neural networks) are inherently opaque, and attempts to simplify into a more transparent process may be of limited value. In my view, regulators can take a balanced approach – requiring documentation, meaningful efforts at explainability and detailed disclosures – without the need for actual algorithmic source code transparency that could be impossible. The goal here is to prevent the non-understanding of the clinicians about how an AI arrives at its conclusions as this could lead to the erosion of

5 FDA, Health Canada and MHRA (n 1).

6 ibid.

7 World Health Organization (n 1) 27.

8 Department of Health & Social Care, 'A Guide to Good Practice for Digital and Data-driven Health Technologies' (*GOV.UK*, 19 January 2021), Principle 1 <https://www.gov.uk/government/publications/code-of-conduct-for-data-driven-health-and-care-technology/initial-code-of-conduct-for-data-driven-health-and-care-technology> accessed 1 October 2025.

9 Article 14 of the EU AI Act.

professional responsibility and trust from patients.[10] In short, while certain challenges still remain in defining just how deep and wide transparency can (or should) go, AI systems have been transplantable into a set of concrete obligations (documentation, labelling, explanation) that render them more inspectable and understandable, if not straightforwardly adopted.

III. Accountability

Accountability, a medical principle stating that a person or entity must be held accountable for clinical decisions made with assistance from AI technology. It calls for clear assignment of responsibility for the development, deployment and use of AI in healthcare.[11] This principle is influencing regulatory instruments that vary from *ex ante* evaluation regimes to *ex post* liability regimes. Therefore, a principal approach is the *risk classification* and *conformity assessment* of AI systems before they are used in clinical practice. By designating most healthcare AI (namely the diagnostic algorithms) as high-risk technologies, regulators can ensure the systems are subject to rigorous third-party oversight. In the European Union, many AI-based medical devices already fall under the provisions of the Medical Devices Regulation 2017/745, and the AI Act adds that AI that has considerable potential influence on health should be considered "high risk" – the device is subject to rigorous requirements for safety, transparency and monitoring.[12] Before a high-risk AI tool can be marketed for clinical use, the provider will need to establish a robust *risk management system* and undergo a *conformity assessment* which will confirm that the system indeed meets all requirements (accuracy, cybersecurity, transparency, etc.). This process takes advantage of the idea of accountability by making the developers accountable for ensuring that the products meet the necessary risk standards, and to perform a third-party audit and certification for their claims.[13] In other words, conformity assessments are a responsibility checkpoint that requires developers to take the ball by the horns before the product can cause harm.

Even after AI systems have been deployed, there is always the question of accountability. Governance measures include pursuing mandatory ongoing monitoring and reporting of practices so that problems can be identified and addressed. For example, EU law obliges deployers (e.g. hospitals using a high-risk AI system) to monitor the performance of the AI they're using and log any incidents or malfunctions, sharing these logs with regulators and the manufacturer.[14] These obligations to maintain records and report incidents result in an audit trail from which it should then be possible to investigate what went wrong when an adverse event occurs (for instance due to a diagnosis error made by an AI) and who was

10 Hannah R. Sullivan and Scott J. Schweikart, 'Are Current Tort Liability Doctrines Adequate for Addressing Injury Caused by AI?' (2019) 21(2) AMA Journal of Ethics E 160–166.

11 World Health Organization (n 1) 28.

12 Leeuwen, Doorn and Gelderblom (n 4).

13 ibid.

14 Article 26(5) of the EU AI Act.

responsible. The principle of accountability also informs new governance bodies and roles. Some hospitals have done the same – adopting AI oversight committees – and the EU AI Act itself predicts that users will have human supervisors who have the power to step in if the AI acts anomalously.[15] By setting aside responsible people ("human oversight" personnel or safety officers), organisations can ensure that there are identified people who are responsible for the action of the AI – they can take action if things go wrong.

Perhaps the most intricate of governance tools under accountability is the *model of liability* for harm caused by AI. For decades, when a doctor made a mistake that harmed a patient, the doctor (and the doctor's employer) could be held liable under the theory of malpractice, and when a medical device malfunctioned, the manufacturer could be held liable under the theory of medical products liability. AI adds layers of complexity to this divide where mistakes can arise from arcane algorithmic processes as opposed to obvious human incompetence or a physical defect in the product. In order to ensure responsibility, legal systems are evolving. Existing tort doctrines in the United States are being stretched: if, in the United States, a physician who relies on AI is considered to have failed to meet the professional standard of care, he could still be found negligent, but if the AI is FDA-approved and the physician uses it as intended, the liability could be placed on the manufacturer based on product liability.[16] Some commentators have identified a potential "accountability gap" arising from AI's lack of explainability, which means that traditional rules will be difficult to apply in cases where AI's decision-making is difficult to understand.[17] In response, policymakers are thinking about new approaches. The White House's blueprint for the 2022 AI Bill of Rights (which, although not law, carries significant implications for those who want to use advanced technologies like AI in the United States) highlighted the importance of AI operators being held accountable for adhering to these principles.[18]

Europe is one step closer to developing a refined liability scheme. The European Commission has proposed an AI Liability Directive to alleviate some of the difficulties that victims of AI face in establishing fault in an AI case.[19] Notably, it would have established a rebuttable presumption of causality: if one can prove that a provider breached a duty of care (e.g. violated safety requirements) and that the output

15 Article 14 of the EU AI Act.

16 George Maliha and others, 'Artificial Intelligence and Liability in Medicine: Balancing Safety and Innovation' (2021) 99(3) The Milbank Quarterly 629–647.

17 Sullivan and Schweikart (n 10).

18 The White House of Washington, 'The Blueprint for an AI Bill of Rights: Making Automated Systems Work for the American People' (October 2022) <https://marketingstorageragrs.blob.core.windows.net/webfiles/Blueprint-for-an-AI-Bill-of-Rights.pdf> accessed 2 October 2025.

19 Proposal for a DIRECTIVE OF THE EUROPEAN PARLIAMENT AND OF THE COUNCIL on adapting non-contractual civil liability rules to artificial intelligence (AI Liability Directive) COM/2022/496 final, 2022/0303 (COD). However, it was withdrawn in 2025, see European Commission, '2025 Commission Work Programme and Annexes' (11 February 2025), Annex IV No. 32 <https://commission.europa.eu/publications/2025-commission-work-programme-and-annexes_en> accessed 19 September 2025.

of an AI system likely caused harm, then the burden shifts to a provider to prove that the link between the cause and the harm is improbable.[20] This proposal was an attempt to make sure that those hurt by opaque AI systems are not left without recourse because they can't untangle the algorithm's inner workings. In its stead, the European Union rewrote general product liability law: the new Product Liability Directive (adopted in 2024) explicitly applies to software and AI and even contains a rebuttable presumption of defect if an AI system is so complex that it becomes unreasonably challenging for the victim to show a defect in the system.[21] In other words, if a product is likely to have caused harm due to the actions of an autonomous diagnostic AI but there's no way to pinpoint any specific "defect", then a court may assume the product was defective unless the manufacturer establishes otherwise. This development reflects a fairness and accountability issue that is shifting tort law in the direction of decreasing the evidentiary requirements from injured patients – holding AI makers more responsible for harms associated with their products.

In the United Kingdom, there is not yet an AI-specific liability Act and liability must be met on an existing statute (negligence and product liability under the Consumer Protection Act 1987). However, UK regulators and professional bodies emphasise that if AI is deployed it does not remove the duty of care for providers of healthcare. NHS advice states that it is important for clinicians using AI decision-support to be responsible for the final decision and not to uncritically defer to the outputs of algorithms.[22] Further, the General Medical Council states that it is a doctor's responsibility to question and validate AI recommendations as part of good practice.[23] These soft-law signals help provide continued support for the accountability principle, most importantly by holding human professionals accountable based on their duty of prudent integration of AI into care, and AI developers will be expected to contribute to the accountability, in several ways, such as providing transparent information and fail-safes. This does bring with it the danger of shared responsibility: if everyone – developer, hospital, clinician – is part-responsible, then there's a danger to fall into the trap that no one in practice will be fully responsible. Thus, a clear division of responsibilities is essential. In all three jurisdictions (EU, UK, US), emerging laws are moving towards defining obligations at every point in the AI lifecycle so that there will be identifiable people, organisations or

20 Petra Holmberg, 'AI in Healthcare and the Liability Vacuum in EU Law' (*Health Law Blog Sweden*, 5 May 2025) <https://healthlawsweden.blogg.lu.se/2025/05/05/ai-in-healthcare-and-the-liability-vacuum-in-eu-law/#_ftn18> accessed 2 October 2025.

21 Directive (EU) 2024/2853 of the European Parliament and of the Council of 23 October 2024 on liability for defective products and repealing Council Directive 85/374/EEC, Articles 9 and 10.

22 Department of Health & Social Care (n 8) Principle 1.

23 General Medical Council, 'Understanding Doctors' Experiences of Using Artificial Intelligence (AI) in the UK: A Qualitative Research Study for the GMC' (November 2024), 27 <https://www.gmc-uk.org/-/media/documents/understanding-doctors--experiences-of-using-artificial-intelligence--ai--in-the-uk_pdf-109934543.pdf> accessed 2 October 2025. See also General Medical Council, 'Good Practice in Proposing, Prescribing, Providing and Managing Medicines and Devices' (18 February 2021, updated 13 December 2024), 7 <https://www.gmc-uk.org/-/media/documents/prescribing-guidance-updated-english-20210405_pdf-85260533.pdf> accessed 2 October 2025.

institutions to hold responsible for the functioning of AI. While it still remains very difficult to account for the chain of accountability when complex AI systems err, the combination of *ex ante* controls (e.g. conformity assessments) and *ex post* liability adjustments is beginning to take shape to shore up the ethical mandate that AI in healthcare be accompanied by accountability and mechanisms for redress.[24]

IV. Human Oversight

Human oversight (sometimes called "human-in-the-loop" or "human-in-command") is an ethic related closely to human autonomy and safety. In the medical context, this means that AI should not be seen as replacing human judgement in clinical decision-making, but should be acting within the human context, under appropriate human governance. As expressed in the WHO's statement, upholding human autonomy in healthcare means humans would have to continue to be in control of healthcare systems and medical decisions even when AI tools are used.[25] This principle ensures that humans are never relied upon too heavily to create automated outputs and that there are responsible humans in place who can step in to avoid harm. Regulatory regimes have codified the tools of control with the intent of human oversight. The EU AI Act specifically calls for high-risk AI systems to be designed and deployed in a manner that ensures effective human oversight is in place.[26] In practice, this means that those developing AI must program in features that allow for human oversight and intervention. For example, a diagnostic assistant could feature a simple interface that presents alerts or levels of uncertainty to the clinicians to give them an idea of when and how to explore an issue further. The system should be designed such that the human user can override or switch off the AI's function if it is not functioning as intended or if it is returning implausible results.[27] Article 14 of the AI Act contains specific provisions for oversight: the AI oversight bodies must be able to understand the limitations of an AI, identify anomalies and mistakes and be able to refuse to use the AI system or otherwise ignore or override its output where applicable.[28] In fact, in some high-stakes applications (an AI automatically recognising patients based on biometric data for example), it is even mandatory by law that no final action be taken without confirmation by two human officials.[29] These measures are implementing the oversight principle through the hard-coding of a role for human judgement in the workflow of AI systems.

Beyond the features of a design, policies and standards help to reinforce human oversight in the clinical field. Many jurisdictions require AI systems for diagnosis or treatment decision-support to be cleared by regulatory bodies not for

24 World Health Organization (n 1) 44–45.
25 ibid, 143.
26 Article 14 of the EU AI Act.
27 ibid.
28 Article 14(4)(d) of the EU AI Act.
29 Article 14(5) of the EU AI Act.

use as a sort of autonomous decision-maker but only for assistive purposes. The US FDA, for example, has cleared AI algorithms on the condition that they are being used as help to a qualified physician, who takes full responsibility for interpreting the results.[30] The FDA's regulatory labels frequently contain text such as "For clinical decision support – not intended to be used as the sole basis for diagnosis or treatment decisions".[31] Such conditions, while not always couched as "oversight" per se, really amount to a human-in-the-loop. Similarly, professional guidelines (i.e. from the AMA as well as from specialty colleges) emphasise the importance of clinicians exercising their own judgement in using AI recommendations, and to be trained in the appropriate use and limitations of the AI.[32] The United Kingdom's NHS Code of Conduct for data-driven health technologies incorporates the principles of "human-centred design", and oversight, to guide the use of AI that is meant to supplement rather than replace clinical staff, and workflows should be designed to ensure professionals can review and, if needed, correct the AI outputs.[33]

Human supervision is also connected to *training* and *competency* needs. Not only is keeping humans in control a technical issue, it is also an issue of human preparedness. The EU AI Act requires that deployers of high-risk AI (such as hospitals) ensure that their staff are trained in the proper use of the AI system; specifically how to read the results and when to intervene or shut down the system.[34] This is part of a governance strategy of empowering human operators to do their overseeing job well. In awareness that supervision is only as successful as the understandings of the user, some institutions within the United States have also started to implement "clinician training programs" for AI systems.[35] By codifying the need for training, regulators put meaning and substance to the human-in-the-loop principle: it's not sufficient to nominally have a human in the loop; that person must be

30 European Society of Radiology, 'Summary of the Proceedings of the International Forum 2021: "A more visible radiologist can never be replaced by AI"' (2022) 13 Insights Imaging 43, 2.

31 See, for instance, 21 CFR § 866.3181 – Cytomegalovirus nucleic acid detection device for congenital cytomegalovirus infection.

32 Federation of State Medical Boards, *Navigating the Responsible and Ethical Incorporation of Artificial Intelligence into Clinical Practice* (April 2024) 5 <https://www.fsmb.org/siteassets/advocacy/policies/incorporation-of-ai-into-practice.pdf> accessed 2 October 2025.

33 National Health Service, *Artificial Intelligence in Health and Care Award 2020 Call for Applications* (15 January 2020) 4 <https://www.england.nhs.uk/aac/wp-content/uploads/sites/50/2020/01/ai-award-2020-call-for-applications-v1.pdf> accessed 2 October 2025. See also British Medical Association, *Principles for Artificial Intelligence (AI) and its Application in Healthcare* (2024) 19 <https://www.bma.org.uk/media/njgfbmnn/bma-principles-for-artificial-intelligence-ai-and-its-application-in-healthcare.pdf> accessed 2 October 2025.

34 Preamble 20 and 91 of the EU AI Act. See also Leeuwen, Doorn and Gelderblom (n 4).

35 See, for example, Patrick Boyle, 'Medical Schools Move from Worrying about AI to Teaching It' (*Association of American Medical Colleges*, 15 May 2025) <https://www.aamc.org/news/medical-schools-move-worrying-about-ai-teaching-it> accessed 2 October 2025; Bobbie Collins, 'New Courses Respond to Rapid Adoption of AI in Health Care' (*Harvard Medical School*, 17 October 2024) <https://hms.harvard.edu/news/new-courses-respond-rapid-adoption-ai-health-care> accessed 2 October 2025.

able to provide meaningful oversight, otherwise oversight becomes a euphemism for a fully automated system that goes unsupervised.

The human oversight principle is a response to widely documented *automation biases*, which are defined as the human propensity to follow an automated recommendation, even when it's incorrect. Governance tools attempt to counter this through both technical and procedural means (e.g. requiring AI systems to signal uncertainty and requiring humans to confirm important AI-driven decisions). Article 14 of the AI Act, for example, specifically states that users should be alerted to the risk of "automation bias" and should not put blind trust in the AI.[36] From an academic perspective, some experts have argued that too much exploitation of human oversight might actually pose a loophole: if there is an underlying safety system that is unsafe, having a human supervisor might not really reduce the risk, if the human is involved in the process and simply defers to the machine.[37] Knowing this, regulators often bundle oversight requirements together with other safeguards (such as accuracy parameters or fail-safety mechanisms) to ensure that oversight achieves its goal.[38]

In summary, the human oversight principle has been translated into the law in the form of an AI's inability to function as an unconstrained autonomous entity in the field of patient care. There would always need to be a capable human in the loop or in some supervisory capacity, with the backing and ability to override AI. This scheme of governance respects the autonomy of human beings and is encoded with the ethical mandate that technology is a tool in the hands of professionals and not a substitute for their judgement.[39] It also gives patients the assurance that they have an accountable human being – bound by professional standards – ultimately responsible for their care on behalf of which their trust in the clinical process is maintained, despite the proliferation of AI tools.

V. Fairness

This principle of fairness in AI for healthcare includes both non-discrimination and fair benefit sharing. It calls for AI systems to be free of biases towards any population, and for all patients to receive a similar standard of care and outcomes through AI-assisted medicine.[40] In particular, there are quite serious concerns that AI algorithms' ability to identify health conditions and risks could be systematically compromised by poor representation in training data and/or underlying societal

36 Article 14(4)(b) of the EU AI Act.

37 For instance, see Ben Green, 'The Flaws of Policies Requiring Human Oversight of Government Algorithms' (2022) 45 Computer Law & Security Review 105681.

38 See, for example, Articles 14 and 15(3)–(4) of the EU AI Act.

39 World Health Organization (n 1) 143.

40 UNESCO, *Recommendation on the Ethics of Artificial Intelligence* (24 November 2021) 20–21 <https://unesdoc.unesco.org/ark:/48223/pf0000381137> accessed 2 October 2025. See also Irene Dankwa-Mullan, 'Health Equity and Ethical Considerations in Using Artificial Intelligence in Public Health and Medicine' (2024) 21 Preventing Chronic Disease E64.

biases in putting these capabilities into practice, resulting in a worsening of health inequalities (e.g. minority ethnic groups or women).[41] Governance tools are therefore becoming more focused on providing bias mitigation and on equitable AI design and deployment. One underlying mechanism is the need for a variety of representative training data. The EU AI Act incorporates this into what it requires for providers of high-risk AI: providers must use training, validation and testing data sets that are sufficiently broad and representative "to the best extent possible" to reduce the amount of algorithmic bias.[42] Data governance provisions of the AI Act require data to be checked for potential gaps and bias and call for appropriate statistical methods to be applied that work to avoid discriminatory results.[43] Likewise, the FDA's review process for AI-based medical devices increasingly looks at performance within various groups of people; an AI model that performs well overall but poorly within a subset group (for instance, a particular demographic) may find itself questioned, or in need of improving, before its medical device is cleared.[44] Such regulatory scrutiny encourages developers to consider fairness issues while developing – e.g. put balanced data into the development or bias correction algorithms.

Another important tool consists in applying formal algorithmic impact analysis for the purpose of non-discrimination requirements. The US Department of Health and Human Services has recently gone a step further: it has published a proposed rule implementing Section 1557 of the Affordable Care Act (the landmark medical discrimination law) that would require the bias auditing of CDS tools (including AI) that are used by health systems and other health-related organisations. Specifically, covered entities "must make reasonable efforts to determine whether their decision support tools use protected traits (like race, sex, or disability) as inputs" and, if so, "must make reasonable efforts to mitigate the risk of discrimination" that might result.[45] Pursuant to this new law, hospitals and insurers would be required to perform bias audits of AI tools they implement, and to implement corrective measures (altering the tool or its policies of use) if disparate impact is deemed possible.[46] The enforcement of this rule, from 2025 on, means that fairness

41 Natalia Norori and others, 'Addressing bias in Big Data and AI for Health Care: A Call for Open Science' (2021) 2(10) Patterns 100347. See also Ziad Obermeyer and others, 'Dissecting Racial bias in an Algorithm Used to Manage the Health of Populations' (2019) 366(6464) Science 447–453.

42 Article 10(3) of the EU AI Act.

43 Article 10(2)(h) of the EU AI Act.

44 FDA, *Artificial Intelligence-Enabled Device Software Functions: Lifecycle Management and Marketing Submission Recommendations* (January 2025) FDA-2024-D-4488, 18–24 <https://www.fda.gov/media/184856/download> accessed 2 October 2025. See also Liz Richardson, 'FDA Review Can Limit Bias Risks in Medical Devices Using Artificial Intelligence' (*Pew Charitable Trusts*, 7 October 2021) <https://www.pew.org/en/research-and-analysis/articles/2021/10/07/fda-review-can-limit-bias-risks-in-medical-devices-using-artificial-intelligence> accessed 2 October 2025.

45 Michelle M. Mello and Jessica L. Roberts, 'Antidiscrimination Law Meets Artificial Intelligence – New Requirements for Health Care Organizations and Insurers' (2024) 5(8) JAMA Health Forum e243397.

46 ibid.

is not a matter of abstract ideals but is, instead, a question of compliance: failure to address types of bias that are identified is potentially risky for institutions in terms of determining that it has committed unlawful discrimination, and is therefore subject to investigation or liability. Importantly, the United States approach holds health providers, rather than AI developers, responsible for ensuring the fairness of AI in practice, thus driving market incentives for AI developers to provide needed data concerning the bias testing of their algorithms.[47] What we should see here is one of the first instances of governance innovation linking the principle of fairness to a pre-existing civil rights law in a way that gives the moral principle legal force.

On the industry side, soft governance mechanisms including best practices and standards are under development to increase the chance of fairness. Organisations such as the Institute of Electrical and Electronics Engineers (IEEE) and the International Organization for Standardization (ISO) are working on technical standards for testing algorithms for algorithmic bias and managing the risk of algorithmic bias. In healthcare specifically, the current international standard IEC 62304 (for health software), as well as recently proposed draft ISO standard on AI risk management, encourage developers to incorporate risk controls for "information bias", backed up with records of performance differences across subgroups in the population.[48] The guidance the United Kingdom's NHS has adopted for AI's uptake has a similar focus on addressing "inequalities": It encourages processes to be in place to ensure that AI is not used in a way that inadvertently under-serves protected communities and recommends that a range of stakeholders are involved in the design and validation of tools.[49] Some NHS trusts have started to ask for proof that a proposed application of AI was tested in populations similar to those seen in the local population, as a condition of procurement. These have the advantage that they ensure inclusion from the outset in a way that is consistent with the fairness principle.

Another government level for ensuring fairness is post-market analysis. We know that even well-intentioned AI has the potential to behave in a manner that's unfair in the field due to correlations or context of deployment that no one identified as an issue until the AI was deployed. As such, the EU AI Act requires operators of high-risk AI systems to implement monitoring and reporting mechanisms that include an oversight capability to monitor for "discriminatory impacts or other adverse effects on fundamental rights".[50] If correctly identified errors for a subgroup persist over time, the provider will be expected to provide corrective action or remove the system. Under the new US rule, the Office for Civil Rights will

47 ibid.

48 ISO, *IEC 62304:2006 Medical Device Software – Software Life Cycle Processes* (2006) <https://www.iso.org/obp/ui/en/#iso:std:iec:62304:ed-1:v1:en> accessed 2 October 2025; AAMI, *CR34971:2022 Guidance on the Application of ISO 14971 to Artificial Intelligence and Machine Learning* (2022) <https://www.accessdata.fda.gov/scripts/cdrh/cfdocs/cfStandards/detail.cfm?standard__identification_no=43891> accessed 2 October 2025.

49 Department of Health & Social Care (n 8) Principle 1.

50 Articles 9 and 72 of the EU AI Act.

examine complaints of bias in AI-enabled clinical decisions,[51] enabling patients or patient advocates to request an investigation when they believe an AI tool is leading to biased results. This enforcement by complaint serves as a backstop to identify fairness problems left undetected by initial testing.

When put to work, however, the fairness principle also collides with certain complexities and controversies. Specifically, proposing operational definitions of "fairness" is difficult. Different measures (e.g. outcomes parity or outcomes for all groups) compete with each other, and have to be balanced with other clinical values such as accuracy. For example, optimising an algorithm's performance for a minority group may have the side effect of hurting overall performance through trade-offs in model optimisation; is this justified? There is ethical justification for this, many people provide positive answer from this perspective, but from the legal angle, the manufacturers are afraid that they will be labelled "defective" if they knowingly choose to release a less accurate model in the name of fairness.[52] Regulators have started to provide guidance: both the EU regulations and the US Office for Civil Rights rules seem to suggest that a desire to avoid unjust discrimination is part of what it means for an AI to be both trustworthy and compliant.[53] Indeed, *diversity* and *non-discrimination* are a specific lens through which to understand the European Commission's ethical guidelines and the concept of "Trustworthy AI", as they are clearly expressed as a core expectation, along with accuracy and privacy.[54] Courts and agencies, it is likely, would regard a grossly biased outcome from AI as inconsistent with the standard of care or as an example of indirect discrimination on the part of the institution deploying the AI.

There is also some debate about whether sensitive attributes should be used in the algorithms. While fairness may justify the inclusion of a patient's race or ethnicity as an input in order to adjust for baseline differences (for example, to prevent a diagnostic algorithm from being biased towards the majority population), anti-discrimination laws are very cautious about the use of characteristics that are protected by law. The US law strikes a balance between the right to use characteristics such as race or age in algorithms which are clinically necessary or otherwise in evidence-based medicine and prohibiting the use of such characteristics if arbitrary or discriminatory.[55] This is an example of an approach to governance that is subtle because not every fact of difference in treatment is unfair, and indeed sometimes there need to be different inputs to bring about fairness in terms of outcomes (the

51 Mello and Roberts (n 45).

52 Paul Ohm, 'Debunking AI's Supposed Fairness-Accuracy Tradeoff' (*Jotwell*, 7 May 2024) <https://cyber.jotwell.com/debunking-ais-supposed-fairness-accuracy-tradeoff/> accessed 2 October 2025.

53 Article 10 of the EU AI Act; Department of Health and Human Services, Office for Civil Rights, *Nondiscrimination in Health Programs and Activities* (Final Rule, published 4 Oct. 2023, effective 2024) <https://www.federalregister.gov/documents/2024/05/06/2024-08711/nondiscrimination-in-health-programs-and-activities> accessed 2 October 2025 (amending 45 CFR 92 to address clinical algorithms).

54 World Health Organization (n 1) 29–30, 54–57 and 67.

55 Mello and Roberts (n 45).

principle of substantive equality). Law and policy are therefore struggling with ways to allow *affirmative fairness measures* (for example, intentionally targeting algorithms towards underserved populations) without contravening the conventions of anti-discrimination.

In conclusion, the ethical imperative of fairness has spawned a strong principle of governance intervention, including required assessment of bias, data standards for representativeness, transparency requirements related to the development of AI (to allow external reviewers to identify biases) as well as legal liability for discriminatory impacts. These interventions in the EU, UK and US contexts aim to ensure that AI tools do no harm in the sense of perpetuating health inequalities – instead, they are ideally supposed to be tools for diminishing human biases and equity. The success or otherwise of these measures will be dependent on strict implementation and the technical capability to identify and correct the effects of bias. Nevertheless, the pattern is obvious: fairness is no longer a vague consideration, but rather an emerging compliance condition, determining how AI in healthcare is developed, tested and regulated, in order to ensure the basic legal and ethical right of equality in healthcare.

VI. Conclusion

From concept to practice, AI governance in clinical healthcare is being reconceptualised based on core ethical values. Transparency, accountability, human oversight and fairness are not some abstract ideals, but are positively directing the creation of laws, regulations and standards that attempt to make AI a trustworthy adjunct to medicine. Each principle maps to concrete legal instruments – be it the explainability and technical documents emerging of transparency; accountability, with its implications in terms of liability reforms and audits; the oversight mechanisms with their mandatory human-in-the-loop control mechanisms, or bias mitigation measures for fairness. As this chapter has demonstrated, such principles have already been enshrined in emerging frameworks such as the EU AI Act, in national policies such as the NHS guidelines and US federal rules, as well as in industry practices. Together, they represent a new but important governing framework of AI in health.

It is clear that ethical principles exert significant normative influence: they set the agenda for policy makers and are the justifying ground for enforcing new obligations for developers and users of AI. However, there are still open questions about how to properly balance these principles in practice. Tensions can arise – e.g. making an AI model fully transparent might go against intellectual property protections, or even security (too much transparency invites gaming of the system). Maximising fairness might entail interventions that make accountability more complex (if multiple stakeholders must coordinate in order to monitor bias, who's accounted for in the event of a failure); sticking to human oversight might slow down processes and make less efficient use of gains in efficiency that might be provided by AI processes. These are problems to the point of continuing critical analysis. Moreover, the enforcement of these governance tools will be important. Good standards in theory do not automatically translate to good AI in practice;

supervisory bodies will need resources and skills to examine adherence (e.g. verifying that documentation is honest or audits around bias are sufficient), and healthcare organisations will need ethics as a culture to back up regulations.

However, the direction is clear: ethical values are gradually finding their way into the binding requirements of the law. This convergence between ethics and governance is particularly prominent in the area of healthcare, where trust is of the utmost importance. By implementing transparency, accountability, human oversight and fairness by law into the framework that surrounds clinical AI, society is making attempts to ensure that these technologies improve care without compromising fundamental rights and professional values. Over the next few years, these governance tools will be tested based on how well they can successfully prevent harm and bias as well as how they can scale with the increased complexity of AI models (like adaptive AI or generative AI in medicine). Persistent refinement based on the empirical results as well as moral introspection will be needed. Chapter 5 will go on to look in more detail at specific case studies and governance challenges, but the groundwork that has been laid here is promising: it's an argument that ethical principles debated at the theoretical level are now catalysing the development of a more responsible and human-centric legal framework for AI in healthcare. While the combination of ethics and governance tools is not only desirable for advancing AI's path to safe and effective application, this coupling is ultimately necessary to ensure the operationalisation of the ideal of "trustworthy AI" in the healing professions.

Part II

Core Legal Risk Domains (Patient-Centred Sequence)

5 Data Governance and Privacy

Abstract

This chapter analyses how AI-enabled clinical care can be made lawful and trustworthy through concrete data-governance techniques rather than slogans. It charts the irresolvable tensions (purpose limitation vs. secondary uses for model training; data minimisation vs performance "data hunger" and de-identification's limits given the risks of re-identification) and sees how these are dealt with under EU (GDPR plus the AI Act's Article 10 data governance duties), UK (UK GDPR/DPA 2018, common law confidentiality and CAG approvals) and US (HIPAA's entity based model; OCR's non-discrimination guidance, and FDA's GMLP, or Good Machine Learning Practice/PCCP lifecycle oversight) frameworks. Building on these frameworks, it makes pragmatic suggestions on how to protect privacy against unintended or unbalanced modes of model performance (e.g. data protection impact assessments, or DPIAs, strong role-based access and retention controls, contractual and cross-border transfer rules, subgroup performance monitoring, continuous bias audit) to ensure that privacy is not sacrificed for safe and equitable model performance. It proposes two important tools (the Privacy Impact Matrix and a concentrate Clinician's Checklist) to translate the doctrine into employable steps for hospitals and developers. The chapter argues for the necessity of good data stewardship as not an ambiguity on innovation, but the degree for trustworthy clinical AI at scale.

I. Introduction

AI systems in clinical care are based on enormous troves of patient data. From the use of diagnostic algorithms in acknowledging health to clinical decision support systems that help to highlight future conditions of patients, these systems offer promises for a better healthcare delivery system only if they are in some way able to manage sensitive information regarding healthcare. Robust data governance and privacy safeguards are therefore not add-ons – they are a part of building patient trust and remaining legal.[1] This chapter provides a critical analysis of

1 New York State Dental Association, 'OCR Issues Guidance on AI in Health Care' (11 January 2025) <https://www.nysdental.org/news-publications/news/2025/01/11/ocr-issues-guidance-on-ai-in-health-care> accessed 21 October 2025.

DOI: 10.4324/9781003785385-7

how issues of privacy and governance of data present in AI-enabled healthcare, and compares regulatory responses in the European Union, United Kingdom and United States. It focuses on the handling of clinical data for AI, including lawful bases for the use of data, risks of re-identification of data, secondary use of data for model training and the tension between data minimisation principles and AI's hunger for big data. Practical tools – including a Privacy Impact Matrix and a Clinician's Data Checklist – are contained so that these issues can be converted into practical issues.

II. Data Governance Challenges in AI-Enabled Clinical Care

AI works best with data: machine-learning models frequently require huge amounts of data (diverse, large and high-quality) in order to generate accurate and unbiased results.[2] In the case of healthcare, it means that algorithms are being fed sensitive personal health information (PHI) from electronic health records, medical images, genomic data, etc. Such large-scale consumption of data presents specific governance challenges. The first issue refers to secondary use and limitation of purpose. Patient data being collected for treatment is now being repurposed for use in training algorithms – a different use than was originally intended for clinical purposes. Privacy regimes such as the European Union's GDPR[3] ensure that purpose limitation is enshrined, i.e. any further processing should be compatible with the original purpose or have a separate legal basis.[4] In practice, utilising clinical data for the development of AI may often amount to a secondary use (e.g. research or product development), which requires careful legal justification (such as patient consent or an exemption for research). The NHS in England, for example, recommends that if AI developers will use patient records to train algorithms, identifiable information should be removed "wherever possible" and any use of confidential patient data without consent should be approved by an independent governance body.[5] This serves as an underline that the reuse of health data for AI is high-risk in itself and often needs some additional oversight.

Another challenge is data minimisation and data hunger. Both GDPR (and UK GDPR) and the US HIPAA codify a principle of collecting and using the minimum

2 Article 10 of the EU AI Act.

3 Regulation (EU) 2016/679 of the European Parliament and of the Council of 27 April 2016 on the protection of natural persons with regard to the processing of personal data and on the free movement of such data (General Data Protection Regulation) OJ L119/1.

4 Article 5(1)(b) of the EU GDPR; see also Mark J. Taylor, 'Health Research, Data Protection, and the Public Interest in Notification' (2011) 19(2) Medical Law Review 267–303, discussing purpose limitation and secondary use in health research, and Gonzalo F. Gállego and Juan Ramón Robles, 'Compatibility Test: Can I Process Lawfully Collected Personal Data for a New Purpose?' (*HoganLovells*, 17 May 2021) <https://www.hoganlovells.com/en/publications/compatibility-test-can-i-process-lawfully-collected-personal-data-for-a-new-purpose_1> accessed 25 October 2025.

5 NHS England, 'Artificial Intelligence' (30 April 2025) <https://transform.england.nhs.uk/information-governance/guidance/artificial-intelligence/> accessed 21 October 2025.

necessary data for a given purpose.[6] AI development, however, tends to benefit from "more data" – giving algorithms a long list of features and examples in order to perform better. This conflict is apparent in the context of the US HIPAA: PHI usage without patient authorisation is fine for the core treatment, payment, or healthcare operations (TPO), but training a new AI model is not readily compatible with TPO. If a hospital or hospital vendor wants to train an AI on large amounts of PHI outside of direct care, HIPAA likely requires the obtaining of each patient's authorization.[7] Scaling consent of such a magnitude to thousands of records is not feasible and may hamper the development of AI tools.[8] Similarly under GDPR, data minimisation [Article 5 (1) (c)] requires that only data "adequate, relevant and limited" to what is necessary be used – a standard which is difficult to reconcile to AI's appetite for exhaustive datasets. This is an issue that has been highlighted by regulators and scholars: how do we determine "how much data is enough" for an AI to work, whilst ensuring that the minimum-use rule is respected?[9] It runs the risk that AI systems will gather or store more personal data than necessary, violating privacy.

Further, the issue of de-identification and re-identification risk is also a concern. One appealing option to address the privacy issue is to anonymise patient data before feeding it into the model to train and validate AI models. Truly anonymous data is not covered by GDPR and HIPAA, removing a lot of legal hurdles. However, in practise "truly anonymised data is rare and the threshold for anonymisation is high".[10] GDPR defines anonymisation quite strictly – data needs to be stripped of personal identifiers irreversibly such that no individual can be identified by "all the means reasonably likely to be used" by any party.[11] AI development makes this more complicated because even if identifiers (such as names) are explicitly removed, all

6 Todd Mayover, 'When AI Technology and HIPAA Collide' (*The HIPAA Journal*, 2 May 2025) <https://www.hipaajournal.com/when-ai-technology-and-hipaa-collide/> accessed 21 October 2025.

7 ibid.

8 ibid.

9 For instance, see International Actuarial Association, 'Actuarial Control Cycle for Narrow Artificial Intelligence' (2024) 5 <https://actuaries.org/app/uploads/2025/05/AITF2024_C5_ModelValidation_narrow-ai-models_DRAFT.pdf> accessed 23 March 2026.

10 Nathalie Moreno and Catriona Melton, 'Training AI on Health Data: Contractual and Data Protection Considerations for Healthtech Providers' (*kennedyslaw.com*, 11 June 2025) <https://www.kennedyslaw.com/en/thought-leadership/article/2025/training-ai-on-health-data-contractual-and-data-protection-considerations-for-healthtech-providers/> accessed 21 October 2025.

11 Recital 26 of the EU GDPR; Information Commissioner's Office, 'How Do We Ensure Anonymisation is Effective?' (28 March 2025) <https://ico.org.uk/for-organisations/uk-gdpr-guidance-and-resources/data-sharing/anonymisation/how-do-we-ensure-anonymisation-is-effective/?search=all%20the%20means%20reasonably%20likely%20to%20be%20used> accessed 25 October 2025. See also Scott Quellhorst and Renata Valkova, 'A Practical Guide to Anonymization Standards across the EU and UK' (*iapp.org*, 24 January 2023) <https://iapp.org/news/a/a-practical-guide-to-anonymization-standards-across-the-eu-and-uk> accessed 25 October 2025, and European Commission, 'Data Protection Explained' <https://commission.europa.eu/law/law-topic/data-protection/data-protection-explained_en> accessed 25 October 2025.

the richness of health datasets (e.g. imaging or genomic patterns) and the power of AI itself can render data re-identifiable. Models can spontaneously memorise unique pieces of data or possibly be probed to release training data. Legal advisers caution that the chance of re-identification, which may arise even after careful de-identification, is still likely.[12] Under GDPR/UK law, if there is any reasonable chance of re-identifying a person in the dataset, the data should be considered personal data, and therefore all the privacy obligations will apply.[13] Similarly, US regulators understand that de-identified data provided for "big data" health research operations may still be problematic to privacy if integrated with other data.[14] In sum, anonymisation is an important goal but cannot be assumed as well – organisations need to have ongoing re-identification testing and safeguards (e.g. masking, aggregation, contractual prohibitions on re-identification) as part of their governance.[15]

More issues include data quality, bias and representativeness. Data governance is not only about privacy – it is also about data quality and their proper use. AI tools trained on biased or unrepresentative data can lead to discriminatory results, which is an especially reflective problem in the case of healthcare. Governance frameworks therefore also require more attention to be paid to the scrutiny of training data for biases and gaps. The EU AI Act puts data governance right in the centre of bias mitigation for high-risk AI. Article 10(3) of the AI Act requires that training, validation and test datasets be relevant, representative, without error and complete to the extent possible, including the measures taken to benefit from awareness of possible bias. Notably, to make AI systems more fair, the Act also exceptionally allows the use of sensitive personal data (such as health data disclosing race or ethnicity) to correct any bias if there are strict safeguards in place.[16] This explains a certain trade-off: to derive equitable AI, developers may require access to attributes of a sensitive nature – but under strict controls (pseudonymisation, distinct rights per role, deletion when it is corrected for bias and so on).[17] In practice, a good approach in building healthcare AI projects is to ensure that data governance plans are in place that include documentation of data provenance, data quality evaluations, bias audits and data monitoring continuously according to the necessary compliance with emerging law. Good governance, therefore, is not just privacy protection, but is also the foundation of model reliability and trust by the public.

12 Luc Rocher, Julien M. Hendrickx and Yves-Alexandre de Montjoye, 'Estimating the Success of Re-identifications in Incomplete Datasets using Generative Models' (2019) 10 Nature Communications 3069; Khaled El Emam and others, 'A Systematic Review of Re-Identification Attacks on Health Data' (2011) 6(12) PLoS ONE e28071. See also Abdallah Al-Ani and others, 'Evaluating the Understanding of the Ethical and Moral Challenges of Big Data and AI among Jordanian Medical Students, Physicians in Training, and Senior Practitioners: A Cross-sectional Study' (2024) 25 BMC Medical Ethics 18.

13 Recital 26 of the EU GDPR. Information Commissioner's Office (n 11).

14 W. Nicholson Price II., 'Problematic Interactions between AI and Health Privacy' (2021) (4) Utah Law Review 925–928.

15 Moreno and Melton (n 10).

16 Article 10(5) of the EU AI Act.

17 ibid.

Having presented these challenges in the most general terms, we now focus on how various jurisdictions respond to (or struggle with) these problems.

III. European Union: GDPR and the AI Act

The European Union has one of the most stringent data protection regimes in the world (GDPR) and it directly applies to the processing of personal health data in AI. Health data in the European Union falls under "special category" personal data in the context of GDPR Article 9, which means that its processing is in principle prohibited unless there is a specific exception. For clinical AI development, explicit consent of the data subject is an example of a common lawful basis (consent that is freely given, informed and specific).[18] However, consent can be problematic for big data uses – it can be withdrawn at any point, and is not often "freely given" in a healthcare context. GDPR does offer other options for the processing: processing, for example, can be permissible if "necessary for reasons of public interest in the area of public health" or for the purposes of scientific research, with strict safeguards.[19] EU countries have national laws that allow for the use of health data for research or innovation, subject to ethical supervision of its use, and this could potentially be applicable to certain AI training activities. Yet these research derogations are narrowly construed and may well not include commercial product development.[20] Companies need to be careful: a medical AI company is unlikely to be able to rely on the original patient consent obtained by the hospital (for treatment) to subsequently use those data in training a diagnostic algorithm – fresh consent or another exception is required in order to comply with the principles of GDPR purpose limitation and fairness.

Beyond lawful basis, where AI is used with EU health data, the key GDPR principles of data minimisation (collect only what is necessary), purpose limitation, storage limitation (don't store data for longer than necessary), integrity and confidentiality (don't keep data in an easy-to-launch format for hackers) and accountability must be adhered to. Regulators anticipate DPIAs for AI projects involving health data because such are likely to be "high-risk" processing activities.[21] A DPIA requires the controller to assess threats to patient rights and record the steps that are taken to avoid them (encryption, access controls, etc.).[22] Moreover, trans-

18 Moreno and Melton (n 10).

19 Article 9(2)(i) and (j) of the EU GDPR.

20 Moreno and Melton (n 10).

21 Articles 5 and 35 of the EU GDPR; European Data Protection Board, *Guidelines on Data Protection Impact Assessment (DPIA) and Determining Whether Processing Is "Likely to Result in a High Risk"* (WP248 rev.01, 2017/18), 9, 11 and 18 <https://ec.europa.eu/newsroom/document.cfm?doc_id=47711> accessed 25 October 2025. See also Marin Milenkoski, 'Conducting a DPIA: Best Practices for AI Systems' (*gdprlocal.com*, updated July 2025) <https://gdprlocal.com/conducting-a-dpia-best-practices-for-ai-systems/> accessed 25 October 2025.

22 Article 35(7) of the EU GDPR; Information Commissioner's Office, *Data Protection Impact Assessments* (17 October 2022) 33–34 <https://ico.org.uk/for-organisations/uk-gdpr-guidance-and

parency and patient rights are critical – patients have rights to information, access, rectification and even erasure of their data, which need to be reconciled with the development of AI (e.g. informing patients if their records are being used to train an AI, and possibly accommodating deletion requests, which can be complex once data is included in a model).[23]

In addition to GDPR, the European Union has the AI Act, a horizontal regulation that imposes other requirements on "high-risk" AI systems – a category which includes most AI that is used in clinical diagnosis or care (likely via classification as medical devices or under health and safety risk domains). The AI Act dedicates an entire provision (Article 10) to the issue of data and data governance. From 2 August 2026 it will require the developers of AI to put into place a comprehensive range of data governance measures, including the documentation of data provenance, relevance and biases. In essence, in order to obtain regulatory approval or CE marking, an AI system has to demonstrate that the training and test data used are of high quality and "sufficiently representative" of the population in which the AI will be used.[24] Any gaps or shortcomings in the data need to be found and addressed.[25] These requirements echo the principles of accuracy and fairness in GDPR, but make them explicit for AI: if an AI is used for detecting skin cancer and for this purpose is trained mostly with data acquired from images of light skin patients, the developer must be aware of the bias and should take steps (collect more diverse data or use bias correction techniques) to ensure that they are compliant with the law. Crucially, under Article 10(5) of the AI Act, when processing sensitive data (e.g. racial or ethnic origin, health status), it is permissible to process such data for the purpose of bias monitoring/correction provided that the processing is "strictly necessary" and is accompanied by appropriate safeguards. Those safeguards include state-of-the-art security, access controls, no onward sharing and quick deletion once the bias issue has been fixed,[26] in addition to GDPR's own requirements. This carve-out was devised as strictly adhering to GDPR could mean that developers can paradoxically limit themselves from using demographic or genetic data that may help to identify bias in an AI model. The European Union is thus attempting to find a balance between privacy and equity in terms of outcome – a nuanced position that reflects the fact that governing data is about both protecting individuals and guaranteeing data quality.

In summary, how it works is that the EU approach combines layers of a comprehensive privacy law (GDPR) that already includes privacy laws covering health

-resources/accountability-and-governance/data-protection-impact-assessments-dpias/> accessed 25 October 2025.

23 Articles 12–17 of the EU GDPR; Information Commissioner's Office, 'Task 2: Collect and Pre-process Your Data in an Explanation-aware Manner' (17 October 2022) <https://ico.org.uk/for-organisations/uk-gdpr-guidance-and-resources/artificial-intelligence/explaining-decisions-made-with-artificial-intelligence/part-2-explaining-ai-in-practice/task-2-collect/> accessed 25 October 2025.

24 Article 10(3) of the EU AI Act.

25 Article 10(2)(h) of the EU AI Act.

26 Article 10(5) of the EU AI Act.

data, consent and individual rights, as well as new programs of regulations for AI (AI Act) focusing on data governance, risk management and transparency. An AI system in healthcare needs to be compliant with both. For example, a future product such as a high-risk AI diagnostic tool will have to register in an EU database, undergo conformity assessment and include in its technical documentation elaborate information on the data it is trained on,[27] all while making sure that any personal data processing during this process complies with GDPR requirements. EU regulators (and European Data Protection Supervisor for EU institutions) are also tightening guidance on AI ethics as well as privacy – anticipate to see harmonised standards (via European Commission and bodies such as European Committee for Standardization/European Committee for Electrotechnical Standardization, or CEN/CENELEC) based on these legal requirements being translated in practical checklists for data management/pace of auditing traceability/privacy-by-designing AI systems.

IV. United Kingdom: UK GDPR, DPA 2018 and Regulatory Guidance

Having left the European Union, the United Kingdom has a very similar regime for data protection – the UK GDPR (which essentially mirrors the EU GDPR as incorporated into UK law)[28] and the Data Protection Act (DPA) 2018 (which supplements the UK GDPR with some specific provisions and exemptions).[29] For healthcare AI, the UK GDPR equally considers health data to be "special category" identically to what the European Union does – so data can only be processed with expressed consent or another requirement from Schedule 1 of the DPA 2018 (e.g. medical purposes and research in the public interest with appropriate safeguards).[30] Thus, the substantive rules about the use of patient data for AI – lawfulness, transparency, data minimisation, security etc. – are aligned with the European Union. A developer or hospital in England must ensure that they have a lawful basis for processing (consent, or a statutory authorisation), and are likely to have to conduct a DPIA if they are truly deploying an AI tool that processes patient data in new ways.

Apart from statutory data protection, UK healthcare providers have a common-law duty of confidentiality to patients. This means that even if data use is legal in the context of UK GDPR (for example, considered "in the public interest"), disclosure of identifiable patient information without consent can be a breach of

27 Annex IV of the EU AI Act.

28 Council Regulation (EU) 2016/679 of the European Parliament and of the Council of 27 April 2016 on the protection of natural persons with regard to the processing of personal data and on the free movement of such data (UK GDPR) <https://www.legislation.gov.uk/eur/2016/679> accessed 23 October 2025.

29 *Data Protection Act 2018*, c.12. <https://www.legislation.gov.uk/ukpga/2018/12/contents> accessed 23 October 2025.

30 Regarding this Schedule 1, see <https://www.legislation.gov.uk/ukpga/2018/12/schedule/1/enacted> accessed 23 October 2025.

confidentiality unless there is an overriding public interest or a specific legal permission.[31] To navigate this, the Health Research Authority is responsible for the operation of a confidentiality advisory group (CAG) which can authorise the use of confidential information from patients in the NHS for medical research or planning without the patient's consent under the provisions of Section 251 of the NHS Act 2006.[32] AI developers typically rely on this mechanism when using NHS data: if the data cannot be completely anonymised and it's impractical to obtain individual consent to their use, one needs CAG approval that this is a justified use and that privacy is adequately protected.[33] The need for CAG (or an equivalent process in each UK nation) highlights an important practical consideration: it is not sufficient just to have a legal basis under data protection law – one must also have to consider confidentiality and ethical approvals in using UK health data for AI. In short, UK institutions must double-hurdle: comply with UK GDPR/DPA 2018 and respect the rules on confidentiality in the NHS.

The United Kingdom's Information Commissioner's Office (ICO) has been proactive in its interpretation of how AI can be applied in line with data protection. In 2022, the ICO revised its intricate Guidance on AI and Data Protection,[34] providing best practice on topics such as fairness, transparency and DPIAs in AI systems. For instance, the ICO (in collaboration with the Alan Turing Institute) produced detailed guidance on AI explainability, recognising data provenance and privacy as an element of developing explainable AI models.[35] NHS bodies have also published practical guides – this guidance by the NHS around 2025 has again emphasised the importance of involving the organisation's data protection officer (DPO) and Caldicott Guardian early on, in order to "support the lawful and safe use of data for AI innovations".[36] Frontline staff are advised that if they see strange

31 The UK Caldicott Guardian Council, 'The Common Law Duty of Confidentiality' <https://www.ukcgc.uk/duty-of-confidentiality> accessed 25 October 2025. See also *W v. Egdell* [1990] Ch 359 (CA), regarding public-interest exception within common law confidentiality, and General Medical Council, *Confidentiality: Good Practice in Handling Patient Information* (2017, updated 13 December 2024) <https://www.gmc-uk.org/-/media/documents/gmc-guidance-for-doctors---confidentiality-good-practice-in-handling-patient-information----70080105.pdf> accessed 25 October 2025.

32 Regarding this Section, see NHS Act 2006 c. 41, Part 13, Patient Information, Section 251 <https://www.legislation.gov.uk/ukpga/2006/41/section/251> accessed 23 October 2025.

33 NHS England (n 5).

34 ICO, 'Guidance on AI and Data Protection' (15 March 2023) <https://ico.org.uk/for-organisations/uk-gdpr-guidance-and-resources/artificial-intelligence/guidance-on-ai-and-data-protection/> accessed 23 October 2025.

35 Information Commissioner's Office (n 23).

36 NHS England (n 5). See also Department of Health and Social Care, *A Guide to Good Practice for Digital and Data-Driven Health Technologies* (2018; updated 19 January 2021) <https://www.gov.uk/government/publications/code-of-conduct-for-data-driven-health-and-care-technology/initial-code-of-conduct-for-data-driven-health-and-care-technology> accessed 25 October 2025 regarding the principles on Information Governance, or IG/DPO and Caldicott engagement; Indra Joshi and Dominic Cushnan, *A Buyer's Guide to AI in Health and Care* (*NHS*, November 2020) <https://webarchive.nationalarchives.gov.uk/ukgwa/20230504130145mp_/https://transform.england.nhs.uk

outputs from an AI (e.g. potential bias or errors) this should trigger a check if the training data might be skewed or inappropriate – essentially integrating data governance reflexes into clinical practice.[37]

On the more macro regulatory level, the MHRA are revamping regulatory laws for medical devices to include AI. The United Kingdom is not following the AI Act-style law, but is instead incorporating AI thinking into the existing legal frameworks. Under proposed reforms, a number of AI software tools will be "up-classified" to a higher risk classification resulting in greater oversight.[38] The MHRA's *Software and AI as a Medical Device Change Programme*, as well as recent strategy statements, emphasise accountability for the data that is used to feed AI models and post-market monitoring of the performance of AI.[39] In a 2024 report, the MHRA commented that in the case of AI-based medical devices, *"accountability and governance are also applicable to the datasets used in the creation of AI models and* [to] *potential changes that occur to the model in post market use"*.[40] This is in line with the EU approach that data is included in the life cycle regulation for the device. While the MHRA is not a regulator for privacy, it coordinates with the ICO and NHS to ensure the approval of products and testing of AI devices in the real world does not trample data protection laws. One concrete example of the United Kingdom being in line with what is essentially best practice worldwide is collaboration between the MHRA, the US FDA and Health Canada to express GMLP principles. These include expectations on data quality, representativeness as well as the mitigation of bias and drift in AI systems.[41] Although the GMLP is guidance and not law, it is a sign to developers that regulators will be looking at the way that datasets were curated and whether privacy and security were maintained during model training. In summary, the way the United Kingdom approaches data governance for AI healthcare is as an incremental guidance-driven program based on a foundation of existing robust laws (UK GDPR) and sectoral regulations (NHS, confidentiality, device regulation). Organisations should adhere

/media/documents/NHSX_A_Buyers_Guide_to_AI_in_Health_and_Care.pdf> accessed 25 October 2025.

37 NHS England (n 5).

38 MHRA, 'Impact of AI on the Regulation of Medical Products: Implementing the AI White Paper Principles' (April 2024) 7 <https://assets.publishing.service.gov.uk/media/662fce1e9e82181baa98a988/MHRA_Impact-of-AI-on-the-regulation-of-medical-products.pdf> accessed 23 October 2025.

39 Regarding the programme, see MHRA, 'Software and AI as a Medical Device Change Programme Roadmap' (*Gov.uk*, updated 14 June 2023) <https://www.gov.uk/government/publications/software-and-ai-as-a-medical-device-change-programme/software-and-ai-as-a-medical-device-change-programme-roadmap#wp-4-post-market> accessed 23 October 2025.

40 MHRA (n 38) 9.

41 Artificial Intelligence/Machine Learning-Enabled Working Group, 'Good Machine Learning Practice for Medical Device Development: Guiding Principles' (*Imdrf.org*, 27 January 2025) <https://www.imdrf.org/sites/default/files/2025-02/IMDRF_AIML%20WG_GMLP_N88%20Final.pdf> accessed 23 October 2025.

to the spirit of both: the privacy of patient data must be maintained rigorously and data integrity ensured throughout the lifecycle of the AI system.

V. United States: HIPAA, OCR Rules and FDA Perspectives

Unlike the European Union and United Kingdom, the United States does not have a single comprehensive data protection law relating to health data. Instead, it uses an uncoordinated collection of laws and guidance on a sector-by-sector basis. The most important of these is the HIPAA Privacy and Security Rules,[42] which provide protection for medical information held by healthcare providers, insurers and their business associates. In the context of AI, the rules of HIPAA will apply if the entity developing or using the AI is a covered entity (e.g. a hospital or clinic) or a business associate handling PHI on behalf of a covered entity.[43] This means many clinical AI tools developed within hospitals or by vendors under contract will be limited in fact by HIPAA's privacy requirements. However, standalone AI health apps offered directly to consumers (without involvement of a provider/insurer) are not covered by HIPAA – a fact that has increasingly been criticised by commentators.[44] Thus, a key difference in the United States is that privacy protections are grounded in who has access to the data and not what the data is.[45] Sensitive health information used by a hospital to create an AI diagnostic is protected by law (HIPAA applies) whereas the same sort of information gathered by a fitness or symptom checker app might have no federal law protecting it (only consumer protection laws or state laws). This inconsistency has been criticised in the age of AI,[46] since it is easy for data to flow between the clinical and commercial contexts.

Where HIPAA does apply, it has a number of relevant governance standards. The first one is for use and disclosure limitations. PHI can be used freely for treatment, payment or healthcare operations, however, other uses (like research or marketing) require explicit patient authorisation or an Institutional Review Board (IRB)/privacy board waiver.[47] Training an AI system is not explicitly listed as a HIPAA "operation" and the common thinking is that the use of AI training

42 For the HIPAA Privacy Rule, see <https://www.hhs.gov/hipaa/for-professionals/privacy/index.html> accessed 23 October 2025; for the HIPAA Security Rule, see <https://www.hhs.gov/hipaa/for-professionals/security/index.html> accessed 23 October 2025.

43 Craig Konnoth, 'AI and Data Protection Law in Health' in Barry Solaiman and I. Glenn Cohen (eds), *Research Handbook on Health, AI and the Law* (Edward Elgar Publishing 2024), 111–129, 113.

44 For instance, see ibid 113–114.

45 ibid 126.

46 ibid 113–114.

47 45 CFR §164.506, regarding HIPAA permitted uses/disclosures for treatment, payment, health-care operations); 45 CFR §164.508, regarding authorisation required for other uses, including marketing; 45 CFR §164.512(i), regarding research and IRB/Privacy Board waiver. See also U.S. Department of HHS, 'How OCR Enforces the HIPAA Privacy & Security Rules' (20 November 2023) <https://www.hhs.gov/hipaa/for-professionals/compliance-enforcement/examples/how-ocr-enforces-the-hipaa-privacy-and-security-rules/index.html> accessed 25 October 2025.

would not be considered part of routine treatment or operations.[48] In fact, the US Department of Health and Human Services (HHS) was fairly clear that the creation of AI models using PHI usually constitutes either research or some secondary purpose, for which individual authorisation is required, unless an exemption applies.[49] HIPAA-covered entities are facing a quandary: getting informed consent from every patient whose data could be used to feed an algorithm is an onerous effort and perhaps impossible; bypassing authorisation could violate federal law. One of the ways around this is de-identification: HIPAA provides a "safe harbour" standard – removal of 18 types of identifiers (names, dates, contacts, etc.) – after which data is no longer regulated as PHI. Many US institutions are attempting to de-identify datasets before they use or share them in their AI projects. But as discussed, de-identification is not foolproof and regulators encourage constant risk assessment to make sure that re-identification risk is very small.[50] Another HIPAA principle is Minimum Necessary use. Covered entities and business associates must restrict the use of PHIs to the minimum required for achieving an intended purpose.[51] This raises tough questions for AI: if in general performance of a model improves with the amount of data, how can one measure the "necessary" amount? HHS' Office for Civil Rights (OCR) – which enforces HIPAA – warns that there must be guards against "data overreach" by AI for controllers of PHI, who should have oversight mechanisms to ensure that it is only using the needed data for training or deployment.[52] In real terms, this may include data curation (to remove unwanted fields), data sampling or monitoring the AI with respect to the access of data.

In late 2023, OCR released a policy "Dear Colleague" letter pointing out ways that occurrences such as the use of AI in healthcare should be handled in compliance with civil rights laws and HIPAA.[53] Under Section 1557 of the Affordable Care Act,[54] it is now explicit that hospitals and insurers cannot use the AI decision tools in ways that discriminate (e.g. an algorithmic triage tool that systematically undertreats certain racial groups would violate the law).[55] The OCR letter recommends that covered entities test their AI for such biases, which are related to a protected class, and manage the harmful effects of any discrimination.[56] It also restates that "privacy and security are equally vital" in the adoption of AI: healthcare enti-

48 Mayover (n 6).
49 ibid.
50 David Williamson, 'Where AI Meets Health Data Privacy: How to Balance Innovation with Risk' (*davant.com*, 28 May 2025) <https://www.datavant.com/hipaa-privacy/where-ai-meets-health-data-privacy-how-to-balance-innovation-with-risk> accessed 23 October 2025.
51 Mayover (n 6).
52 ibid.
53 New York State Dental Association (n 1).
54 Regarding this Section 1557, see U.S. Department of Health and Human Services, 'Section 1557: Protecting Individuals Against Sex Discrimination' (*hhs.gov*, 3 November 2020) <https://www.hhs.gov/civil-rights/for-individuals/section-1557/fs-sex-discrimination/index.html> accessed 23 October 2025.
55 New York State Dental Association (n 1).
56 ibid.

ties should be investing in strong safeguards and proving HIPAA compliance as they adopt AI.[57] This emphasis implies that US regulators view privacy as more than a box to be co-ticked and see it as part of ensuring that the public maintain trust in AI innovations. For now, enforcement of AI-related privacy issues comes through traditional avenues – OCR can investigate breaches of or improper PHI disclosures by AI vendors, and the Federal Trade Commission (FTC) can sanction companies (even non-HIPAA ones) for misleading consumers about the data practices of AI products. On the horizon, extension of privacy to health data held by tech companies is being considered by some US states (e.g. California, with the California Consumer Privacy Act[58]) with federal ideas for health data privacy and AI accountability being debated as well. But as of 2025, the United States depends largely on HIPAA plus patchwork regulations, leaving large gaps behind in regulation of the AI developers who sit outside of the healthcare establishment.[59]

The FDA, which is responsible for approving medical devices, including some systems using software/AI, has been looking at how best to test the safety and efficacy of AI algorithms. While the FDA's mandate is product safety/effectiveness (not privacy per se), data governance factors into its assessments in an indirect way. For instance, in order to approve an AI diagnostic tool, the FDA is expecting proof of clinical validation and this requires working with high-quality datasets. If the training dataset was too narrow or biased, then that can undermine the claims to effectiveness in supporting different groups of patients. In 2021, the FDA (with MHRA and Health Canada) has published ten guiding principles of GMLP.[60] These principles promote practices such as involving "multi-disciplinary expertise" throughout the development of an AI, ensuring "data relevancy" and "data quality" and monitoring the performance of AI looking for the introduction of concept drift or emergent biases over time.[61] One of the GMLP principles explicitly advocates paying due consideration to the data that is fed into algorithms including proper partitioning into training/test datasets and that the data represents the intended patient population.[62] Another principle emphasises the importance of transparency – AI developers should keep documentation on the development processes of the model, including source of data and preprocessing procedures, which can be reviewed by either the regulators or users.[63] From the privacy side, FDA approvals have sometimes required that companies demonstrate how they anonymise patient data or how consent of the patient to using data in the device development process

57 ibid.

58 California Consumer Privacy Act, Cal Civ Code § 1798.100 et seq. <https://leginfo.legislature.ca.gov/faces/codes_displayText.xhtml?division=3.&part=4.&lawCode=CIV&title=1.81.> accessed 23 October 2025.

59 Konnoth (n 43).

60 Artificial Intelligence/Machine Learning-Enabled Working Group (n 41).

61 ibid.

62 ibid Principle 3.

63 ibid Principle 9.

was obtained (particularly if the data was sourced from clinical trials).[64] Moreover, the FDA's post-market monitoring may overlap with privacy: production of AI devices depends on feedback from real-world data; it requires companies to gather new patient data to adjust models (somewhat referred to as "continuous learning" algorithms). The framework the FDA proposed for PCCP (for learning AI devices) states that manufacturers should explain how they will utilise real-world data in a safe and lawful manner.[65] In short, while the FDA is not policing privacy like the OCR, it is indirectly pushing for good data governance (data integrity, no incorrect biases), as part of what makes an AI tool "safe and effective".

VI. Comparative Reflections

A comparative analysis shows both the convergence and divergence between the EU, UK and US approach to data governance for AI in healthcare, particularly when it comes to the following: (1) breadth of coverage, (2) lawful basis and consent, (3) data minimisation and quality and (4) accountability and enforcement.

In terms of breadth of coverage, EU (and UK) privacy laws apply to all personal health data regardless of the type of entity that is processing it, and in the US privacy laws apply primarily based on what type of entity is doing the processing. As a result, a patient in Europe has legal protections and rights over an AI usage of that patient's health data (i.e. a right to withdraw consent or request deletion), whereas, in America, an individual's rights as a patient hinge on whether a HIPAA-covered care provider is involved. This means that AI startups not operating within traditional healthcare in the United States can sometimes bypass strict privacy controls – a regulatory gap that the European Union/United Kingdom does not have. Policymakers in the United States have begun to take notice of this gap,[66] but currently patients are safer (privacy-wise) in jurisdictions with omnibus laws.

The second aspect is the lawful basis and consent. All regions are aware of the difficulties of operationalising informed consent for facilitating large-scale data use. GDPR/UK law nominally favour explicit consent to using health data, but have some work-arounds (public interest, research exemption) to bypass consent fatigue and allow medical research. The United States, by contrast, does not, in general, require consent for treatment uses of data (implied consent is assumed in healthcare delivery), but HIPAA does effectively require consent (authorisation) for non-treatment uses, such as training an AI model – unless the data is de-identified or authorisation is waived by an IRB pursuant to the Common Rule (for

64 21 CFR Part 50, regarding the protection of human subjects: informed consent for clinical investigations supporting device submissions. See also FDA, *Use of Electronic Health Record Data in Clinical Investigations* (Guidance for Industry, July 2018) 9–10 <https://www.fda.gov/media/97567/download> accessed 25 October 2025.

65 FDA, *Marketing Submission Recommendations for a Predetermined Change Control Plan (PCCP) for AI/ML-Enabled Device Software Functions* 28 (4 December 2024, updated 18 August 2025) <https://www.fda.gov/media/166704/download> accessed 26 October 2025.

66 Konnoth (n 43).

research). In reality, EU/UK and US institutions alike are also considering ways in which data may be used without constantly burdening the patient again: broad consent for future research (allowed under revised US Common Rule and under discussion in Europe) and dynamic consent platforms are examples. Each approach must balance between individual autonomy and special societal interest in medical innovation.

In terms of data minimisation and quality, the principle of data minimisation is enshrined in EU/UK law and the minimum necessary rule in HIPAA law. Yet, all jurisdictions struggle with what this means in the context of AI. The EU AI Act leans towards requiring data quality rather than pure minimisation, in essence accepting that it may be necessary to use more data (of the right kind) to improve its accuracy and minimise bias.[67] GDPR is flexible on this point: it allows taking into account the necessity of data for the purpose – if there is a genuine need for a larger data set to apply the AI in a medically safe way then this may be permitted, but controllers should document why and make sure that no irrelevant data is included. The US HIPAA method is less granular (it lacks an AI-specific nuance); covered entities must make good faith decisions as to what is "minimum necessary", and are liable if they obviously stockpile too much PHI without justification. In all regions, data governance thus requires documentation and moves that data oversight in the following proper direction: internal committees or DPOs should vet AI data requests and make sure they're not grabbing more identifying data or records than necessary. Techniques such as data sampling, feature selection and early stopping can tie the development of models to the minimisation principles.[68] At the same time, regulators are sending a signal that it is not just about minimisation when it comes to data governance: it is about using appropriate and representative data.[69] This is very subtle and important, especially in the European Union – making sure that data protection law does not inadvertently undermine model performance or model fairness.

With respect to accountability and enforcement, the European Union's approach is very regulatory – formal steps in the process of compliance (DPIAs, technical documentation, possible audits by Data Protection Authorities or new AI Act authorities) and heavy weights for violations (GDPR fines, and the AI Act will introduce its own fines for non-compliance of data governance rules).[70]

67 Article 10 of the EU AI Act.

68 European Data Protection Board, *Guidelines 4/2019 on Article 25 Data Protection by Design and by Default* (20 October 2020) 12–14 and 21–23 <https://www.edpb.europa.eu/sites/default/files/files/file1/edpb_guidelines_201904_dataprotection_by_design_and_by_default_v2.0_en.pdf> accessed 26 October 2025; National Institute of Standards and Technology (NIST), *AI Risk Management Framework (AI RMF 1.0)* (January 2023) 17 <https://nvlpubs.nist.gov/nistpubs/ai/nist.ai.100-1.pdf> accessed 26 October 2025.

69 Article 10 of the EU AI Act; Artificial Intelligence/Machine Learning-Enabled Working Group (n 41).

70 Article 83 of the EU GDPR, regarding administrative fines and accountability/audits; Articles 72–76 and 99 of the EU AI Act, regarding post-market monitoring, conformity documentation and penalties for non-compliance.

The United Kingdom is similarly tough on paper but is thinking of a more proportionate and innovation-friendly approach to its AI regulation policy (e.g. the 2023 UK AI White Paper is in favour of guidance and voluntary compliance in sectors like health rather than new hard rules[71]). The United States is reliant on enforcement of existing rules (OCR is able to impose fines for HIPAA breaches or to refer cases to the Department of Justice if there is misconduct involved,[72] and the FTC is able to take action against companies for data practices ruled "unfair or deceptive"[73]). Notably, discrimination or bias as a consequence of AI use is now explicitly a legal risk both in the United States (under civil rights law) and the European Union (the AI Act forbids AI leading to forbidden bias).[74] This is an area where data governance (proper training data) is directly related to legal liability.

In all jurisdictions, best practices are converging around some key governance measures: conducting privacy risk assessments prior to the deployment of AI systems (DPIA or similar), having multi-disciplinary oversight (legal, clinical, IT, ethics), ensuring technical safeguards such as encryption, accessing control and audit logs and ensuring transparency around the nature of data use of AI systems (both to regulators and to the people affected – patients, as appropriate).

VII. Proposing Privacy Impact Matrix and Clinician's Checklist

This chapter suggests two tools that provide a more practical distillation of some of these practices. Table 5.1 (Privacy Impact Matrix) gives a high-level framework to assess the privacy implications of an AI healthcare project. It matches key factors (data attributes and processing context) with relative levels of impact, to help decide which uses of AI on the data are low risk, and which are really high risk and therefore requiring stringent protections or even avoidance. If an AI project falls more in the column "Lower Privacy Impact" (e.g. using de-identified and small-scale data for direct care purposes only, with high levels of protections), the privacy impact is relatively small – standard steps for compliance with privacy requirements may suffice. If there are many factors in the column "Higher Privacy

71 Secretary of State for Science, Innovation and Technology, *A Pro-Innovation Approach to AI Regulation* (updated 3 August 2023) Command Paper Number: 815 <https://www.gov.uk/government/publications/ai-regulation-a-pro-innovation-approach/white-paper> accessed 26 October 2025.

72 45 CFR pt 160 Subpart C–D, regarding enforcement and HIPAA civil money penalties; 42 USC §1320d-6, regarding criminal penalties and Department of Justice prosecutions upon OCR referral).

73 15 USC §45 (FTC Act s 5), regarding "unfair or deceptive acts or practices"; *In the Matter of GoodRx Holdings, Inc* (FTC, Decision and Order, 2023) <https://www.ftc.gov/legal-library/browse/cases-proceedings/2023090-goodrx-holdings-inc> accessed 26 October 2025, regarding the enforcement over deceptive health-data practices.

74 US Department of Health and Human Services, Office for Civil Rights, *Nondiscrimination in Health Programs and Activities* (Final Rule, 2024), codified at 45 CFR Part 92 <https://www.govinfo.gov/content/pkg/FR-2024-05-06/pdf/2024-08711.pdf> accessed 26 October 2025, addressing algorithmic bias in clinical decision tools; Articles 9–10, 71–72 of the EU AI Act, regarding risk management and fundamental rights safeguards, including non-discrimination, for high-risk AI.

Table 5.1 Privacy Impact Matrix

Factor	*Lower Privacy Impact (Example)*	*Higher Privacy Impact (Example)*
Data Identifiability	Data fully anonymised (no reasonable re-identification possible)	Direct identifiers or easy to link pseudo-anonymous Data
Data Sensitivity	General data of health (e.g. vital signs) without detailed information about the personal context	Highly sensitive content (e.g. mental health notes, genetic profiles)
Purpose of Use	Institution-level direct patient care or quality improvement (primary purpose)	Secondary use for AI model training/ research which is not related to original care context
Volume & Scope of Data	Small and well-focused dataset (minimal fields, relevant population)	Massive collect of datasets from many sources (big data pooling)
Data Recipients	Internal applications by treating provider team or In-house AI developers	Shared with third-party AI vendors or cross-border (external use)
Retention & Control	Use for a limited period of time with data promptly deleted or kept in secure form	Indefinite retention of raw data; unclear policies for the data deletion
Safeguards in Place	Good security (encryption, access controls), DPIA carried out, contractual restrictions on use	Lack of encryption and/or no specific access controls; no documented risk assessment

Impact" (e.g. training a diagnostic AI on identifiable and comprehensive databases of patients, for a new purpose with external parties), then the privacy impact is high – requiring extensive safeguards: explicit patient consent or authorisation, independent ethical approval, heavy reliance on security considerations, ongoing monitoring for adherence and perhaps reframing of the project to reduce exposure of data. This matrix can be used as a quick-check tool (for clinicians, data scientists and compliance officers) to identify high-impact aspects of an AI initiative as early as possible during planning.

On the other hand, frontline clinicians and health IT teams are an important part of maintaining data governance when adopting AI tools. Table 5.2 (Clinician's Checklist) is a practical checklist for healthcare professionals to ensure that privacy and data protection are baked into healthcare where using AI is enabled. Following this checklist is a way that clinicians and healthcare teams can help to ensure that the introduction of AI in care does not breach the trust that underpins the relationship between patients and their providers. Data governance in practice means putting privacy considerations into day-to-day workflows – including, from an AI project's conception, through the project's rollout and continued utilisation.

Table 5.2 Clinician's Checklist

Checklist Item	*Summary Action*
Data Protection & Privacy Compliance	Ensure the use of AI data is done in compliance with regulations (e.g. GDPR/HIPAA) and preserving patient confidentiality and security
Data Governance & Quality	Go through the steps to achieve data governance, i.e. assigning stewards, quality checks and limiting data use
Informed Consent & Legal Basis	Get informed consent from patients or other legal basis for using AI patient data
Transparency & Communication	Consider how AI is used, and the way that data is handled, and make this understood by patients, staff and regulators
Ongoing Monitoring & Oversight	Constantly monitor performance and compliance of AI; have a clear overseeing responsibility to take charge of issues
Reporting Duty	Report to the medical institution in case of violation of personal health data to minimise the damage.

VIII. Conclusion

AI's potential to change clinical care does exist along with the equally powerful duty: to ethically and legally govern data. Strong privacy and data governance frameworks do not impact innovation but are the key part in ensuring that they can flourish in a sustainable manner. The comprehensive approach of the European Union, the blended advice and legislation in the United Kingdom, and the sectoral mosaic in the United St all have lessons to learn. Taken together they point to a time in the future when data stewardship will be an integral competency for any healthcare initiative involving AI. The key is to incorporate privacy by design – anticipating problems such as consent, minimisation, bias and security, for example, from the outset – as opposed to scrambling to address compliance issues later.

6 Patient Autonomy and Informed Consent

Abstract

This chapter examines how AI technology affects the traditional concept of an individual's consent before being treated in the health sector. Due to the historical roots planted from the concept of patient self-determination, informed consent requires persons to have knowledge of, and to consent to, medical treatment. However, arising challenges include issues of algorithmic transparency and potential variance in the accuracy of the outcomes generated by AI, particularly in clinical decision-making. These challenges complicate a traditional notion of a physician's role in presenting factual, clear and relevant information, which is crucial to the informed consent process. This chapter considers the potential applicability of informed consent to AI as the means of meeting the ethical issues that it raises. It underlines the necessity of the organisation's openness concerning the use of AI in decision-making processes. That is why the modification of the "reasonable physician standard" in favour of ensuring that patients receive adequate information about AI's functions and limitations should be matched by the modification of the "reasonable patient standard". When reconsidering the legal and moral angles of the contribution of patients, the chapter calls for a more nuanced understanding of informed consent that would protect patients' autonomy together with the specificity of AI in medicine.

I. Introduction

The idea of informed consent has been a component of medical practice and research from the beginning; it ensures patients' autonomy and makes sure they give their valuable consent after being informed about the particular treatment they agree to undergo. In its historical perspective, this theory has advanced along with advancements in the medical field, at the same time bearing the impact of legal and ethical norms that have been framed in order to protect the rights of individuals. However, the arrival of AI in the healthcare industry has led to the development of new challenges. These problems stem from features of so-called "expert" function AI systems such as machine learning, deep learning and other forms of AI that are increasingly being incorporated into clinical decision-making, diagnostics and treatment planning.

DOI: 10.4324/9781003785385-8

As has been observed, AI has the potential to revolutionise healthcare and give positive outcomes like none other; nonetheless, it has complexities that the standard system of informed consent is unable to effectively address. Such features as algorithmic impermeability, concerns over the privacy of the data and decreased liability for physicians raise doubts regarding the sufficiency of consent processes that exist currently. As healthcare is becoming advanced and technology-based, it is essential to reconsider the process of obtaining consent from the patient as the patient is losing a significant amount of control to AI.

This chapter aims at exploring the meaning of informed consent in relation to AI in healthcare delivery. It will examine if a change in the existing doctrine of informed consent should be made, or the consent criteria enlarged to meet the ethical issues posed by the AI technology. In view of the changing conditions of informed consent in line with the increasingly complex and transformative nature of the use of informatics in healthcare, this chapter shall discuss informed consent historically and theoretically, followed by an evaluation of the specific issues of AI in the field.

II. The Doctrine of Informed Consent

Informed Consent is a concept that has been used in many fields, such as healthcare, medical research and clinical trials, data privacy, transactions between retailers and customers and the like, even though other terms rather than "informed consent" can be adopted in a particular field. In a healthcare setting, physicians should obtain oral or, in certain cases, written informed consent from patients before medical interventions; otherwise, they may be subject to legal liability. It should be obtained also in a medical research setting. This is because informed consent, legally speaking, has been a fundamental principle either in international law or in internal law, and in the latter, it exists not only in common law systems but also in civil law systems. Taking international law as a reference, the value of informed consent has been demonstrated by the growing formalisation of international law, which includes the Nuremberg Code of 1947, the Declaration of Helsinki of the World Medical Association of 1964, the Convention on Human Rights and Biomedicine of 1997 and the Charter of Fundamental Rights of the European Union of 2009.[1]

In this section, I will focus primarily on two parts, namely historical review and theoretical review before integrating the AI concept into the traditional doctrine of informed consent, given that they are a premise of understanding the complex problems that can result from the mentioned integration.

1 Emmanuel Betta, 'Between Law and Profession: The Origins of Informed Consent (1840–1900)' in M. Malatesta (ed.), *Doctor and Patients. History, Representation, Communication from Antiquity to the Present* (University of California Medical Humanities Press 2015) 108.

A. Historical Review

By reviewing the history of medical practice, the year of 1957 was a turning point for the appearance of the concept of informed consent. It is correct to say the case law since 1957 is important to understand the current doctrine of informed consent. Nonetheless, a historical review, especially before 1957, is also fundamental to capture what had happened before and why this concept only appeared in the 20th century.

Before the 19th century, especially during the times of ancient Greece, the Middle Ages and the Enlightenment, paternalism had been applied in medical settings, in which patients could not participate in decision-making for medical treatment.[2] It was Hippocratic authoritarianism, or the so-called "beneficence model", that dominated throughout these periods, in which patients had to obey the commands and decisions made by physicians, who in turn had a duty of benefiting the sick and preventing patients from harm and injustice.[3] As a result, the information provided by physicians during these periods differs from what should be provided under the current doctrine of informed consent since lying or deception was often acceptable, particularly when it benefited the clinical condition of a patient.

For a better understanding of the problems of truth-telling between the time of ancient Greece and the 19th century, especially in the codes and treatises from Hippocrates to the AMA, a summary of the content written by Tom L. Beauchamp and Ruth R. Faden is beneficial (see Table 6.1).[4] This summary demonstrates clearly that the communication in the physician-patient relationship before and during the first half of the 19th century had followed Hippocratic authoritarianism, namely the "beneficence model",[5] instead of the "autonomy model".[6] It implies patients were not the ones who decided for their own bodies, and the (occasionally deceptive) information they received was not intended to inform consent, but to provide medical benefit.

Throughout the course of the 20th century, the paternalistic attitude to healthcare transformed into a more patient-centred attitude, and patients began to be the decision-makers for their own bodies.[7] The case *Schloendorff v. The Society of New York Hospital*[8] raised, in 1914, the question of consent to medical treatment for the

2 Peter M. Murray, 'The History of Informed Consent' (1990) 10 The Iowa Orthopaedic Journal 104.

3 Ruth R. Faden and Tom L. Beauchamp (in collaboration with Nancy M. P. King), *A History and Theory of Informed Consent* (Oxford University Press 1986) 61–62.

4 ibid 60–74.

5 As these authors put it, this model "depicts the physician's responsibilities of disclosure and consent-seeking as established by the principle of beneficence, in particular through the idea that the physician's *primary* obligation (surpassing obligations of respect for autonomy) is to provide *medical* benefits", ibid 59.

6 For the same authors, this model "is the view that the physician's responsibilities of disclosure and consent-seeking are established primarily (perhaps exclusively) by the principle of respect for autonomy", ibid.

7 Murray (n 2) 109. After providing an overview of some of the most important cases of the 20th century, the author explored how these decisions influenced the development of the modern theory of informed consent, ibid 104–109. See also *Natanson v. Kline*, 350 P2d 1093 (1960).

8 *Schloendorff v. The Society of New York Hospital*, 105 N.E. 92, 211 N.Y. 125 (1914).

Table 6.1 Summary of the Model of Communication between Ancient Greece and 19th Century

	Representative(s)	*Model of Communication*
Ancient Greece	Unknown authorship *Corpus Hippocraticum*	Hippocratic Authoritarianism (Beneficence Model): skilled communication in healthcare and respect for the patient's choices did not exist, except communication that could be used to persuade or build confidence for a treatment plan
Middle Ages	Frenchman Henri de Mondeville (ca. 1260–1325) *On the Morals and Etiquette of Surgeons*	Hippocratic Authoritarianism (Beneficence Model)
Enlightenment	Benjamin Rush (1745–1813) • *On the Vices and Virtues of Physicians* • *Medical Inquiries and Observations* • *Sixteen Introductory Lectures*	Hippocratic Authoritarianism (Beneficence Model) He recommended providing truthful and comprehensive information, but only for patients to understand physician's recommendations and be motivated to comply
	John Gregory (1724–1773) *Lectures on the Duties and Qualifications of a Physician*	Hippocratic Authoritarianism (Beneficence Model)
Modern British & American Medicine	Thomas Percival (1740–1804) *Medical Ethics* (1803)	Hippocratic Authoritarianism (Beneficence Model)
	American Medical Association *Code of Medical Ethics* (1847)	Hippocratic Authoritarianism (Beneficence Model), but criticised by: • Worthington Hooker, *Physician and Patient* (1849) and *Lessons from the History of Medical Delusions* (1850) • Austin Flint, *Medical Ethics and Etiquette* (1883) • Nathan Davis, "Do Moral Principles Changes?" (1883)

first time in our history, even though it did not require that the consent be informed. In this case, the judge Benjamin Cardozo ruled that:

> Every human being of adult years and sound mind has a right to determine what shall be done with his own body; and a surgeon who performs an operation without his patient's consent commits an assault for which he is liable in damages. This is true except in cases of emergency where the patient is unconscious and where it is necessary to operate before consent can be obtained.[9]

9 ibid.

The term "informed consent" was coined only in the 1950s, especially in *Salgo v. Leland Stanford Jr., University Board of Trustees* of 1957,[10] In this case, the judge Absalom F. Bray wrote that:

> A physician violates his duty to his patient and subjects himself to liability if he withholds any facts which are necessary to form the basis of an intelligent consent by the patient to the proposed treatment. Likewise the physician may not minimize the known dangers of a procedure or operation in order to induce his patient's consent.[11]

Hereafter, courts in the common law system began requiring not only simple consent, but "knowledgeable consent" or "informed consent".[12] The notion that physicians alone should determine what and how much information to provide to patients, namely the beneficence model, was clearly rejected by the Salgo case, as it emphasised the idea that patients have to be well-informed enough to make deliberate decisions regarding their medical care.[13] In other words, physicians started having duties other than just obtaining simple consent. Accordingly, the 20th century is a period that recorded the basis of patient autonomy as a principle through judicial rulings.[14]

Nonetheless, disclosures made prior to 1957 had different objectives and content than those made after 1957. As Ruth R. Faden and Tom L. Beauchamp notice, the "beneficence model" had guided disclosures made until 1957, whereas the "autonomy model" has governed disclosures made after 1957 about their objectives and content.[15] That is, disclosures before 1957 were made with the purpose of ensuring patients' medical benefits, but those after 1957 have focused on patients' autonomy.[16] According to their understanding, "[t]he consent practices emerging from this context [beneficence model] were *not meaningful exercises of autonomous decisionmaking*".[17] Nowadays, adhering to the "autonomy model" is appropriate, since it entails disclosing relevant information to secure free consent, as opposed to the "beneficence model" which involves persuading or even pressuring the patient to make a decision that the physician deems optimal for them. This is the reason why the "autonomy model" has been adopted by the current doctrine of informed consent.[18]

10 *Salgo v. Leland Stanford Jr., University Board of Trustees*, 154 Cal App 2d 560, 317 P2d 17 (1957).

11 ibid.

12 Roger M. Rose, 'Informed Consent: History, Theory, and Practice' (1986) 7(1) The American Journal of Otology 82.

13 Betta (n 1) 109.

14 Lydia A. Bazzano, Jaquail Durant and Paula Rhode Brantley, 'A Modern History of Informed Consent and the Role of Key Information' (2021) 21(1) Ochsner Journal 81.

15 Faden and Beauchamp (n 3) 59.

16 ibid.

17 ibid 60.

18 The principle of respect for autonomy is a cornerstone of developing not only the concept of informed consent, but also the concept of advance directives (ADs), which can be defined as "a

B. Theoretical Review

1. Autonomy as a Cornerstone

By adopting the "autonomy model" in the current doctrine of informed consent, the concept of autonomy, defined as "steering the direction of one's life, determining how to behave, and deciding what projects to engage in",[19] has been regarded in the literature as a cornerstone of informed consent.[20] In other words, the requirement of obtaining informed consent in medical settings is based on the principle of respect for autonomy. Without this principle, it would not have any possibility of requiring physicians to obtain informed consent from patients, which implies returning from the "autonomy model" to the "beneficence model".

At first glance, it could appear that understanding the term "autonomy" is simple, but this is in fact not the case. "Autonomy" is a complex term that has been used by many philosophers in different contexts and for different natures or meanings. Important philosophers' various perspectives on the concept of autonomy, such as those of John Rawls, Thomas Scanlon, Robert P. Wolff, Bruce Ackerman and Ronald Dworkin, were collected by Gerald Dworkin.[21] As this author puts it:

> It is apparent that, although not used just as a synonym for qualities that are usually approved of, 'autonomy' is used in an exceedingly broad fashion. It is used sometimes as an equivalent of liberty (positive or negative in Berlin's

---

statement in which a competent person makes an advance decision in matters concerning their health and welfare, which is to be implemented in the event that the person becomes incompetent (loses capacity) in the future", see Daisy Cheung, Michael Dunn and Richard Huxtable, 'Introduction' in Daisy Cheung and Michael Dunn (eds), *Advance Directives Across Asia: A Comparative Socio-Legal Analysis* (Cambridge University Press 2023) 1. The difference between informed consent and ADs can be demonstrated, among others, by the fact that the former is applied in a current moment, whereas the latter in the future, especially when a person becomes incompetent. However, the concept of ADs will not be discussed in this chapter as my focus will be on informed consent. For more information about this concept, see, for example, Daisy Cheung and Michael Dunn (eds), *Advance Directives Across Asia: A Comparative Socio-Legal Analysis* (Cambridge University Press 2023); Hui Yun Chan, *Advance Directives: Rethinking Regulation, Autonomy & Healthcare Decision-Making* (Springer 2018); Man Teng Iong, *Directivas antecipadas de vontade: um regime existente em Macau?* (Novas Edições Acadêmicas 2017); Vera Lucia Raposo, 'To Act or Not to Act, That Is the Question: Informed Consent in a Criminal Perspective' (2012) 19(4) European Journal of Health Law 388–390; André Pereira, 'Advance Directives: Binding or Merely Indicative? Incoherence of the Portuguese National Council of Ethics for the Life Sciences and Insufficiencies of Newly Proposed Regulation' (2009) 16(2) European Journal of Health Law 165–171.

19 Thomas May, *Bioethics in a Liberal Society: The Political Framework of Bioethics Decision Making* (Johns Hopkins University Press 2009) 39.

20 See, for instance, Faden and Beauchamp (n 3) 235; James Stacey Taylor, 'Autonomy and Informed Consent: A Much Misunderstood Relationship' (2004) 38(3) Journal of Value Inquiry 383; Lucie White, 'Understanding the Relationship Between Autonomy and Informed Consent: A Response to Taylor' (2013) 47(3) The Journal of Value Inquiry 483; Jonathan Pugh, *Autonomy, Rationality, and Contemporary Bioethics* (Oxford University Press 2020) 149; Man Teng Iong. *Responsabilidade Civil na Medicina Tradicional Chinesa* (Almedina 2024) 176.

21 Gerald Dworkin, *The Theory and Practice of Autonomy* (Cambridge University Press 1988) 3–6.

> terminology), sometimes as equivalent to self-rule or sovereignty, sometimes as identical with freedom of the will. It is equated with dignity, integrity, individuality, independence, responsibility, and self-knowledge. It is identified with qualities of self-assertion, with critical reflection, with freedom from obligation, with absence of external causation, with knowledge of one's own interests. It is even equated by some economists with the impossibility of interpersonal comparisons. It is related to actions, to beliefs, to reasons for acting, to rules, to the will of other persons, to thoughts, and to principles.[22]

As a way to prevent any conceptual ambiguity, authors in the current literature normally identify a nature of autonomy that can fit well to their studies. For instance, Tom L. Beauchamp and James F. Childress adopt "choice", "action" or "authorization" rather than "capacity" as the nature of autonomy for their study;[23] by contrast, Gerald Dworkin[24] and Thomas Ploug[25] adopt "capacity" as the concept's nature for their studies. As a result, my study also needs to identify a suitable nature of the concept for the purpose of avoiding any conceptual ambiguity.

For this purpose, especially for better understanding the nature of autonomy in the relationship between this concept and informed consent, it seems suitable to demonstrate the distinction, drawn by Faden and Beauchamp, between autonomous persons (agent as nature of autonomy) and autonomous actions (action as nature of autonomy). Hence, these two concepts can be viewed as two different natures of autonomy. For these authors, autonomous persons refer to "persons who qualify to choose and consent precisely because they are autonomous", whereas autonomous actions are the actions satisfying the following conditions: (1) intentionality, (2) substantial understanding and (3) lack of substantial controlling influence by others.[26] Under this distinction, autonomous persons might act, or not act, auton-

22 ibid 6.

23 Tom L. Beauchamp and James F. Childress, *Principles of Biomedical Ethics* (Oxford University Press 2001) 58.

24 Dworkin (n 21) 3–20.

25 Thomas Ploug and Soren Holm, 'Doctors, Patients, and Nudging in the Clinical Context – Four Views on Nudging and Informed Consent' (2015) 15(10) The American Journal of Bioethics 24.

26 Faden and Beauchamp (n 3) 235, 238. For a detailed explanation of these three conditions, ibid 241–262.

Faden and Beauchamp, when analysing the three conditions, defend the idea of degrees of autonomous action, claiming that, even though there is no degree involved in the first condition "intentionality", the second and third conditions are a matter of degree. For their understanding, acts can be either intentional or non-intentional, whereas the conditions of "understanding" and "lack of controlling influence by others" can be fulfilled to a different extent. This is the reason why only in the second and third conditions we can see the expression "substantial", ibid 237–262.

However, this position can be criticised by defending an inexistence of extent or degrees in the second and third conditions. Regarding the second condition, I hold that a patient either understands or doesn't understand the relevant information provided by a physician. There is no such thing as half understanding, less than half understanding, more than half understanding, more and less understanding or any other similar expressions that represent an extent of understanding. If information is relevant according to the adopted disclosure standard (such as the "reasonable patient omously. The same occurs for non-autonomous persons. It depends on whether these (autonomous or non-autonomous) persons' actions do or do not satisfy the conditions above. Hence, it is possible for a situation to occur in which autonomous persons might not act autonomously, whereas non-autonomous persons might act autonomously. For instance, autonomous persons, who are legally qualified to give informed consent, might fail to act autonomously when their actions do not meet any of the abovementioned conditions, such as understanding the relevant information provided by their physicians; in contrast, non-autonomous persons (e.g. those under legal age) might act autonomously by fulfilling the required three conditions, namely by acting intentionally, understanding the relevant information given by their physicians and lacking any controlling influences by others (e.g. a lack of coercion), even though their decisions should not be regarded as legally binding.

Concentrating on "autonomous actions" (action as nature of autonomy), the current literature indicates that the three conditions, defended by Faden and Beauchamp, can be subject to criticism or controversy, especially the second (substantial understanding) and third conditions (lack of substantial controlling influence by others). The second condition, "substantial understanding", especially in part of the research ethics literature,[27] can be seen as an unnecessary condition. It means a consent to clinical trial is valid even though a person does not understand the research project in question. Besides, the third condition "lack of substantial controlling influence by others" can be criticised, especially when "it fails to offer a sufficient account of the sorts of influences that can undermine our decisional autonomy", as Jonathan

---

standard" or the "reasonable physician standard"), its (complete) understanding is essential to make informed consent. For instance, if a patient has 70%, 80% or 90% of understanding regarding the relevant information *X*, it means he/she doesn't understand *X*. Any partial understanding of *X*, even though its percentage is high, means, from my perspective, is non-understanding, because the patient doesn't capture the whole picture of *X*, which is very important for making a decision. What the physician needs to do is guarantee the patient's complete understanding by simplifying the complexity of *X* or using other communication methods.

In regard to the third condition, Faden and Beauchamp claim that there are three main forms of influence (coercion, manipulation and persuasion). For them, manipulation is a continuum concept with extent between coercion and persuasion; coercion is always completely controlling influence; and persuasion is always completely non-controlling influence, ibid 258–259. However, instead of defending three forms of influence, namely two polar extreme influences (coercion and persuasion) and one influence with extent (manipulation, that includes sub-forms, such as deception, indoctrination, seduction, etc.), why don't we identify directly which fact is seen as controlling influence for a particular patient in a specific situation? Coercion surely should be seen as controlling influence. However, instead of using an upper-level concept "manipulation", why don't we analyse directly if, for example, deception can directly influence the decision-making of a particular patient in a specific situation? If this argument is feasible and valid, there will be no such terms as "substantially controlling influence" and "substantially non-controlling influence", as Faden and Beauchamp defend.

After providing these arguments, I argue that there is no degree of autonomous action.

27 For instance, see Franklin G. Miller and Alan Wertheimer, 'The Fair Transaction Model of Informed Consent: An Alternative to Autonomous Authorization' (2011) 21(3) Kennedy Institute of Ethics Journal 215.

Pugh puts it.[28] This author further claims that, according to compatibilist theories, "autonomy is understood to be compatible with the truth of causal determinism; on these views, not all forms of determining influence are understood to undermine autonomy".[29] This claim, from my perspective, should be accepted and followed. Not all forms of influence can be regarded as controlling influences, only the ones that have a causal relationship, namely the ones as a decisive antecedent to affect the decision-making of a person. Even with controversy or criticism in the current literature, I hold that the three conditions, upheld by Faden and Beauchamp, are the basis for the principle of respect for autonomy, based on which the literature can discuss what constitutes a better connotation for the second and third conditions according to the different cultures or backgrounds of each jurisdiction.

In order to connect autonomy to informed consent, the nature of autonomy that we should adopt should be "choices", "actions" or "authorizations" rather than "agents" when discussing autonomy as "agents" (autonomous persons) or, instead, as "choices", "actions" or "authorizations" (autonomous actions).[30] This is because informed consent, in its nature, is a concept that relates to "choices", "actions" or "authorization", not to "agents". Although the concepts seem to be interchangeable, "autonomous authorization" and "informed consent" are not, and should not be, the same. It implies that the two concepts are not synonymous, contrary to what could be understood apparently. As mentioned by Faden and Beauchamp, informed consent, especially in one of its two senses defended by these authors, can be seen as "a specific kind of autonomous choice (or action), an "autonomous authorization" by patients or subjects".[31] This assertion clearly points out the difference in breadth between the two expressions. "Autonomous authorization" has a broader dimension than informed consent has, including other kinds of autonomous choice or action, such as informed rejection.

2. Nature and Requirements of Informed Consent

So, what is the nature of informed consent? Concerns around safeguarding and promoting patients' or research subjects' autonomous or self-determining choice are the foundation of informed consent. Since I adopted "choices", "actions" or "authorization" as the appropriate nature of autonomy in the preceding analysis to connect this concept with informed consent, it seems clear that informed consent and autonomy share the same nature. This claim can be true, but only if the nature of autonomy is determined to be the one that can share with informed consent, not

28 Pugh (n 20) 10. See also Rebecca L. Walker, 'Medical Ethics Needs a New View of Autonomy' (2008) 33(6) The Journal of Medicine and Philosophy 601.

29 Pugh (n 20) 10.

30 I choose "choices", "actions" or "authorizations" as the nature of autonomy in my study not because it is the best in the literature according to my understanding, or it is better than any other natures of the mentioned concept. It is solely because it is, among others, the most appropriate nature for the subject of my current study, which is informed consent.

31 Faden and Beauchamp (n 3) 277.

any of the others.[32] Nonetheless, our analysis should not end here; more investigation into the nature of informed consent is necessary to see the whole picture.

In their analysis of informed consent, Faden and Beauchamp propose two different senses of informed consent in their study, which implies the following two different interpretations with different justifications of the concept: (1) informed consent in the first sense, that refers to an "autonomous authorization", that is, "an autonomous action by a subject or a patient that authorizes a professional either to involve the subject in research or to initiate a medical plan for the patient (or both)"; and (2) informed consent in the second sense, which alludes to an "effective consent", namely "to a legally or institutionally effective (sometimes misleadingly called valid) authorization from a patient or a subject".[33] Both senses are not always overlapping in terms of requirements since informed consent in the first sense can fail to obey relevant policy and institutional rules required by informed consent in the second sense, and on the contrary, informed consent in the second sense may not correspond with informed consent in the first sense, especially when the former does not require compliance with certain requirements of the latter.[34] Despite the non-overlapping relationship, the requirements of informed consent in the first sense can serve as a model or benchmark for evaluating the moral adequacy of the requirements of informed consent in the second sense.[35] We can understand that both senses involve two doctrines of informed consent, that is, the moral one and the legal one. The legal one tends to correspond with the moral one as a means of better protecting personal autonomy in a moral way. However, this correspondence is not always necessary since each jurisdiction has its own moral considerations that can diverge from the moral doctrine of informed consent. This is the reason why the legal doctrine of informed consent varies from one to another state in the common law system in terms of requirements. Taking the United States as a reference, New York statute[36] requires alternatives, reasonably foreseeable risks and benefits involved as disclosure elements, which are different from the ones required by New Georgia statute,[37] which include diagnosis, nature and purpose of surgical and diagnostic procedure, material risks, likelihood of success, practical alternatives and prognosis. In case law, as Peter H. Schuck notices, over half the states in

32 In addition to "autonomy-based justifications of informed consent" (expression originating from Pugh (n 27) 155), I surely admit the existence of other arguments that can justify the duty of obtaining informed consent from physicians, such as the arguments from relational continuity, conflicts of interest, inequalities of power and information and utility. Regarding these arguments, including the one from individual autonomy, see Peter H. Schuck, 'Rethinking Informed Consent' (1994) 103(4) The Yale Law Journal 924–938, even though this author has some reservations relating to these arguments and admits that "powerful dynamics in the health care system that are pushing physician-patient relationships in a more cost-conscious, bureaucratic direction are at once undermining some of these arguments and reinforcing others", ibid 924.

33 Faden and Beauchamp (n 3) 277.

34 ibid 283.

35 ibid 284.

36 New York Public Health Law, s 2805-d (2014).

37 Georgia Code § 31-9-6.1 (2022).

the United States adopt the "reasonable physician standard" as the legal standard for disclosure, whereas other states apply the "reasonable patient standard" for the same purpose.[38] This explains why there are no unifying legal or institutional requirements for all jurisdictions.

Despite this, the discussion of the moral doctrine of informed consent is not without value. As I will demonstrate below, it may need to change to protect personal autonomy in a moral way when integrating the concept of AI. Hence, understanding the requirements of the moral doctrine of informed consent is a prerequisite in order to analyse what requirement(s) need to be changed or improved to face the challenges of AI to personal autonomy. According to Faden and Beauchamp, the following requirements can be derived from informed consent in the first sense (or I would rather call this "the moral doctrine of informed consent"): (1) substantial understanding, (2) substantial lack of control by others, (3) intentionality and (4) authorisation or refusal for a professional to act.[39] The current literature normally summarises and integrates these conditions into the following three requirements: (1) disclosure, (2) understanding (or "comprehension") and (3) decision free from undue influence (or "voluntariness"/"voluntary decision").[40] It should be emphasised that the requirement of "competence" is not mentioned here since it is a problem addressed in the context of informed consent in the second sense rather than the first sense.[41] That is to say, the competence of a person providing an authorisation in accordance with a legal policy or psychiatric standard is not important based on the idea of informed consent in the first sense.

III. Informed Consent for AI-Driven Healthcare

What has been discussed and analysed above relates to the doctrine of informed consent without integrating the concept of AI. As AI-driven healthcare has brought us not only benefits (e.g. providing more accurate diagnoses than physicians do) but also challenges or ethical considerations (e.g. opacity from inputs to outputs in CDSSs), it is fundamental to analyse if the doctrine of informed consent should be changed and improved to face the existing challenges in AI-driven healthcare settings in order to better protect personal autonomy in a moral way. Therefore, in this section I will discuss the new challenges that can appear when applying informed consent in AI-driven healthcare settings, proposing solutions to address the potential problems.

38 Schuck (n 32) 916. This author cites some landmark decisions to support his statement, such as *Chapel v. Allison*, 785 P.2d 204 (1990) and *Henning v. Thomas*, 366 S.E.2d 109 (1988) for states adopting "reasonable physician standard", and *Canterbury v. Spence*, 464 F.2d 772 (1972) for states adopting "reasonable patient standard".

39 Faden and Beauchamp (n 3) 278.

40 See, for instance, Ploug and Holm (n 25) 30–31; Kerry A. Sherman and others, 'Adequacy of Measures of Informed Consent in Medical Practice: A Systematic Review' (2021) 16(5) PloS ONE e0251485.

41 Faden and Beauchamp (n 3) 287, 290–291.

A. New Challenges

AI technologies have played a significant role in healthcare. Previous studies demonstrate that certain AI technologies, such as machine learning (especially its neural networks and deep learning), natural language processing, rule-based expert systems, physical robots and robotic process automation, are relevant to healthcare settings.[42] This can explain why many areas of medicine thus far have benefited from the development of AI technologies. For example, one area where AI technologies are beneficial is precision medicine, which particularly benefits from its machine learning techniques. Machine learning approaches can solve the existing challenges faced by precision medicine, which involve, among others, the fact that a specific treatment may only assist a small number of patients, while other patients may not benefit at all or may even experience unfavourable side effects.[43] As Zeeshan Ahmed and others put it, machine learning approaches can "[bridge] multiple domains in a secure environment for heterogeneous healthcare data analysis and visualization".[44] This could resolve the issue where certain treatments only work for some patients, not all patients.

Nonetheless, it's important to ask if applying informed consent in AI-driven healthcare will bring any new challenges. The premise for answering this question is determining the existing challenges in healthcare without an AI background. Not surprisingly, there have been challenges existing in the traditional context of clinical informed consent.[45] These challenges can relate to factors resulting not only from physicians (or medical institutions) and patients, but also from values protected by certain cultures.

For instance, low health literacy of vulnerable people, such as those who are unemployed, disabled, retired, less educated, with low income and minority ethnic groups,[46] can be a challenge during the informed consent process,[47] especially in

42 See, for instance, Thomas Davenport and Ravi Kalakota, 'The Potential for Artificial Intelligence in Healthcare' (2019) 6(2) Future Healthcare Journal 94–95.

43 Zeeshan Ahmed and others, 'Artificial Intelligence with Multi-functional Machine Learning Platform Development for Better Healthcare and Precision Medicine' (2020) 2020 Database: The Journal of Biological Databases and Curation baaa010.

44 ibid.

45 There are two models of informed consent, namely the clinical model and the research model, in which information disclosure of the former differs from that of the latter. The differences are justified by the differences in their goals, that is, helping patients in the clinical model and producing useful knowledge in the research model. See Christine Grady, 'Enduring and Emerging Challenges of Informed Consent' (2015) 372(9) The New England Journal of Medicine 857. Here in my study, I only concentrate on the clinical model of informed consent since my study will relate only to healthcare settings, not also to research settings. Nonetheless, for information about challenges of the research model of informed consent, see, for instance, Rashmi Ashish Kadam, 'Informed Consent Process: A Step Further towards Making it Meaningful!' (2017) 8(3) Perspectives in Clinical Research 108–109; Lokesh P. Nijhawan and others, 'Informed Consent: Issues and Challenges' (2013) 4(3) Journal of Advanced Pharmaceutical Technology & Research 138.

46 Suzanne E. Mitchell and others, 'Health Literacy and 30-day Postdischarge Hospital Utilization' (2012) 17(sup 3) Journal of Health Communication 325.

47 Isaac KS Ng, 'Informed Consent in Clinical Practice: Old Problems, New Challenges' (2024) 54(2) Journal of the Royal College of Physicians of Edinburgh 154.

terms of understanding the relevant information given by their physicians. It seems obvious that the level of health literacy is proportional to the level of understanding. If patients have poor health literacy, they may have more difficulties in understanding the relevant information provided by physicians, compared to the patients with a higher level of health literacy. Sometimes, people can be regarded as vulnerable not only due to the abovementioned reasons, but also to psychiatric illness and cognitive impairment, such as psychiatric patients and elderly persons,[48] who may have limited mental capacity that can affect their understanding during the informed consent process. On the other hand, sociocultural factors present another challenge for clinical informed consent. Certain cultures in our world have more collectivistic traditions, where family members are more involved in patient care and health-related decision-making, in contrast to Western countries that place greater emphasis on a patient's autonomy.[49] In those cultures, like the Japanese one,[50] the process of obtaining informed consent may involve the patients and their family, or, in more serious cases, only the family. This can affect individual preferences and values that personal autonomy recognises. The following instances show that certain cultural values prevail over personal autonomy: (1) in traditional African communities, older family members' preferences or opinions prevail over younger patients' decisions on medical treatment; (2) in certain societies, women do not have the right of medical decision-making, as it belongs to their husband; (3) in Arab culture, collective, family, tribal or community level make decisions rather than individuals; and (4) family-based healthcare decisions also serve as the primary guiding principle in some Hispanic communities in the United States, particularly those headed by elder members who may be less assimilated.[51] In addition, the fact that patients appear to have numerous options, when in fact they have none, is a further challenge for clinical informed consent. For a patient facing multiple treatment options but lacking medical insurance, the capacity for autonomous decision-making becomes irrelevant, as the absence of necessary resources precludes the ability to effectively pursue any chosen course of action.[52] For instance, we can consider a patient diagnosed with a chronic condition that can be managed through various treatment methods, such as medication, physical therapy, or surgery. However, due to the patient's lack of medical insurance, he/she is unable to afford any of these treatments. Despite having the autonomy to choose the most suitable option for their condition, this decision-making power becomes meaningless because the financial barriers prevent him/her from accessing the necessary care.

48 ibid 156.

49 ibid 155. See also Patrick W. Corrigan and Eun-Jeong Lee, 'Family-Centered Decision Making for East Asian Adults With Mental Illness' (2020) 72(1) Psychiatric Services 114–116.

50 Michael D. Fetters, 'The Family in Medical Decision Making: Japanese Perspectives' (1998) 9(2) The Journal of Clinical Ethics 132–146.

51 Regarding these examples, see Marcela G. Del Carman and Steven Joffe, 'Informed Consent for Medical Treatment and Research: A Review' (2005) 10(8) The Oncologist 638.

52 ibid 637–638.

On the basis of the existing challenges, if combined with AI, will clinical informed consent encounter new challenges? It seems that, whether it is combined with AI, there is nothing worth discussing at the level of informed consent if physicians can comply with the legal requirements, such as the duties of providing relevant information to patients, guaranteeing understanding of the information provided and obtaining consent free from any undue influence.[53] This assertion is correct only if the legal requirements of informed consent are met, but this does not always occur in AI-driven healthcare, especially in terms of requiring physicians' disclosure duty or, on the opposing side, patients' right to obtain relevant information from a physician.

The disclosure duty may face challenges when using CDSSs powered by AI. CDSSs, among many facets of AI-driven healthcare, are the ones that can be linked to clinical informed consent. The clinical decision process, which comprises the following steps: (1) choosing suitable diagnostic tests, (2) determining the patient's diagnosis, (3) choosing the most effective form of treatments and (4) predicting the patient's prognosis, is often used by physicians to make decisions on patient diagnosis and treatment.[54] Since the 1970s, particularly when the development of the decision support systems has coincided with the rise of AI or machine learning, CDSSs have been used to aid with this type of decision-making.[55] It can be viewed as an efficient means of enhancing patient safety by giving physicians access to information that has been intelligently filtered or presented at the right moments to improve health and healthcare.[56] Nonetheless, physicians may have questions pertaining to whether they have a duty to disclose how inputs generate outputs when employing CDSSs, that is, how CDSSs generate the medical treatments the systems consider "the most effective". Even though this question can be solved by legally requiring the mentioned duty, the problem is that in certain cases physicians (or developers) cannot explain to patients how CDSSs generate the treatment suggestions, especially when facing black-box algorithms. It should be emphasised here that a "cannot explain" case, which involves "algorithms that are inherently black box", is different from a "do not explain" case, which involves "algorithms that are deliberately black box".[57] In the latter case, the problem can be easily resolved by using legal tools to require physicians to disclose or explain; otherwise, they can be subject to legal liability. However, the problem in the former case ("algorithms that are inherently black box") is not easy to solve and it can raise other questions: (1) should physicians be (legally and morally) obliged to explain how CDSSs

53 When I express "legal requirements" here, it refers to informed consent in the second sense. Hence, the conditions may include others rather than the mentioned ones, such as legal capacity.

54 Dimitrios Zikos and Nailya DeLellis, 'CDSS-RM: A Clinical Decision Support System Reference Model' (2018) 18:137 BMC Medical Research Methodology 2.

55 I. Glenn Cohen, 'Informed Consent and Medical Artificial Intelligence: What to Tell the Patient?' (2020) 108(6) Georgetown Law Journal 1430.

56 Zikos and DeLellis (n 45) 1; see also Reed T. Sutton and others, 'An Overview of Clinical Decision Support Systems: Benefits, Risks, and Strategies for Success' (2020) 3(17) npj Digital Medicine 1.

57 W. Nicholson Price II, 'Regulating Black-Box Medicine' (2017) 116(3) Michigan Law Review 430.

produce treatment suggestions, even though they are not able to explain it; (2) or, on the contrary, do patients need to bear the risks that can appear when adopting the treatment suggestions generated by CDSSs with algorithms that are inherently black box? In addition to the challenge of opacity or non-transparency generated by black-box algorithms, AI-guided decision-making is prone to inaccuracies and suboptimal outcomes due to measurement errors from flawed data, selection bias from skewed training datasets affecting underrepresented groups and feedback-loop bias that perpetuates systemic healthcare disparities.[58] For instance, an AI model used to predict patient outcomes might perform poorly for minority groups (such as racial and ethnic minorities, LGBTQ+, people with rare diseases, elderly populations, low-income or rural populations, etc.) if the training data primarily comes from a majority population, leading to biased predictions and reinforcing healthcare inequalities.

B. New Moral Requirement

The first question we must address is what information should be disclosed. The content of disclosure duty varies from one jurisdiction to another. To be sure, it is inappropriate to require physicians to provide patients with all information, including unimportant or irrelevant information, as this requirement is unrealistic; similarly, it is inadequate to allow physicians to disclose less information than they should, as patients may make different decisions based on the missed relevant information. What should be disclosed, in fact, depends on the disclosure standard adopted by a particular jurisdiction. The current literature indicates two applicable disclosure standards, that is, "reasonable physician standard" and "reasonable patient standard" (with subjective and objective standards).[59] The "reasonable physician standard" assesses a physician's actions based on whether they align with what a competent professional in the same field would consider acceptable practice, whereas the "reasonable patient standard" requires physicians to disclose information that a typical patient would find material[60] (objective standard) or what the specific patient would personally consider significant (subjective standard).[61] If a jurisdiction adopts a disclosure standard that does not demand notification of whether physicians use AI-guided CDSSs or how these systems generate medical treatment recommendations, then the jurisdiction undoubtedly will not face the challenges originating from black-box algorithms. In this case, it is unnecessary to discuss if physicians should be obliged to explain how CDSSs produce treatment

58 Sharona Hoffman and Andy Podgurski, 'Artificial Intelligence and Discrimination in Health Care' (2020) 19(3) Yale Journal of Health Policy, Law, and Ethics 1–23; Ng (n 47) 156–157.

59 Ng (n 47) 154.

60 "Material information is information which the physician knows or should know would be regarded as significant by a reasonable person in the patient's position when deciding to accept or reject a recommended medical procedure", *Wheeldon v. Madison*, 374 N.W.2d 367 (1985).

61 Ng (n 47) 154. For more discussion about disclosure standards, see Faden and Beauchamp (n 3) 305–316.

suggestions or patients should bear the risks of uncertainty that black-box algorithms cause. But this doesn't always happen, particularly when it's morally required to inform patients whether physicians employ AI-driven CDSSs and how these systems generate recommendations of medical care, under either "reasonable physician standard" or "reasonable patient standard". From my perspective, this can be regarded as a new moral requirement in the doctrine of informed consent, especially in its disclosure duty, since it would not have appeared if AI technologies were not integrated in the healthcare context.

However, the question is when will this moral requirement of disclosure appear? If AI-driven CDSSs can produce the same diagnoses and medical recommendations as physicians, or even better and more accurate diagnoses and medical recommendations than physicians, it seems unnecessary to require physicians to disclose to patients that they have used AI technologies to provide medical advice, as neither physicians nor patients seem to find the information relevant under both disclosure standards. The mentioned moral requirement, in my opinion, ought to arise when certain deficiencies in AI-guided CDSSs, such as opacity and inaccuracies of outcomes, may increase treatment risks and, consequently, influence a patient's decision-making. In this case, patients may choose to follow human-made treatment recommendations instead of AI-generated ones if they are informed about the possible opacity or inaccuracies of AI-driven CDSSs in a given situation.

C. Justifications

Either under the "reasonable patient standard" or the "reasonable physician standard", there are arguments that can justify the new moral requirement, that is, the one that requires physicians, while facing opacity and inaccuracies of outcomes, to disclose to patients whether they have employed AI-driven CDSSs and how these systems have produced recommendations for medical treatment. As not all jurisdictions adopt the same disclosure standard, it is valuable to justify, with strong arguments, the necessity of the new moral requirement under both disclosure standards.

1. Arguments for the "Reasonable Physician Standard"

As I mentioned above, "reasonable physician standard" evaluates a physician's conduct by determining whether they are consistent with what a qualified expert in the same area would regard as appropriate practice.[62] The application of AI-powered CDSS under this disclosure standard can raise special ethical considerations that demand disclosure as required by professional obligation, especially when physicians are morally required to inform patients whether they employ AI-driven CDSSs and how these systems generate medical treatment suggestions, which refers to the new moral requirement emphasised above.

62 Ng (n 47) 154.

The first argument that can justify the new moral requirement based on this standard refers to a necessity of standard of care development that aligns with AI development. As we know, AI is revolutionising healthcare and its impact on clinical practice is continuous.[63] It means AI technologies are changing healthcare settings. Although there are immeasurable benefits while applying AI in medical care (for instance, increasing diagnostic accuracy), its disadvantages, such as the new challenges, also need to be taken into account. Inevitably, the standard of care evolves and changes with AI integration in healthcare settings. If AI may present limitations in specific contexts, such as black-box algorithms or inaccuracies of outcomes generated from data bias, the standard of care should make corresponding changes according to these shortcomings in order to guarantee patient safety. In this context, a reasonable physician should disclose the use of AI-driven CDSSs, so patients are at least aware of AI involvement and its limitations throughout the whole treatment process. Therefore, this disclosure duty should be included in the traditional standard of care.

Another argument for justifying the new moral requirement pertains to avoiding increased risks of treatment failure. We certainly cannot require physicians to guarantee accuracies for diagnoses and treatments, given that they are subject to an obligation of conduct (namely, an obligation "to endeavour or to strive to realise a certain result"), instead of an obligation of result (namely, an obligation "to heal or cure the patient").[64] Nonetheless, it seems a reasonable physician, before making a judgement or medical treatment recommendations, should disclose in a particular case to a patient the employment of AI-driven CDSSs and the potential deficiencies that can increase treatment risks. If any physician, placed in the same position as the physician in a particular situation, understands that the patient must be informed of the use of AI technologies and their shortcomings (e.g. uncertainty of generated outcomes) during the decision-making process, failure to notify puts the patient at risk of making an incorrect decision, which may increase the risk of treatment failure and health damage. For that reason, if any physician considers this information relevant or material for the patient's decision-making, it should be a moral requirement included in the disclosure duty under the "reasonable physician standard".

2. Arguments for the "Reasonable Patient Standard"

According to the "reasonable patient standard", physicians must disclose information that either the patient individually would deem significant (subjective standard) or that a typical patient would find material (objective standard).[65] Like the

63 Shuroug A. Alowais and others, 'Revolutionizing Healthcare: The Role of Artificial Intelligence in Clinical Practice' (2023) 23 BMC Medical Education 689.

64 Regarding these two obligations, see Pierre-Marie Dupuy, 'Reviewing the Difficulties of Codification: On Ago's Classification of Obligations of Means and Obligations of Result in Relation to State Responsibility' (1999) 10(2) European Journal of International Law 375.

65 Ng (n 47) 154.

"reasonable physician standard", there are strong arguments to support the new moral requirement under both the objective and subjective standards.

Avoiding impact on decision-making is one of the main arguments to justify the new moral requirement. Patients should have a right to know how AI is affecting their diagnosis and treatment plan in addition to the involvement of the physician. If patients are unaware that AI is being employed, they may mistakenly believe that their physician's judgement is the only factor considered when making decisions. In this situation, if they are not informed about AI engagement, their autonomy may be impacted to varied degrees. This situation seems to correspond to the so-called "ghost" surgery, which occurs "when someone other than the attending surgeon (who obtained consent) performs an operative or other invasive procedure without the patient's knowledge".[66] As I. Glenn Cohen notices, the "ghost" surgery case law can be used as a foundation to apply analogically to AI-driven healthcare, by claiming that:

> This might seem like a particularly good analogy to the AI/ML [Machine Learning] world, because patients may be unaware of the role of AI/ML in only a particular part of their treatment. For example, the physician performs the surgery herself, but it is based on an AI/ML recommendation of which surgical technique to use in this specific case.[67]

Another argument that can be used for the same purpose, from my perspective, is the opportunity for patients to balance risks and benefits. The environment we live in is full of risks. Sometimes we need to accept certain risks to obtain the benefits we want. As Sven Ove Hansson puts it, "[a] risk is acceptable if and only if it is outweighed by a greater benefit".[68] Nonetheless, to have the opportunity to balance risks and benefits, patients should be informed of any potential risks that could have a detrimental impact on their health. Patients are unable to weigh the risks and benefits of medical treatments generated by AI-driven CDSS against those made by physicians if they are not informed of opacity or potential inaccuracies in the recommendations. Incorrectly balancing risks and benefits can lead to decisions that involve more risks than benefits. Therefore, it is important to integrate the new moral requirement into the disclosure duty under the "reasonable patient standard" when either a particular patient would consider the information significant regarding the opacity or inaccuracies of outcomes (subjective standard) or when a typical patient would find it material (objective standard).

66 Debra Dunn, 'Ghost Surgery: A Frank Look at the Issue and How to Address It' (2015) 102(6) AORN Journal 603.

67 Cohen (n 55) 1439. This author cites *Grabowski v. Quigley*, 684 A.2d 610 (Pa. Super. Ct. 1996) to support the mentioned analogy. In addition to "ghost" surgery, this author tries to find the mentioned analogy also in the following informed consent cases: (1) provider experience and qualification; (2) financial conflicts of interest, ibid 1435–1441.

68 Sven Ove Hansson, 'Weighing Risks and Benefits' (2004) 23(2) Topoi 145.

3. Choosing the Most Suitable Standard: My Perspective

Although the "reasonable physician standard" has relevant arguments to justify the new moral requirement, such as those raised above, I do not think it is a suitable one to protect patient autonomy. This is because patient autonomy can be affected if a reasonable physician does not disclose information that a reasonable patient or a particular patient finds relevant or material. In other words, the patient would have made a different decision if the information had been disclosed. It seems we return a little to the "beneficence model", even though patients do not need to obey the physician's decisions nowadays. In this context, although patients still have the right to consent, at least their right to obtain relevant or material information can be affected. If this right is affected, we do not face a true concept of informed consent as the patient's autonomy is under certain control of a physician.

Thus, in my opinion, the best standard to ensure patient autonomy is the "reasonable patient standard", particularly the subjective one. Although the objective standard takes into account a reasonable patient's necessity, it may disregard a specific patient's necessity. A physician, while adopting the objective standard, may propose a one-size-fits-all approach, which, although fits well to a reasonable patient's situation, may ignore a particular patient's preferences and concerns. In my view, physicians can only truly apply the concept of informed consent in healthcare settings when they consider the needs of a specific patient, not the needs of a reasonable patient. Even though courts can encounter difficulties in proving a particular patient's state of mind,[69] I think this kind of evidence can be obtained in various ways, such as the previous behaviour of a particular patient, communications with relatives to know his/her inner thoughts, etc. If these difficulties continue, at least the objective standard should be adopted, instead of the "reasonable physician standard".

IV. Conclusion

With advances in the use of CDSSs as AI-based tools, the doctrine of informed consent is under pressure as never before and requires reconsideration of its remit. Some of the distinguishing features of AI involve issues such as how to address the fact that the logic used to make decisions is often black-boxed, how to manage potential bias built into algorithms and how to explain the impact of these advanced data algorithms, as most of the time users do not understand how they arrive at a particular conclusion.

This chapter has demonstrated why the "reasonable patient standard" and the "reasonable physician standard" require broadening of the disclosure duty of the use of AI in clinical decision support. Patients must be aware of the fact that AI is being used and be given details of this role in the provision of medical advice,

69 Recognising these difficulties, see Vera Lúcia Raposo, 'Wrongful Birth and Wrongful Life Actions (The Experience in Portugal as a Continental Civil Law Country)' (2017) 3(2) Italian Law Journal 442.

and the restrictions encountered in the software. In this way, the regulations of autonomy, transparency and accountability are ensured, and patients are able to have more options regarding their healthcare.

In conclusion, medical technology today, especially AI, has developed to another level, and so has the warrant for legal and ethical development. The problem with current informed consent is that it does not consider the use of AI in medicine, which is why a more expanded concept of informed consent has to be adopted to sustain the trust between the patient and the healthcare provider, and to guarantee patients' rights in the context of digital healthcare. Decisions that are based on powering sophisticated computers and algorithms supported by AI are bound to redefine informed consent legally and ethically as healthcare initiatives are defined in the future.

7 Bias, Fairness and Algorithmic Accountability

Abstract

This chapter examines how algorithmic bias occurs and functions in clinical AI systems used in the area of diagnoses, clinical decision support and surgical robotics. It identifies key sources of bias including unrepresentative training data, flawed models of proxy targets and context-dependent loss of model accuracy, which together generate subgroup discrimination along aspects of race, gender and age. In order to combat such harms, this chapter assesses new audit tools, transparency frameworks and performance disaggregation techniques designed to help identify and address unfair outcomes. A comparative study of the different regulatory responses in the European Union, United Kingdom and United States reveals divergent approaches: whilst the EU AI Act introduces strict ex ante bias-mitigation duties, the United States' regulatory approach is based on achieving guidance from the FDA as well as civil rights regulatory enforcement, and the United Kingdom adopts a principles-based approach with both NHS initiatives and equality law. Persistent accountability gaps have remained, particularly in terms of apportioning liability for biased or opaque algorithmic decisions. The chapter thus proposes a set of reforms, such as mandatory audits of bias, a certification of fairness, strengthening mechanisms for legal redress, developing a higher duty of care for developers and inclusive data governance. It concludes that clinical AI will only be fair and accountable through coordinated regulatory oversight, ethical approaches to development and adequate mechanisms to ensure equitable patient outcomes.

I. Introduction

Clinical AI promises to make a transformation in diagnostics, clinical decision support and even surgical robotics. Yet to these benefits comes one very real cause of concern – algorithmic bias can creep into clinical AI programs, and perpetuate or exacerbate gaps in healthcare provision.[1] Unlike human clinicians, AI tools are capable of learning from data – and if the data is biased and the same historical

1 Mirja Mittermaier, Marium M. Raza and Joseph C. Kvedar, 'Bias in AI-based Models for Medical Applications: Challenges and Mitigation Strategies' (2023) 6 npj Digital Medicine 113. See also

DOI: 10.4324/9781003785385-9

inequities or imbalances are reflected in data, it is possible for the AI to lead to systematically unfair possibilities. For instance, an AI risk predictor model that was trained mostly on male patients did not work well for women because of the skewed dataset.[2] Such biases affect the fairness of clinical AI and result in healthcare disparities for subgroups in terms of accuracy and quality of care. This chapter takes a critical look at the ways in which bias can occur in clinical AI systems, the repercussions of the issues for matters of fairness and patient outcomes and the need for greater accountability. It compares new regulations and standards in the European Union, United Kingdom and United States, and suggests regulations and policies that can make algorithms more fair and accountable in healthcare.

II. Types and Sources of Bias in Clinical AI Systems

Bias in clinical AI can happen at any of the stages in the model development lifecycle. Biased or unrepresentative training data is one of the main sources of bias. If the data used to train a diagnostic algorithm does not represent the diversity of the patient population, then the performance of the model may be inferior for underrepresented groups of people. For example, researchers discovered an AI model for predicting kidney function decline had been trained on data from a Veterans Affairs hospital where 94% of the patients were men, so the algorithm was far less accurate at predicting decline in kidney function in women.[3] Similarly, if certain ethnic groups or age groups are under-included in data being used to train a tool, the tool can make systematic errors when applied to those groups. Data bias can also happen due to measurement errors or historical prejudices: clinical data may carry the implicit bias of providers (e.g. making certain minorities more likely to be under-documented as having certain pain levels[4]), and these patterns are learned by the AI.

Another source of this risk is label bias, also known as target bias – when the outcome that an AI is trained to predict is itself a poor proxy. One of the most striking examples is an algorithm that has become widely used in US hospitals to identify patients for management with extra care. Its goal was ostensibly to identify those with complex health needs, but the model was trained to predict healthcare costs as a proxy for need. Due to the disparity in access, Black patients often had lower costs for their greater underlying illness, and therefore the algorithm systematically assigned them a lower risk score.[5] This design bias meant

Michael D. Abràmoff and others, 'Considerations for Addressing bias in Artificial Intelligence for Health Equity' (2023) npj Digital Medicine 170.

2 Liz Richardson, 'FDA Review Can Limit Bias Risks in Medical Devices Using Artificial Intelligence' (*Pew.org*, 7 October 2024) < https://www.pew.org/en/research-and-analysis/articles/2021/10/07/fda-review-can-limit-bias-risks-in-medical-devices-using-artificial-intelligence> accessed 29 November 2025.

3 Richardson (n 2).

4 Abràmoff and others (n 1).

5 Richardson (n 2); Abràmoff and others (n 1).

that at the same level of predicted risk, Black patients were actually much sicker than White patients on average – a hidden bias that results in underserved Black patients. Algorithm design choices (such as objective functions, feature selection or assumptions) can therefore incorporate bias if they are manifestations of biased proxies or societal inequalities.

Biases may also introduce themselves during the model development and deployment. Choice of model architecture and training (e.g. optimising overall accuracy with no regard to minority errors) may result in algorithmic bias in which error rates vary across groups. Even if a model is trained using fair data, it may have bias when it is deployed in another context – a diagnostic AI might get it wrong in another country's health system due to different patient demographics or practises.[6] In surgical robotics, if an AI-guided system is calibrated based on the data of limited patient demography or surgeon group, it might perform poorly for other body types or skill levels, exhibiting "under skilling" or "over skilling" biases as to how to evaluate the performance of surgeries.[7] In sum, bias in clinical AI can occur from the data collection process through the design and implementation of the AI model. These biases stand to destroy fairness, as similarly situated patients have different quality of care, based on such characteristics as race, gender, or age – an affront to the ethical principle of justice.[8]

III. Subgroup Disparities in AI Performance

The real-world impact of bias is that clinical AI systems may work disproportionately for or against subgroups in their actions and result in different outcomes. Studies have found that there are significant performance gaps linked to sensitive attributes. For example, an algorithm which was designed for the management of high-risk care was found to systematically underestimate risk for Black patients. Among those patients who were identified by the tool as being in the "high-risk" category, Blacks on average had 26% more chronic illnesses than their white counterparts with the same risk score.[9] In practice, this meant many Black people who required enhanced care ended up being overlooked – a clear case of a poor and biased AI making inequality in the healthcare sector even worse. Similarly, racial distances in medical imaging have been demonstrated with AI models: for example, one study found an AI for predicting future breast cancer risk had higher false negative rates with Black women compared to white women, possibly attributed to

6 Mittermaier, Raza and Kvedar (n 1).

7 ibid.

8 Abràmoff and others (n 1); see also Danton S. Char, Michael D. Abràmoff and Chris Feudtner, 'Identifying Ethical Considerations for Machine Learning Healthcare Applications' (2020) 20(11) The American Journal of Bioethics 7–17, and Michael D. Abràmoff et al., 'Foundational Considerations for Artificial Intelligence Using Ophthalmic Images' (2022) 129(2) Ophthalmology e14–e32.

9 Starre Vartan, 'Racial Bias Found in a Major Health Care Risk Algorithm' (*scientificamerican.com*, 24 October 2019) < https://www.scientificamerican.com/article/racial-bias-found-in-a-major-health-care-risk-algorithm/> accessed 29 November 2025.

imbalances in training data and also differences in care context.[10] The result is that Black women were more often misclassified as "low-risk" and missed for follow ups, adding more serious consequences to the outcome.[11]

The phenomenon of disparities is not simply limited to race. Gender bias has been seen, for example, in the kidney function predictor example where women were given less accurate predictions.[12] Age-based inequalities could emerge if an AI system is developed based mainly on middle-aged people and then used on paediatric or geriatric patients for whom physiology differs.[13] In the case of clinical decision support tools, there has been concern that the algorithms may fail to consider sex-specific presentations of disease (extra-typical symptoms of heart attacks in women, for example) and this could hinder the accuracy of the tool or delay diagnoses for one gender group.[14] Intersectional biases – where combinations of the attributes (e.g. older ethnic minorities) experience compounded error rates – are another concern, although often understudied.[15] These subgroup disparities cause distrust of AI systems and bring into serious question the safety and equity of care. In the context of surgical robotics and AI-assisted procedures, any bias in the algorithm's training (using data from primarily surgeries on one demographic, for instance) could translate to super uneven surgical outcomes or complications rates across the demographics of patients,[16] although more research is needed in this emerging area.

IV. Auditing and Ensuring Fairness in Clinical AI

To overcome those issues, some powerful mechanisms for algorithmic auditing and fairness assessment are essential. One basic step is disaggregation of performance by demographic groups in model evaluation.[17] Developers and regulators should insist that AI models are tested separately for accuracy, sensitivity and

10 Mittermaier, Raza and Kvedar (n 1).

11 ibid.

12 Richardson (n 2).

13 Adam Hadhazy, 'Stanford Ethicists Developing Guidelines for the Safe Inclusion of Pediatric Data in AI-Driven Medical Research' (*HAI Stanford University*, 6 September 2023) <https://hai.stanford.edu/news/stanford-ethicists-developing-guidelines-safe-inclusion-pediatric-data-ai-driven-medical> accessed 29 November 2025; Charlene H. Chu et al., 'Age-Related bias and Artificial Intelligence: A Scoping Review' (2023) 10 Humanities and Social Sciences Communications 510.

14 Andrea Downey, 'Criado-Perez: Men Are Not a Standard Women Fail to Live Up To' (*digitalhealth.net*, 4 March 2020) <https://www.digitalhealth.net/2020/03/criado-perez-men-are-not-a-standard-women-fail-to-live-up-to/> accessed 29 November 2025. See also Isabel Straw, Geraint Rees and Parashkev Nachev, 'Sex-Based Performance Disparities in Machine Learning Algorithms for Cardiac Disease Prediction: Exploratory Study' (2024) 26 Journal of Medical Internet Research e46936.

15 Abràmoff and others (n 1).

16 Jim McCartney, 'AI Is Poised to "Revolutionize" Surgery' (*facs.org*, 7 June 2023) <https://www.facs.org/for-medical-professionals/news-publications/news-and-articles/bulletin/2023/june-2023-volume-108-issue-6/ai-is-poised-to-revolutionize-surgery/> accessed 29 November 2025. See also Ava G. Chappell and Chad M. Teven, 'How Should Surgeons Consider Emerging Innovations in Artificial Intelligence and Robotics?' (2023) 25(8) AMA Journal of Ethics E589–597.

17 Mittermaier, Raza and Kvedar (n 1).

specificity across, for example, different racial groups, genders and age groups. Such "accuracy disaggregation" can expose hidden biases – if the sensitivity of an AI to detect a disease has a 90% success rate for one group, but only a 70% success rate for another group, for instance, it's something that needs to be flagged and removed from the equation.[18] Indeed, experts urge AI developers to undertake basic bias audits – in terms of checking parity of predictions across groups – before any product reaches real patients.[19] If gaps are discovered, the onus is either on developers to gather more diverse data to retrain (correcting a data bias) the model or to correct the algorithm's design (e.g. change its decision threshold or objective) in order to mitigate the bias.[20]

A number of different technical fairness measures as well as toolkits now exist to measure the algorithmic bias in healthcare models.[21] These range from statistical measures of difference in error rate or predictive values by group to more involved measures of "equalised odds" or "calibration" in subpopulations. Alongside measures on metrics, transparency measures are gaining vogue as a means of ensuring fairness. For example, model documentation frameworks such as Model Cards have been proposed to accompany clinical AI tools in order to document the use of the tool, its respective performance possibilities including subgroup performance, as well as known limitations or biases.[22] The *Lancet Digital Health* "STANDING Together" consortium recently released 29 different consensus recommendations for recording information in a health dataset to better deal with issues of transparency and bias.[23] Key recommendations include ensuring the demographic make-up of a dataset and any gaps or skew are fully reported, so that consumers of an AI model (clinicians, hospitals, regulators) are aware of its applicability limits.[24] By improving the transparency of datasets such standards try to detect and reduce algorithmic biases at the origin.[25]

Independent algorithmic auditing is also becoming a practice. Hospitals and health systems are starting to test third-party AI tools (and even their own in house models) for bias before they are put to work. In the United Kingdom, for example, researchers have created platforms to more systematically evaluate commercial AI algorithms for the NHS to ensure that they are "fit for purpose" and that they do not unduly disadvantage any patient group.[26] These audits and bias impact assess-

18 ibid.
19 Vartan (n 9).
20 ibid.
21 Abràmoff and others (n 1).
22 Margaret Mitchell and others, 'Model Cards for Model Reporting' (2019) *FAT* '19: Proceedings of the Conference on Fairness, Accountability, and Transparency* 220–229.
23 Joseph E. Alderman and others, 'Tackling Algorithmic bias and Promoting Transparency in Health Datasets: The STANDING Together Consensus Recommendations' 7(1) The Lancet Digital Health e64–e88.
24 ibid.
25 ibid.
26 Phil Taylor, 'Platform Tests Commercial Algorithms for NHS Use for Bias' (*pharmaphorum.com*, 27 November 2025) <https://pharmaphorum.com/news/platform-tests-commercial-algorithms-nhs-use-bias> accessed 29 November 2025.

ments have the potential to give an external check on industry claims and flag issues, which internal testing might miss. Ultimately, a multi-pronged approach – things that include rigorous validation on a diversity of data, continuing to monitor AI performance in the field and transparency of reporting – is needed in order to build fairness into clinical AI. Keeping "humans in the loop" is another safeguard: clinicians can be trained to pay attention to when a decision support tool is likely making biased recommendations (for example, flagging up the fact that a decision support tool is systematically under-predicting risk in minority patients), and intervene accordingly.[27] Such human oversight, however, should complement (not replace) upstream fixes; the aim is for the AI itself to be as fair and unbiased as it can be at the design time.

V. Regulatory Duties for Bias Mitigation: European Union, United Kingdom and United States

It is increasingly realised by regulators in different jurisdictions that algorithmic bias across healthcare AI needs to be managed proactively. Approaches differ in the European Union, United Kingdom and United States, but there is a general trend emerging: imposing duties upon developers and users of AI to assure fairness and safety.

A. European Union: The EU AI Act and Medical Device Regulations

The EU AI Act is one of the most comprehensive attempts to regulate AI, which has particular implications for the clinic. It categorically defines AI systems that are destined for medical applications (such as AI for diagnosis or treatment choices) as "high-risk" AI and, as a result, subject to stringent requirements.[28] These include requirements with respect to the governance of data: providers of high-risk applications using AI should ensure that training and testing data sets are broad and representative enough, and devoid of errors, in order to limit discriminatory impacts.[29] Article 10 of the EU AI Act requires an assessment of data for potential biases which could pertain to health and safety, and that developers take the "geographical, contextual, behavioural or functional setting" of use to ensure the AI performs equitably in context.[30] In essence, EU law requires the makers of clinical AI to try to actively identify and mitigate the risks of bias during development.

In addition, high-risk AI systems must be subject to conformity assessments and must keep extensive technical documentation proving their compliance.[31] This

27 Mittermaier, Raza and Kvedar (n 1).

28 Article 6 and Annex II of the EU AI Act.

29 Mateo Aboy, Timo Minssen and Effy Vayena, 'Navigating the EU AI Act: Implications for Regulated Digital Medical Products' (2024) 7 npj Digital Medicine 237.

30 Article 10(4) of the EU AI Act.

31 Articles 11 and 43 of the EU AI Act.

means that design decisions, the source of data and metrics on performance are to be recorded, and disaggregated along relevant groups (if relevant).[32] The goal is a lifecycle effort of quality and fairness bolstered by post-market monitoring obligations (providers must track for emerging problems with safety or bias once the AI is implemented and notify the official regulatory authority of serious incidents).[33] Notably, the EU AI Act is done in tandem with existing EU medical device regulations. AI-based diagnostic or decision tools do not only need CE certification under the MDR (which focuses on safety and performance) but also must comply with AI Act requirements in regard to fairness, transparency and human oversight.[34] The stated aim of the policy is specifically to provide for AI not to cause unlawful discrimination or harm to fundamental rights.[35] As the chief architect of the Act explained, EU lawmakers aim to enshrine in law provisions to ensure that AI systems "meet minimum standards of safety and don't lead to undesired impacts (such as illegal discrimination)" and build public trust.[36]

Beyond the AI Act, the European Union also attempted to change its liability regime to aid injured parties in their claims for redress against harms caused by AI. Even though it was withdrawn, a proposed AI Liability Directive – alongside an updated Product Liability Directive – had at its core the aim of addressing the "liability gap", easing the burden of proof on victims in cases where damage is caused by AI systems.[37] For example, when a biased clinical algorithm causes harm to a patient, these measures would enable them to gain compensation by assuming causality if the user of the AI has obviously breached safety requirements. Although the AI Liability Directive was withdrawn, it appears that the trend in the European Union is towards *ex ante* regulation (preventing bias through design and testing requirements) as well as *ex post* accountability (facilitating legal remedies for unfair outcomes).

B. United States: FDA Guidance and Civil Rights Enforcement

In the United States, the regulation of bias in clinical AI is still relatively piecemeal but is moving very quickly. The FDA – which is responsible for medical devices, including many software-based AI tools – has realised that it needs to

32 Article 11(1) and Annex IV of the EU AI Act.
33 Aboy, Minssen and Vayena (n 29).
34 ibid.
35 IESE Business School, 'Artificial Intelligence in Europe: Balancing Innovation with Regulation' (*iese.edu*, 1 August 2024) <https://www.iese.edu/insight/articles/artificial-intelligence-europe-innovation-regulation/> accessed 29 November 2025.
36 ibid.
37 Philipp Hacker, *Proposal for a Directive on Adapting Non-Contractual Civil Liability Rules to Artificial Intelligence: Complementary Impact Assessment* (European Parliament, September 2024) 1 <https://www.europarl.europa.eu/RegData/etudes/STUD/2024/762861/EPRS_STU(2024)762861_EN.pdf> accessed 29 November 2025; Richard Summerfield, 'Risks and Responsibilities: Exploring AI Liabilities' (Financier Worldwide, May 2025) <https://www.financierworldwide.com/risks-and-responsibilities-exploring-ai-liabilities> accessed 29 November 2025.

consider fairness aspects in their review process.[38] Historically, many of the medical devices equipped with AI were cleared by the FDA without much transparency on the demographic performance. A recent study found that 95.5% of AI devices approved by the FDA between 2015–2022 did not report the outcomes of the devices in their demographic subgroups in the approval summaries.[39] This means that there is a gap in accountability: developers were not making an effort to show that their algorithms work equitably across populations. The FDA is now working to close that gap. It has issued guidance that urges manufacturers to include diverse groups of patients in clinical trials and also to evaluate device performance by race, sex and age.[40] Regulators possess broad powers to require such data; however, experts point out that the FDA is within its rights to deny authorisation of an AI product if subgroup analysis shows unacceptable bias in effectiveness.[41] In practice, vital steps that were highlighted in the Good Machine Learning Practice principles, which are co-released by the FDA and the other regulators, include using representative datasets and monitoring to identify the presence of bias over time as AI models are learning or adapting.[42] While not yet binding rules, these principles provide a hint that focusing on bias is a part of getting devices filtered out as "safe and effective" – the threshold of device approval.

Crucially, the United States is also using civil rights legislation to advance fairness in clinical AI. In 2024, the Department of HHS published a final rule on Section 1557 of the Affordable Care Act, under which discriminatory use of biased algorithms in healthcare by health providers or insurers can be considered unlawful.[43] Section 1557 forbids discrimination relating to race, sex, ethnicity, etc. under federally funded health programs.[44] The new rule (which has been in force since 2025) explicitly requires hospitals, clinics and insurance plans to evaluate their clinical decision support tools (including AI) for bias. If an AI tool is based on protected characteristics or has disparate impacts, then "reasonable efforts" must be made by the organisation to ensure that the risk of discrimination is reduced.[45]

38 Abràmoff and others (n 1).

39 John C. Lin and others, 'Benefit-Risk Reporting for FDA-Cleared Artificial Intelligence–Enabled Medical Devices' (2025) 6(9) JAMA Health Forum e253351.

40 FDA, *Evaluation and Reporting of Age-, Race-, and Ethnicity-Specific Data in Medical Device Clinical Studies: Guidance for Industry and Food and Drug Administration Staff* (FDA, 12 September 2017) <https://www.fda.gov/media/98686/download?attachment> accessed 30 November 2025.

41 Richardson (n 2).

42 FDA, Health Canada and MHRA, *Good Machine Learning Practice for Medical Device Development: Guiding Principles* (October 2021) <https://www.fda.gov/media/153486/download> accessed 30 November 2025.

43 Michelle M. Mello and Jessica L. Roberts, 'Antidiscrimination Law Meets Artificial Intelligence – New Requirements for Health Care Organizations and Insurers' (2024) 5(8) JAMA Health Forum e243397.

44 US Department of HHS, Section 1557: Protecting Individuals Against Sex Discrimination (3 November 2020) <https://www.hhs.gov/civil-rights/for-individuals/section-1557/fs-sex-discrimination/index.html> accessed 30 November 2025.

45 Mello and Roberts (n 43).

Regulators (the HHS OCR) have the authority to investigate and enforce compliance, and patients who are subjected to discrimination have the private right of action.[46] This is a huge step: even with no AI-specific law coming from Congress, current anti-discrimination law is being used to hold users of AI accountable for algorithmic bias in healthcare. However, there is a notable gap in that these rules are focused on the deployers (health providers) rather than the developers of the AI technology, due to jurisdictional limits.[47] Developers are indirectly being pressured to create fairer tools since providers will favour AI that is certified as mitigating against bias. In parallel, other US agencies have started to come up with standards – for example, the US Department of Health and Human Services' Office of the National Coordinator for Health Information Technology (ONC) updated its program for certifying healthcare technology with requirements for AI transparency and equity-conscious design for clinical decision software.[48] Although the United States does not have any comprehensive AI Act, this mix of FDA guidance, sectoral certification and anti-discrimination enforcement is steadily building a patchwork of clinical AI bias accountability.

C. United Kingdom: Principles-Based and Existing Frameworks

The United Kingdom, having left the EU regulatory regime, is striking out for itself and so far taking a position that focuses more on guidance than on new laws. In 2023 the UK government issued a white paper aiming at a "pro-innovation" approach to AI regulation, where no new single statute is developed and instead the requirement should be placed on existing regulators to respond to issues related to AI within their sphere of responsibility. Fairness is one of the core principles identified for all regulators – along with safety, transparency, accountability and contestability.[49] The idea is that bodies such as the MHRA (for medical devices), the Care Quality Commission (for healthcare services) and the Equity and Human Rights Commission (EHRC) interpret and enforce fairness within their spheres. The white paper explicitly points out that "fairness is embedded across many areas of law" in the United Kingdom – from equality and human rights law (which prevents discrimination in the delivery of services, including healthcare) to data protection and consumer protection.[50] Rather than new legislation, it is expected that regulators will produce guidance in order to articulate how to ensure that AI-driven

46 Malwina Anna Wójcik-Suffia, 'Algorithmic Discrimination in M-Health: Rethinking the US Non-discrimination Legal Framework Through the Lens of Intersectionality' (2024) (1) BioLaw Journal 367–388.

47 Mello and Roberts (n 43).

48 ibid.

49 Department for Science, Innovation & Technology, *A Pro-innovation Approach to AI Regulation* (March 2023) 26–33 <https://assets.publishing.service.gov.uk/media/64cb71a547915a00142a91c4/a-pro-innovation-approach-to-ai-regulation-amended-web-ready.pdf> accessed 30 November 2025.

50 ibid 29.

decisions do not infringe these standards that already exist in legislation.[51] For instance, the MHRA has been collaborating with international partners on developing good machine learning practice and the NHS has published an AI Code of Conduct for AI developers which emphasises the importance of representative data and bias testing for AI solutions in the NHS.[52] The EHRC in 2024 does state their intent to use their powers under the Equality Act to investigate and enforce against discriminatory AI – and this indicates that an NHS trust or vendor could exactly be held to account if an algorithm is found to be exposing a protected group in its disproportionate manner.[53]

In practice, the United Kingdom is supplementing its traditional frameworks in order to address the problem of AI bias. The NHS AI Lab has set up an AI Ethics Initiative and is funding research into the topic of algorithmic fairness in the field of health. Tools to audit AI efficiency for the NHS (as mentioned earlier) are part of this effort for the operationalisation of fairness checks.[54] While the United Kingdom currently does not have any binding rules as detailed as the European Union's, its regulators have the flexibility to act quickly and place conditions upon the use of AI. For example, the MHRA can require evidence of clinical efficacy in a variety of patient groups as part of the approval of an AI-based diagnostic device. And under the Equality Act 2010, patients could in theory bring claims if an AI-influenced decision amounted to unlawful indirect discrimination (although no such case has yet been tested in courts).[55] The approach in the United Kingdom is therefore principles-based, based on general duties (e.g. the duty not

51 ibid 29.

52 FDA, Health Canada and MHRA (n 42); Department of Health & Social Care, 'A Guide to Good Practice for Digital and Data-Driven Health Technologies' (*GOV.UK*, 19 January 2021) <https://www.gov.uk/government/publications/code-of-conduct-for-data-driven-health-and-care-technology/initial-code-of-conduct-for-data-driven-health-and-care-technology> accessed 30 November 2025.

53 Tom Whittaker, 'AI's Impact on Equality and Human Rights: Equality and Human Rights Commission Sets out its Strategic Plan' (*Burges Salmon*, 9 September 2022) <https://www.burges-salmon.com/articles/102hwg7/ais-impact-on-equality-and-human-rights-equality-and-human-rights-commission-se/> accessed 30 November 2025. See also Clare Fletcher and David Rintoul, 'Equality in AI: The EHRC's Updated Approach to Regulating AI in the Workplace' (*thelens.slaughterandmay.com*, 23 May 2024) <https://thelens.slaughterandmay.com/post/102j87q/equality-in-ai-the-ehrcs-updated-approach-to-regulating-ai-in-the-workplace> accessed 30 November 2025.

54 Department of Health & Social Care, 'Policy Paper: Government Response to the Report of the Equity in Medical Devices: Independent Review' (*GOV.UK*, 11 March 2024) <https://www.gov.uk/government/publications/government-response-to-the-report-of-the-equity-in-medical-devices-independent-review/government-response-to-the-report-of-the-equity-in-medical-devices-independent-review> accessed 30 November 2025. See also, NHS, 'Building Confidence in Clinical Use of AI' (*digital.nhs.uk*, 21 July 2025) <https://digital.nhs.uk/services/ai-knowledge-repository/nhs-lab-ai-ethics-initiative/building-confidence-in-clinical-use-of-ai> accessed 30 November 2025.

55 See Section 19(1) and (2) of the Equality Act 2010. See also Alex McHugh, 'The Interplay between the Equality Act 2010 and the use of AI in Recruitment' (*Pump Court Chambers*, 19 June 2023) <https://www.pumpcourtchambers.com/2023/06/19/the-interplay-between-the-equality-act-2010-and-the-use-of-ai-in-recruitment/> accessed 30 November 2025; Daniel Gray, 'Has Analysis of AI Systems' Potentially Discriminatory Impact Been too Narrow?' (*Mishcon de Reya*, 30 June 2023)

to discriminate, the duty of care in medicine) to cover AI bias issues, supplemented by guidance and voluntary compliance. Critics point out that this patchwork approach could create gaps – and without any explicit rules perhaps some developers might not prioritise dealing with bias – but the government is sure that this agile approach will ensure that the process does not restrict innovation while still maintaining fairness.[56]

VI. Accountability Gaps and Legal Solutions

Despite these regulatory developments, there are still large accountability gaps in the field of ensuring fair and unbiased AI in clinical settings. One challenge is allocating responsibility when that is caused by an algorithm. If an AI misdiagnosis or biased recommendation causes patient injury, who would be legally responsible – the software manufacturer, clinician that relied on the tool, the hospital that deployed the tool or all of the above? Traditional tort and product liability law have a hard time dealing with the complexity of AI. For example, under existing product liability rules in the United States, a manufacturer may be held liable for any injury caused by a defective product.[57] But is an AI model "defective" if it works well for the majority of patients but badly for a subset of patients? From the view of an injured patient given such substandard care based on algorithmic bias, the damage is real, but it is onerous to prove the algorithmic defect or negligence when such bias may be latent and the inner workings of the AI may be opaque. The European Union's effort to reverse the burden of proof for AI harms is one effort to rebalance this, forcing the provider of a high-risk AI system to demonstrate they didn't cause the harm in the case where certain violations of the law (in this case, not meeting the requirements of bias mitigation) were found.[58] This sort of reform can provide incentives for rigorous bias mitigation as non-compliance is effectively to take on liability in a court case.

Another gap exists in terms of transparency and explainability. Many clinical AI algorithms are proprietary "black boxes", making it difficult for affected patients and/or regulators to review how a decision was reached. If a patient is

<https://www.mishcon.com/news/has-analysis-of-ai-systems-potentially-discriminatory-impact-been-too-narrow> accessed 30 November 2025.

56 Department for Science, Innovation & Technology (n 49) 6 and 12.

57 See Del Cid v. Beloit Corp., 901 F. Supp. 539 (E.D.N.Y. 1995), and also Finerty v. Abex Corp., 2016 NY Slip Op 3411, 27 N.Y.3d 236, 51 N.E.3d 555, 32 N.Y.S.3d 44 (N.Y. 2016).

58 Even though the AI Liability Directive has been withdrawn since 6 October 2025 (see EU, *Proposal for a DIRECTIVE OF THE EUROPEAN PARLIAMENT AND OF THE COUNCIL on Adapting Non-contractual Civil Liability Rules to Artificial Intelligence (AI Liability Directive)*, COM/2022/496 final <https://eur-lex.europa.eu/legal-content/EN/ALL/?uri=CELEX:52022PC0496> accessed 30 November 2025), Article 10 of the revised Product Liability Directive has been clear about reversing the burden of proof for AI harms, see EU, *Directive (EU) 2024/2853 of the European Parliament and of the Council of 23 October 2024 on liability for defective products and repealing Council Directive 85/374/EEC*, PE/7/2024/REV/1 <https://eur-lex.europa.eu/legal-content/en/TXT/?uri=CELEX%3A32024L2853> accessed 30 November 2025.

denied a certain treatment because an AI-based decision support tool deemed this unnecessary, it may become very difficult to challenge this decision without gaining insight into the model. This lack of transparency makes accountability difficult because potential bias is not transparent. Legal scholars have argued for a "right to explanation" in AI – some mechanism for patients to know the basis of algorithmic decisions in their care.[59] The EU AI Act has pushed in this direction by requiring transparency to users for high-risk AI (including notifying patients when they are interacting with an AI system and providing information on the system's capabilities and limitations).[60] In the United States, the ONC's new rules around certification require developers to reveal some source attributes and performance data,[61] in an attempt to bring to light what might otherwise be obscured by bias. Ensuring algorithmic transparency without undermining intellectual property is a delicate balance which regulators are trying to strike because ultimately, transparency is fundamental for external audit as well as for the trust of patients.

Ethically, there is also the issue of accountability for outcomes. If a biased AI leads to a systematic under-treatment of a minority group (as with the care management algorithm that deprived many Black patients of extra care[62]), this poses questions of justice that current healthcare quality oversight may not detect. Such disparities might fail to raise immediate safety alarms as there is no one dramatic incident; yet cumulatively they create unfair, suboptimal care. Holding organisations accountable for such statistical harms is difficult. The HHS anti-discrimination rule under Section 1557 is a novel attempt: it is a way for regulators and private litigants to focus on even non-intentional disparate impacts as a form of discrimination in healthcare.[63] However, as one study points out, US courts are divided on whether private lawsuits for disparate impact (unintentional discrimination) should be permitted, which could limit this avenue.[64] In other jurisdictions, too, enforcement of the concept of fairness may hinge more on regulatory oversight than it may based on individual lawsuits. This suggests that public accountability mechanisms – audits, certification, monitoring by watchdog agencies – will play a major role in conjunction with traditional litigation.

Finally, there is a gap in the ethical accountability of AI developers. Developers are not, as a general rule, directly treating patients and, thus, are not subjected to the fiduciary duties imposed on clinicians. Yet their design choices can have major implications on patient outcomes. Some have called for a clearer "duty of care" to be placed on developers of AI for medical tools, similar to the ones shouldered by

59 For instance, see Elanor Taylor, 'Explanation and the Right to Explanation' (2024) 10(3) Journal of the American Philosophical Association 467–482.
60 Article 50 of the EU AI Act. See also Aboy, Minssen and Vayena (n 29).
61 Mello and Roberts (n 43).
62 Abràmoff et al (n 1).
63 Mello and Roberts (n 43).
64 ibid.

medical device manufacturers.[65] Industry standards are starting to take this under consideration: for instance, the ISO has published a set of guidelines to emphasise the need for risk management of bias in AI tools.[66] But without the force of law, such standards depend on corporate goodwill. The regulatory approval process (the FDA's or European Union's) is the power point to make developers accountable, by way of requiring bias mitigation as a condition to access to the market. As these processes strengthen, developers who overlook fairness do so at the risk of their product not being accepted, or of it being withdrawn from the market by an imperative from post-market surveillance if an inequitable performance is found.

VII. Towards Fair and Accountable AI: Prescriptions for Reform

Ensuring fairness and accountability in clinical AI will represent an ongoing struggle on many fronts. Law and policy must evolve in tandem with technology, to allow protection of patients and promotion of equity in care. Based on the analysis above, a number of prescriptive steps can be suggested.

The first step includes *mandatory bias audits and reporting*. Regulators should ensure that any high-risk clinical AI system is bias audited as part of the pre-market evaluation process and continuing use of the system. This means that developers need to test and report the performance of the model across important demographic groups (e.g. by race, sex, age) through validation studies.[67] Regulatory bodies (FDA, MHRA, EMA in Europe) should not allow AI tool approval or certification if clinically significant differences in performance exist, which are not given adequate justification and cannot be prevented. Further, post-market surveillance programs need to monitor the performance in the real world by subgroup; otherwise, biases might be present only at scale or in novel settings. Public disclosure of these audits – through model cards or through transparency reports – will allow them to be scrutinised by the outside scientific world and by affected groups.

The second step refers to *standards and certification of fairness*. The creation of unambiguous technical standards for algorithmic fairness is important. Efforts, such as ISO/IEC TR 24027:2021, where procedures for evaluating bias in AI systems throughout their lifecycle are offered,[68] are a good start. Expanding on this, governments can introduce certification programs where AI systems which pass a test of some sort related to fairness and transparency can receive an "AI fairness" seal or faster approval. The US ONC's certified Health IT program, which now has

65 Bryan H. Choi, 'AI Malpractice' (2024) 73 DePaul Law Review 301; See also Dale Jobson, Victoria Mar and Ian Freckelton, 'Legal and Ethical Considerations of Artificial Intelligence in Skin Cancer Diagnosis' (2022) 63(1) Australasian Journal of Dermatology e1–e5.

66 See ISO/IEC TR 24027:2021, 'Information Technology – Artificial Intelligence (AI) – Bias in AI Systems and AI Aided Decision Making (*iso.org*, November 2021) <https://www.iso.org/standard/77607.html> accessed 30 November 2025.

67 Richardson (n 2).

68 ISO/IEC TR 24027:2021 (n 66).

a big push for transparency and equity considerations,[69] is a perfect example of voluntary certification promoting industry norms. In the European Union, conformity assessments under the AI Act are used for a similar purpose, since they vet a product's compliance with fairness requirements.[70] Making these certifications visible (for example, an NHS procurement requirement that any AI system used in NHS care will be audited and certified for bias) will provide an incentive for developers to try to focus on fairness from the start.

Third, there should be a greater need to *strengthen legal recourse and oversight.* Patients that suffer from biased AI decisions need to have avenues to seek redress. Anti-discrimination laws and consumer protection laws need to be interpreted (and if necessary, amended) in a way that covers algorithmic decision-making in healthcare expressly. The European Union's steps to shift the burden of proof in situations of harm related to AI can be a model for other jurisdictions on how to lower the procedural hurdles for patients.[71] In the United States, having regulations such as the Section 1557 rule[72] with teeth – perhaps by making it clear that disparate impact lawsuits are permitted – will be important so that healthcare organisations take their compliance duties seriously. Regulatory bodies also must be properly resourced to be able to carry out algorithmic audits and enforce penalties. For example, health regulators could have "algorithm audit units" that regularly review AI systems in operation (in the same way as financial regulators audit banks). These units would be capable of checking for adherence to the standards of fairness, and require fixes or removal of systems that demonstrate biased outcomes.

Fourth, *developer accountability and ethical duties* are important as well. It is important to foster an ethics culture in AI developers in medicine. Professional guidelines (from bodies like the American Medical Informatics Association or the British Computer Society's health division) should be updated to incorporate obligations around bias mitigation – taking it as an essential part of patient safety and quality of care. One proposal is requiring an "Algorithmic Impact Assessment" submitted by developers along with clinical evidence, describing how developers have addressed any potential biases and what the residual risks of bias are. This would work in much the same way as an environmental impact assessment for new projects but with a focus on social impacts, such as equity. Developers could also be legally required to keep audit logs in order and to make interpretability features in the models that can help later investigation if something goes wrong. Crucially, multi-disciplinary oversight boards (operating with a team of clinicians, data scientists, ethicists and patient representatives) can be put in place within the healthcare organisations to review and approve any new AI tool to have a human perspective on fairness before it is deployed.

69 Mello and Roberts (n 43).
70 Aboy, Minssen and Vayena (n 29).
71 Article 9(4) of the Product Liability Directive.
72 US Department of HHS (n 44).

The fifth measure points to the concept of *inclusive design and diverse data.* From a policy perspective, one of the most proactive strategies is to make sure that appropriate clinical AI training data is as inclusive and high quality as possible. Laws and grants can help drive efforts to build diverse, representative health data sets – such as helping to fund the collection of health data in communities that are underrepresented or stating that clinical trial data using AI must have suitable representation for underserved minorities. The FDA is already running guidance that urges diversity in clinical studies;[73] this could be extended to particular AI training data. Policymakers could build data-sharing centres or federated learning networks to break down data silos which commonly lead to AI learning on narrow populations. Ensuring that social determinants of health are captured in data may help algorithms figure out what the real need is instead of using biased proxies as well. In short, it is all about data governance, and if the input is fair and comprehensive, the output is much more likely to be fair.

Last but not least, the *empowerment of users and affected groups* is also an important step. Fairness can be enhanced by providing a greater voice to those affected by clinical AI. Patient advocacy groups and communities should have a role in evaluating AI systems that are used in their care – for example, participating in the setting of thresholds for acceptable error balance between sensitivity and specificity. Providing patients with notice and explanation when AI is used in their treatment can serve as a mechanism for enabling them to ask questions or request a second opinion, or serve as a check against blind overreliance on algorithms. Moreover, frontline healthcare workers are in need of training to be aware of AI limitations and biases; an informed clinician will be more likely to identify when an AI's suggestion seems not to be right for a particular patient, and can mitigate the potential harms. Regulators could require AI tools to be accompanied by user education modules related to the correct use of the tool and known bias issues.

VIII. Conclusion

In conclusion, algorithmic bias of clinical AI is not something that we have to accept. It is a challenge to be faced with purposeful protection, strict supervision and adherence to the basic medical moral principle of justice. As this chapter has demonstrated, the European Union, United Kingdom and United States are working on frameworks – from the European Union's hard law requirements to the United States' combination of regulation and civil rights enforcement, to the United Kingdom's principles-led approach – to ensure that AI-driven healthcare does not compromise fairness. Yet regulation will not be enough; there needs to be a culture of accountability and ethical responsibility among a host of stakeholder communities – including AI developers, clinicians and healthcare institutions. By ensuring that bias mitigation measures are implemented, regular audits are conducted and

73 FDA (n 40).

legal accountability is increased for inequitable outcomes, it is possible to ensure that the benefits of clinical AI are realised instead of fomenting bias. The solution is quite clear: only vigilant and ongoing oversight accompanied by equitable design will allow us to fulfil AI's potential in healthcare, namely better outcomes for all patients and not only for a highly privileged few.

8 Liability, Safety and Oversight

Abstract

This chapter analyses the changing frameworks of liability, safety and oversight as AI becomes embedded in clinical practice in the European Union, United Kingdom and United States. It analyses how traditional doctrines – product liability, medical negligence and professional malpractice – are struggling to accommodate for harm caused by diagnostic algorithms, autonomous robotic systems and generative AI tools. The chapter highlights both the doctrinal challenges between AI mistakes as product defects and professional misjudgement and discusses the evidentiary challenges to patients over many complex, nontransparent and technically involved systems. It then examines regulatory methods to safety as well as post-market monitoring, such as algorithm drift detection, change management obligations and new models for supervising adaptive or continually learning AI. Institutional responsibilities are analysed in terms of the roles of clinicians, hospitals and AI developers, who have different responsibilities in a common ecosystem of accountability. Finally, the chapter assesses the reform proposals – from strict liability expansion and clinical safe harbours to national AI registries and no-fault compensation funds – and argues that legal systems must have a dynamic capacity to ensure innovation while at the same time protecting patients. Through the method of comparative legal analysis, the chapter outlines an agenda for developing credible and trustworthy governance of AI-powered healthcare.

I. Introduction

AI is slowly being integrated into the clinical decision-making and patient care process from the use of diagnostic algorithms and surgical robots to generative AI solutions such as medical chatbots and medical documentation assistant tools. These innovations offer the potential of a new level of efficiency and accuracy, with the further consequences of blurring traditional boundaries of responsibility. When an AI system works in error – when, for example, it misdiagnoses a cancer or provides an unsafe strategy for treatment – this challenges existing legal frameworks when it comes to medical liability and patient safety. Policymakers around the European Union, United Kingdom and United States are struggling with how to assign liability over harm caused by AI systems, and how to supervise

DOI: 10.4324/9781003785385-10

the safety of systems that can evolve over time. This chapter examines, in a critical way, comparative approaches in these jurisdictions with regard to liability allocation, ongoing safety/performance monitoring (including managing algorithm drift), regulation of adaptive or continuously learning AI and responsibility of key actors (clinicians, hospitals and AI developers). Examples ranging from diagnostic AI to generative medical chatbots indicate the gaps that exist in the frameworks. The chapter ends with proposals for reform – including revised liability models, enhanced duties of care and regulatory changes – in efforts to ensure accountability and patient safety in an age of healthcare powered by AI.

II. Allocation of Liability for AI-Related Harm

A. Product Liability and Medical Negligence

When an AI system causes harm – for instance, when a diagnostic algorithm misses a tumour or a robot surgeon injures a patient – liability may fall under product liability law (holding those who make products responsible for a defective product) or under medical negligence law (holding those who provide medical care responsible for failing to provide substandard care to a patient). In the European Union, one traditional rule is that the manufacturer is strictly liable for injuries caused by an erroneous product, under the Product Liability Directive 1985.[1] This strict liability does not require that the producer's fault be proven – just that the product was defective, and that it caused damage.[2] However, the classic directive dates back before the dawn of modern AI software and was left ambiguous as to whether standalone software or algorithms are "products". Recognising this gap, the European Union in 2022 proposed a revised Product Liability Directive[3] in order to explicitly cover software, AI systems and AI enabled services.[4] The United Kingdom, while having inherited the European Union's 1987 Consumer Protection Act (which implemented the original Product Liability Directive), also imposes strict liability on the producer of a faulty medical product, and is considering updates to the UK regime in step with EU reforms to ensure AI software is not

1 EU, Council Directive 85/374/EEC of 25 July 1985 on the approximation of the laws, regulations and administrative provisions of the Member States concerning liability for defective products (25 July 1985) <https://eur-lex.europa.eu/LexUriServ/LexUriServ.do?uri=CELEX:31985L0374:EN:HTML> accessed 8 December 2025.

2 European Commission, 'Commission Staff Working Document Impact Assessment Report' (28 September 2022) 13 <https://www.eu.dk/samling/20221/kommissionsforslag/KOM(2022)0495/forslag/1911579/2630183.pdf> accessed 8 December 2025.

3 EU, Proposal for a DIRECTIVE OF THE EUROPEAN PARLIAMENT AND OF THE COUNCIL on liability for defective products, COM/2022/495 final <https://eur-lex.europa.eu/legal-content/EN/ALL/?uri=CELEX:52022PC0495> accessed 30 November 2025.

4 The proposal was adopted by Directive (EU) 2024/2853 of the European Parliament and of the Council of 23 October 2024 on liability for defective products and repealing Council Directive 85/374/EEC <https://eur-lex.europa.eu/legal-content/en/TXT/?uri=CELEX%3A32024L2853> accessed 25 March 2026.

out of the scope of "product" liability.[5] In practice, UK courts have yet to test these principles on AI, but an injured patient in the United Kingdom can in theory sue an AI tool's developer under product liability or sue their clinician/hospital under negligence – or both.[6]

In the United States, product liability is covered under state tort law instead of under a common statute, but in general the manufacturers of medical devices or tools can be held strictly liable for defective design, manufacturing or inadequate warnings.[7] A key difference in the United States is the learned intermediary doctrine, under which manufacturers of prescription medical products (including AI diagnostic software that is classified as a medical device) are often shielded from liability to patients. Under this doctrine, the duty of warning for risks is not owed to the patient but to the physician, who is considered a "learned intermediary" who makes the assessment and communicates with the patient on the basis of the recommendations suggested by the AI.[8] Essentially, the physician – not the patient – is considered the end-user of an AI diagnostic aid, taking into consideration the notion that the physician is in a better position to interpret the output of the tool and weigh the risks and benefits.[9] If the AI system makes a recommendation that leads to unfavourable patient consequence, the manufacturer can assert that they fulfilled their duty by telling or training the doctor, and that any failure to identify the error rests with the doctor (resulting in a malpractice claim against the doctor).[10] This doctrine, however, is critically being re-examined in the area of AI. Some scholars point out that it can "prevent plaintiffs from suing medical device manufacturers directly" even when an algorithm was flawed, as a way to de facto shift liability to physicians.[11] By contrast, in the European Union, there is no formalised learned intermediary rule for product liability – a patient can sue a manufacturer of AI directly if the AI is considered to be a defective product, even if a doctor was involved. Still, in both EU and UK practice, a clinician's error in applying the AI could amount to contributory negligence or a separate issue in malpractice. Thus,

5 Russell Williamson, 'Legal Alert: Law Commission Announces Review of the UK's Product Liability Regime' (*Bird & Bird*, 17 October 2025) <https://www.twobirds.com/en/insights/2025/uk/legal-alert-law-commission-announces-review-of-the-uks-product-liability-regime/> accessed 8 December 2025.

6 Andrew Austin and others, 'UK Product Liability Reform – New Redress Rules for AI Systems?' (*Freshfields*, 5 August 2025) <https://riskandcompliance.freshfields.com/post/102kz0x/uk-product-liability-reform-new-redress-rules-for-ai-systems> accessed 8 December 2025.

7 Hannah R. Sullivan and Scott J. Schweikart, 'Are Current Tort Liability Doctrines Adequate for Addressing Injury Caused by AI?' (2019) 21(2) AMA Journal of Ethics E160–166.

8 ibid. See also, Jessica S. Allain, 'From Jeopardy to Jaundice: The Medical Liability Implications of Dr. Watson and Other Artificial Intelligence Systems' (2013) 73(4) Louisiana Law Review 1049–1079.

9 Sullivan and Schweikart (n 7) and Allain (n 8).

10 Clara Cestonaro and others, 'Defining Medical Liability When Artificial Intelligence is Applied on Diagnostic Algorithms: A Systematic Review' (2023) 10 Frontiers in Medicine 1305756.

11 For instance, see Allain (n 8).

throughout jurisdictions there is a tension between considering AI-caused injury a product issue versus a professional negligence issue.

B. Medical Malpractice and Shared Fault

Clinicians are at the core of liability analyses as AI is often used in healthcare as a tool to enhance human decision-making, rather than replace it. In all three jurisdictions, a physician can be held liable in negligence if the use of an AI results in care which falls below the professional standard. The standard of care is basically reasonable physician conduct under the circumstances.[12] The advent of AI begs the questions on how standards evolve. For example, does a doctor have a duty not to use an available, highly accurate AI diagnostic tool? Or on the other hand, is it negligent to trust an AI recommendation without independent verification? Courts have not yet come to a definitive answer regarding these questions, but the likely approach is context-dependent. If an AI is widely accepted and proven to improve outcomes (e.g. an AI that catches diabetic retinopathy better than the human average), failing to use it could eventually be considered to be falling below standard care. On the other hand, blindly following the output of an AI against one's own clinical judgement – especially if the AI is known to have limitations – could be considered negligent. Indeed, literature points out the danger of "automation bias" where less experienced clinicians may "blindly trust" AI diagnoses,[13] which could make malpractice determinations difficult in a scenario where both the healthcare professional and AI developer contributed to an error. Malpractice law in the United States and United Kingdom would tend to hold the clinician liable if no reasonable practitioner would have acted as they did (e.g. rely on obviously implausible diagnosis based on an AI-generated result). Hospitals could also be sued directly for failing to properly train personnel on the AI or for deploying an improper system. Furthermore, under the principles of vicarious liability, the healthcare institutions in the common law jurisdictions can be held liable for the negligence of their employees when they use AI tools in their patient care.[14] A hospital that encourages physicians to use a clinical AI decision support system, for instance, could be vicariously liable if an employed doctor's misuse of that system could harm a patient.[15]

C. Challenges of Proving Defects and Causation

One of the major challenges in determining liability for harm done by AI systems is the opacity and complexity of the machines. Advanced machine learning models

12 Sullivan and Schweikart (n 7).

13 Cheuk To Chung and others, 'Clinical Significance, Challenges and Limitations in using Artificial Intelligence for Electrocardiography-based Diagnosis' (2022) 23(1) International Journal of Arrhythmia 24.

14 Allain (n 8).

15 Cestonaro and others (n 10).

(e.g. deep neural networks) are so-called "black boxes" with inner reasoning that is not transparent.[16] This makes it difficult for an injured patient to identify a specific "defect" in the algorithm and to demonstrate that the AI's flaw (as opposed to human error) caused the harm. In reaction, the European Union is leading the way in adjusting the rules regarding the burden of proof. Even though the revised AI Liability Directive has been withdrawn recently,[17] the revised Product Liability Directive provides for courts to presume that a product was defective, or that a defect caused the harm, where it is "excessively difficult" for the claimant to prove these given the technical complexity of an AI product.[18] These measures represent a policy choice aimed at assuring that injured parties do not suffer without being able to seek a remedy solely because AI systems are complex and inscrutable. The United Kingdom has not yet adopted similar presumptions, but it seems that the country's Law Commission and policymakers will study whether current concepts of torts are adequate for AI and therefore need to be adapted. In the United States, absent new legislation, courts could rely on traditional legislation (e.g. res ipsa loquitur or imposing liability for defect on the basis of malfunction) to assist plaintiffs; however, this remains untested in the AI context.

D. Emerging Liability Doctrines and Proposals

The novelty of AI in the field of healthcare has led to the proposal of rethinking liability allocations. One proposal from legal scholarship is to consider all the main actors – the AI manufacturer, the clinician using the AI and the hospital – a "common enterprise" with respect to liability.[19] Rather than holding just one party or the other under negligence or strict liability, this enterprise liability would have joint strict liability on the group as a whole on the theory that they are collectively responsible for introducing and managing the AI tool into patient care.[20] Proponents argue this distributed responsibility would provide strong incentives for each actor to monitor and check on the others (developers improving safety, hospitals training staff, clinicians using judgement).[21] Although enterprise liability is not yet law in any jurisdiction, it does reflect recognition that AI-driven harm more often than not

16 ibid.

17 EU, Proposal for a DIRECTIVE OF THE EUROPEAN PARLIAMENT AND OF THE COUNCIL on Adapting Non-Contractual Civil Liability Rules to Artificial Intelligence (AI Liability Directive), COM/2022/496 final <https://eur-lex.europa.eu/legal-content/EN/ALL/?uri=CELEX:52022PC0496> accessed 30 November 2025.

18 Article 10 of the revised Product Liability Directive has been clear about reversing the burden of proof for AI harms, see EU, Directive (EU) 2024/2853 of the European Parliament and of the Council of 23 October 2024 on Liability for Defective Products and Repealing Council Directive 85/374/EEC, PE/7/2024/REV/1 <https://eur-lex.europa.eu/legal-content/en/TXT/?uri=CELEX%3A32024L2853> accessed 30 November 2025.

19 Benny Chan, 'Applying a Common Enterprise Theory of Liability to Clinical AI Systems' (2021) 47(4) American Journal of Law & Medicine 351–385.

20 ibid.

21 ibid.

has multiple contributing causes. Another discussed idea – though more controversial – is to give legal personhood to AI systems so that the AI agent itself could be sued and forced to compensate harm (perhaps via an insurance fund).[22] This concept of an "electronic person" has emerged during discussions in the European Union and largely been rejected as hindering human responsibility. A more feasible reform, borrowing from vaccine-injury compensation programmes, is the establishment of a no-fault compensation fund for injuries caused by certain medical AI.[23] Such a fund (financed by AI manufacturers or healthcare providers) could rapidly provide compensation to patients without even needing to prove negligence or defect, but at the cost of the industry as a whole to cover the unavoidable mistakes. No jurisdiction has thus far established an AI-specific compensation scheme, although it is likely that calls for patient compensation mechanisms will increase if the occurrence of injury involving AI becomes more frequent and high-profile in nature. In sum, although existing doctrines of product liability and medical malpractice offer a starting point (with some tweaks in the European Union), truly novel approaches may be required to achieve fair apportionment of responsibility in the age of the autonomous or semi-autonomous clinical AI.

III. Safety and Performance Monitoring of AI Systems

The paramount duty for the continuous safety and performance of AI in healthcare does not stop once the system is deployed. In fact, a defining feature of AI systems – in particular those that learn from new data – is that their performance can vary over time. Even a fixed algorithm could have algorithmic drift if the patient population or environment changes from the one under which the algorithm was previously validated. Therefore, regulatory authorities and healthcare institutions are focusing on adequate post-market clinical surveillance and performance monitoring for AI. The EU MDR (MDR 2017/745) already requires healthcare device manufacturers, including those for AI software, to have post-market surveillance plans and to collect data on the performance of their devices or AI software and adverse events at all times.[24] These obligations require an AI developer to monitor

22 See, for instance, Pascal Nitiéma, 'Artificial Intelligence in Medicine: Text Mining of Health Care Workers' Opinions' (2023) 25 Journal of Medical Internet Research e41138; Jonathan Lee Mezrich, 'Is Artificial Intelligence (AI) a Pipe Dream? Why Legal Issues Present Significant Hurdles to AI Autonomy' (2022) 219(1) American Journal of Roentgenology 152–157; Jonathan Lee Mezrich, 'Demystifying Medico-Legal Challenges of Artificial Intelligence Applications in Molecular Imaging and Therapy' (2022) 17(1) PET Clinics 41–49.

23 Søren Holm, Catherine Stanton and Benjamin Bartlett, 'A New Argument for No-Fault Compensation in Health Care: The Introduction of Artificial Intelligence Systems' (2021) 29(3) Health Care Analysis: HCA: Journal of Health Philosophy and Policy 171–188.

24 EU, Regulation (EU) 2017/745 of the European Parliament and of the Council of 5 April 2017 on Medical Devices, Amending Directive 2001/83/EC, Regulation (EC) No 178/2002 and Regulation (EC) No 1223/2009 and Repealing Council Directives 90/385/EEC and 93/42/EEC (Text with EEA relevance), Chapter VII <https://eur-lex.europa.eu/eli/reg/2017/745/oj/eng> accessed 7 December 2025.

how their algorithm actually functions in real-life clinical situations and report any serious occurrences or so-called "near-misses" to authorities. The EU AI Act is strengthening this requirement by giving providers of high-risk AI systems (to which most of the AI used in diagnostics or treatment belongs) an obligation to have a post-market monitoring system in place and to periodically review the compliance of the AI with safety requirements in the real world.[25] Similarly, in the United States, the FDA expects the continuous oversight of AI/ML-based medical devices as part of the life-cycle of the device. The FDA's AI/ML Software as a Medical Device Action Plan which was released in 2021 emphasised the importance of monitoring the performance of algorithms as they are used, and responsible reporting of any safety issue or malfunction of devices.[26] The PCCPs of the FDA not only allow for updates (discussed below) but also require manufacturers to explain how they are going to conduct ongoing performance monitoring and risk management follow each modification.[27] Indeed, the FDA now recommends that AI device makers include in their regulatory submissions a plan for conducting post-market safety and effectiveness surveillance which includes how they will detect degradations or biases in performance that occur over time.[28]

From the standpoint of delivering healthcare, algorithm drift is a matter of concern. For instance, an AI sepsis prediction model might work well in one hospital, but when clinical procedures, patient demographics or even pathogens change, the model could become less accurate unless retrained. If not monitored, such drift could result in greater false negatives or false positives, which could jeopardise patient safety. As a result, many commentators call for post-market performance monitoring for AI to be "pro-active, systematic and an essential condition of deployment".[29] A report by UK experts underlined the importance of scaling up post-market surveillance of AI to be a precondition for reaping the benefits of the technology in a safe manner.[30] Along with this, it stated enhanced safety monitoring infrastructure "is essential if we are to enable the potential benefits of these new technologies, whilst also ensuring that deteriorations in performance can be

25 Article 72 of the EU AI Act.

26 FDA, 'Artificial Intelligence/Machine Learning (AI/ML)-Based Software as a Medical Device (SaMD) Action Plan' (January 2021) 6 <https://www.fda.gov/media/145022/download> accessed 8 December 2025.

27 Regarding the guidance, see FDA, 'Marketing Submission Recommendations for a Predetermined Change Control Plan for Artificial Intelligence-Enabled Device Software Functions' (*FDA*, August 2025) <https://www.fda.gov/media/166704/download> accessed 7 December 2025.

28 Rachel Stauffer, 'FDA Issues Final Guidance on Predetermined Change Control Plans for AI-Enabled Devices' (*McDermott+*, 20 December 2024) <https://www.mcdermottplus.com/insights/fda-issues-final-guidance-on-predetermined-change-control-plans-for-ai-enabled-devices/> accessed 7 December 2025.

29 Regulatory Horizons Council, 'Report on the Regulation of AI as a Medical Device' (November 2022) 9 and 49 <https://assets.publishing.service.gov.uk/media/6384bf98e90e0778a46ce99f/RHC_regulation_of_AI_as_a_Medical_Device_report.pdf> accessed 7 December 2025.

30 ibid.

quickly identified and acted on".[31] This implies that healthcare providers should not blindly trust an AI tool indefinitely once purchased; they need mechanisms in place (such as periodic audits, performance checks in use or feedback loops) to know when an AI's suggestions become less trustworthy. In practice, this could mean periodically auditing some samples of AI-generated outputs for quality, monitoring patient outcomes associated with AI usage and creating ways for frontline clinicians to report errors or anomalies with AI. Regulators in all jurisdictions are moving towards demanding such vigilance.[32]

A related safety issue is changing management for an AI – how updates or modifications to an AI system are managed. Many AI models need to be periodically updated: e.g. they may need new clinical guidelines to be incorporated into a system that provides decision support, or new information in the form of imaging data may need to be used to retrain a diagnostic algorithm to become accurate for a new analysis situation. Each change has the risk of introducing new errors. Best practice is therefore to have a formal change management process: validating the updated software on test data, documentation of changes and communicating to the users. In the instance of regulated medical AI there is an important question of when a change is significant enough to require re-approval by regulators. The EU MDR states that a "substantial change" in how the device is used or of the core algorithm used by the device can lead to the device needing to undergo a new conformity assessment with a notified body, thereby effectively considering the updated AI as a new device.[33] Manufacturers must therefore be careful to evaluate if a software update is minor (e.g. tweaking of the user interface) or major (including an effect on clinical performance) and to liaise with regulators appropriately. The approach for the United Kingdom is also likely to be similar, with guidance rather than specific rules about what constitutes substantial change, with responsibility resting with manufacturers to err on the side of patient safety.[34] In the United States, the FDA has historically required new submissions for significant changes that might impact safety or effectiveness, and this could hamper the improvement of AI in an iterative process.[35] However, as described further below, the FDA has

31 ibid 48.

32 For instance, the UK regulator has moved to require such vigilance, see The Medical Devices (Post-Market Surveillance Requirements) (Amendment) (Great Britain) Regulations 2024 <https://www.legislation.gov.uk/uksi/2024/1368/made> accessed 7 December 2025.

33 Medical Device Coordination Group, 'Guidance on Significant Changes Regarding the Transitional Provision under Article 120 of the MDR with Regard to Devices Covered by Certificates According to MDD or AIMDD' (May 2023) MDCG 2020-3 Rev.1, 13 <https://health.ec.europa.eu/system/files/2023-09/mdcg_2020-3_en_1.pdf> accessed 8 December 2025.

34 British Association of Dermatologists, *Guidance for Reporting Design Changes to Artificial Intelligence* <https://www.bad.org.uk/clinical-services/artificial-intelligence/guidance-for-reporting-design-changes-to-artificial-intelligence> accessed 8 December 2025.

35 FDA, 'Artificial Intelligence in Software as a Medical Device' (*fda.gov*, 25 March 2025) <https://www.fda.gov/medical-devices/software-medical-device-samd/artificial-intelligence-software-medical-device> accessed 8 December 2025.

introduced PCCPs to help manage this by pre-authorising some modifications.[36] Regardless of which jurisdiction is involved, there seems to be a growing consensus that safety monitoring cannot be an afterthought – it has to be a component built into the deployment of AI in healthcare. This includes not only the vigilance of the manufacturer, but the users too: hospitals and clinics should have internal oversight committees to review the performance of AI tools and protocols to stop use if problems arise. In sum, continuous performance monitoring and agile response to any problems that may be detected (including the issuance of software patches or even product recall in the case of unsafe AI systems) are now recognised as fundamental elements of AI governance in healthcare.

IV. Oversight of Adaptive and Continuous Learning AI Systems

Perhaps the most novel regulatory challenge faced by AI in healthcare is that of adaptive or continuously-learning AI systems – those that have the capacity to modify their own models in response to new data or feedback, potentially in real-time. Traditional medical device regulation (in both the European Union and the United States) is based on static products whose characteristics do not vary in an unexpected way after approval. A learning algorithm inverts this premise, in that it evolves by use. Regulators have begun to find ways of building oversight to cope with such AI without inhibiting innovation. The United States FDA has been leading the way with a proposed "total product lifecycle" regulatory paradigm for AI/ML software. After proceeding to circulate discussion papers and get inputs from the industry, the FDA in 2023–2024 rolled out a framework for PCCPs.[37] Under a PCCP, an AI developer, at the time of initial FDA clearance or approval, can state the types of changes to the algorithm that they expect to make (such as periodic re-training of the model with new data or improvements in performance to cover edge cases), as well as a modification protocol that describes how those changes will be developed, validated and tested for safety.[38] If the PCCP is authorised by the FDA, the manufacturer may make those changes in the future with no need to submit a new marketing application for them each time.[39] This is a huge change from the past, and can now be considered adaptive AI which can constantly learn within guardrails. The latest guidance by the FDA (2024) on PCCPs makes clear that the manufacturer primarily has to still ensure each change remain within the approved boundaries, and pay attention to updating of device labelling and

36 FDA, 'Marketing Submission Recommendations for a Predetermined Change Control Plan for Artificial Intelligence/Machine Learning (AI/ML)-Enabled Device Software Functions: Guidance for Industry and Food and Drug Administration Staff' (18 August 2025) <https://www.fda.gov/media/166704/download> accessed 8 December 2025.

37 FDA, 'Predetermined Change Control Plans for Medical Devices: Draft Guidance for Industry and FDA Staff' (August 2024) <https://www.fda.gov/media/180978/download> accessed 7 December 2025.

38 Stauffer (n 28).

39 FDA (n 37) 13–16.

user communications with each implemented change.[40] Notably, the FDA expects PCCPs to focus on how the developer is going to mitigate such risks as bias or decreased performance if the AI learns on new data.[41] This approach tries to fit the regulatory expectations to the technical realities of continuous learning of AI.[42]

Europe is pursuing an equivalent path. The EU AI Act explicitly addresses the issue of continuous learning. If an AI system is intended to learn after being placed on the market, such changes are not always required by the conformity assessment regulation as long as the changes were "predetermined by the manufacturer and pre-assessed at the time of the initial conformity evaluation".[43] In other words, similar to the FDA's PCCP concept, the EU AI Act envisions a regime in which developers specify the extent of the permissible changes that a model will go through and then have that assessed by regulators or notified bodies in advance. Changes that fall within the pre-approved range (e.g. model fine-tuning on additional data that was foreseen in the original risk assessment) would not count as a "substantial modification" with the need for recertification.[44] This approach is destined to be combined with regulation at sectoral level: the European Parliament proposed that after implementation of the AI Act, sectoral legislation, such as the MDR, could be adapted to include AI-specific elements, to provide a harmonised legal framework.[45] Until these laws fully come into effect (the rules of the AI Act should take effect after a transition period, likely by 2026), Europe is relying on existing mechanisms – in effect, considering any significant change to an algorithm as a new version of the device. Meanwhile European standards bodies (CEN/CENELEC and ISO/International Electrotechnical Commission, or IEC) are working on technical standards for AI lifecycle management, in order to provide for the regulatory framework.[46] The United Kingdom, outside of the European Union, has expressed its preference for a "light-touch, standards-driven" approach to adaptive AI. A report sponsored by the government called for the use of non-legislative guidance and international standards as a way to try to grapple with the ongoing learning AI, rather than trying to script out detailed rules in statute.[47] The United

40 ibid 12.

41 Charley F. Brown and Gregory Szewczyk, 'FDA Issues Guidance on AI for Medical Devices' (*ballardspahr.com*, 21 August 2025) <https://www.ballardspahr.com/insights/alerts-and-articles/2025/08/fda-issues-guidance-on-ai-for-medical-devices> accessed 8 December 2025.

42 Taylor Esser, 'The FDA vs. EU AI Act: What Regulatory Teams Must Know Now' (*regdesk.co*, 28 July 2025) <https://www.regdesk.co/blog/the-fda-vs-eu-ai-act-what-regulatory-teams-must-know-now/> accessed 8 December 2025.

43 Katerina Demetzou and Vasileios Rovilos, 'Conformity Assessments Under the Proposed EU AI Act: A Step-By-Step Guide' (*fpf.org*, November 2023) 13 <https://fpf.org/wp-content/uploads/2023/11/OT-FPF-comformity-assessments-ebook_update2.pdf> accessed 8 December 2025.

44 ibid.

45 Eva von Mühlenen, 'Europe's Regulatory Approach to Continuous Learning AI' (*Sidley*, 16 October 2023) <https://goodlifesci.sidley.com/2023/10/16/europes-regulatory-approach-to-continuous-learning-ai/> accessed 8 December 2025.

46 ibid.

47 Regulatory Horizons Council (n 29) 36.

Kingdom's Medicines and Medical Devices Act (post-Brexit) provides the MHRA flexibility for the act to adjust requirements by regulations and the MHRA has been actively involved in international working groups (like the International Medical Device Regulators Forum) focusing on the application of machine learning in relation to medical devices.[48] Thus, it is expected that the UK regulators follow the principles from the FDA and European Union, which require upfront transparency of adaptive algorithms and the insistence of rigorous human supervision of any AI that holds the ability to change itself.

The concept of human oversight requires emphasis. Both the EU AI Act and a variety of national guidelines emphasise the need for human control points even in a highly autonomous AI. Article 14 in the EU AI Act requires high-risk AI systems to be equipped with mechanisms for human intervention – e.g. for a clinician to override a suggestion made by an AI or to turn off a system if it is acting dangerously. In a continuously learning system, there may be a need for human oversight, such as a safety officer or multidisciplinary committee to review the new rules or outputs of the AI system on a periodic basis. This is particularly relevant for adaptive AI which could start to work outside the envelope of its original performance. An example which is illustrative here is an AI based insulin pump which adjusts doses based on patient data: if this keeps being able to learn from every individual patient's glycaemic response, then there should be safeguards (alerts or human review) to make sure that it is not drifting into unsafe dosage recommendations over time. Regulators are effectively asking that "the loop" is never fully closed – a human health professional is responsible at some level to monitor the evolution of the AI.[49] Generative AI systems for healthcare raise other oversight questions on the table. Large language models such as ChatGPT, when deployed as medical chatbots or to assist medical documentation, are general-purpose AI which are not specially trained under the regulations of a medical device. The EU AI Act makes a distinction for such a "general purpose AI" and has produced a Code of Practice to help make responsible use of them until more formal rules are in place.[50] For example, in the case of an AI chatbot that provides health advice, the ideal would be for it to be limited by the fine-tuning it has performed on verified medical knowledge and/or by the fact that a licenced professional is supervising or at least validating the recommendations issued. In late 2023, OpenAI (maker of ChatGPT)

48 Laura Squire, 'Med Tech Regulatory Reform: The First Steps towards a New Framework for Medical Devices in the UK' (*gov.uk*, 13 February 2024) <https://medregs.blog.gov.uk/2024/02/13/med-tech-regulatory-reform-the-first-steps-towards-a-new-framework-for-medical-devices-in-the-uk/> accessed 8 December 2025. See also Medicines & Healthcare products Regulatory Agency, 'Impact of AI on the Regulation of Medical Products' (*gov.uk*, 30 April 2024) <https://www.gov.uk/government/publications/impact-of-ai-on-the-regulation-of-medical-products/impact-of-ai-on-the-regulation-of-medical-products> accessed 8 December 2025.

49 European Commission, 'Artificial Intelligence in Healthcare' <https://health.ec.europa.eu/ehealth-digital-health-and-care/artificial-intelligence-healthcare_en> accessed 8 December 2025.

50 Regarding the Code of Practice, see European Commission, 'The General-Purpose AI Code of Practice' <https://digital-strategy.ec.europa.eu/en/policies/contents-code-gpai> accessed 8 December 2025.

themselves barred ChatGPT from providing medical or legal guidance, taking into account the serious liability and safety concerns that lay users of the unvetted outputs will face.[51] This type of self-regulation by AI vendors points to the fact that without any proper oversight, generative AI could easily produce harmful medical content (e.g. incorrect medication instructions or misdiagnoses). Going forward, it can be that regulators decide that any use of a generative model in patient-facing roles should either be approved as a medical device or should be used in an assistive capacity with clear disclaimers and professional oversight. To summarise, oversight of adaptive AI is an evolving or mosaic piece: any oversight the FDA and European Union impose on AI has to allow for controlled learning under regulatory eye, but both have the caveat of planning, transparency and human control in the spirit of managing the unique risks of AI that change themselves.

V. Institutional Responsibilities in AI-Driven Healthcare

Introduction of AI into healthcare settings does not diffuse the responsibilities of traditional actors – if anything, there are new layers of responsibilities added to each. Those who use AI in their clinical work must still retain their primary role as the ultimate advocates for their patient's welfare. Professional standards give clear examples that a tool, regardless of how good it is, is no substitute for clinical judgement. A doctor depending on AI outputs has to be aware of the aim of those outputs and their limitations as well as verify or corroborate the critical recommendations. For example, if a CDS system recommends that the drugs be given in an erroneously high dosage, the physician is expected to question this and not to simply accept the system's suggestion. Failure to do so could be a breach of the physician's duty of care. In the legal sense, the physician should approach AI as a sophisticated assistant – like seeking the opinion of a colleague or a reference – rather than an infallible oracle. As mentioned, US law already places the physician as the "learned intermediary" between manufacturers of AI devices and patients.[52] This means a responsibility to interpret and filter the AI information in a way that is beneficial for the patient. In practical terms, clinicians may be in need of training in basic AI literacy: understanding concepts such as sensitivity vs. specificity or knowing when the AI itself is less reliable (e.g. when it is known that a diagnostic AI has higher error rates for some minority populations when they were not well represented in the training data); and knowing what course of action to take when the output of such an AI contradicts other clinical evidence. Some professional bodies are working on guidelines for the use of AI. For example, the AMA has warned doctors that it is dangerous to rely on tools such as ChatGPT to

51 TED Law, 'OpenAI Bans ChatGPT's Legal and Health Advice' (4 November 2025) <https://www.tedlaw.com/chatgpt-legal-health-advice-ban-liability-ethics/> accessed 8 December 2025. See also Matthew Chun, 'Who's Liable for Bad Medical Advice in the Age of ChatGPT?' (*The Petrie-Flom Center*, 5 June 2023) <https://petrieflom.law.harvard.edu/2023/06/05/whos-liable-for-bad-medical-advice-in-the-age-of-chatgpt/> accessed 8 December 2025.

52 Sullivan and Schweikart (n 7).

make clinical decisions and should be used with a lot of caution and verification, if used at all.[53] In the United Kingdom, the General Medical Council could in future update their Good Medical Practice guidance to include AI – for instance, to advise that doctors will be responsible for ensuring that any decision-support AI that they use is appropriately validated and that patients are informed when AI is materially involved in their care. A further proposition is the obligation to explain to patients: while previous chapters address the issue of informed consent, it is worth underlining that ethically, clinicians should inform patients when a recommendation by an AI is playing a role in any diagnosis or treatment, particularly in cases when there is doubt or controversy. This transparency is part of the process of trust in the doctor-patient relationship of an AI era.

There is a great deal of responsibility that falls on hospitals and healthcare institutions, as the ones procuring, deploying and governing AI systems in the clinical workflow. A hospital has a duty to provide a safe environment and safe equipment for the care of its patients; this has now spread to digital tools.[54] Hospitals need to put in their due diligence when adopting AI systems – taking into consideration their approval by relevant regulatory bodies, their accuracy and their appropriateness for the patient population. Incorporating AI into practice requires the formation of governance structures: for example, many large hospitals have created AI or digital health committees to manage the introduction of AI tools in a hospital, establishing policies (e.g. which department can use which AI and under which conditions) and monitoring outcomes.[55] If a hospital does not adequately train their staff on how to use a new AI diagnostic aid and a mistake happens, the hospital may be deemed negligent for inappropriate implementation or supervision. There is also a responsibility for maintenance and updating: just as hospitals are responsible for maintaining medical devices (calibrating imaging machines, for example), they require processes to ensure that AI software is updated to the latest safe version and to remove (or patch) systems that are found to be unsafe.[56] Notably, if a hospital undertakes local customisation of an AI – for example, re-training an algorithm using its own data in order to improve performance for its patients – it may legally step into the shoes of a "manufacturer". Under the European Union's amended liability rules, for example, a hospital which customises an AI system could be deemed liable as a producer for defects that arise.[57] This gives the institutions an

53 Changyu Wang and others, 'Ethical Considerations of Using ChatGPT in Health Care' (2023) 25 Journal of Medical Internet Research e48009.

54 George Maliha and others, 'Artificial Intelligence and Liability in Medicine: Balancing Safety and Innovation' (2021) 99(3) Milbank Quarterly 629–647.

55 Hospital and Healthsystem Association of Pennsylvania, 'Testimony: Joint State Government Commission, Use of AI in Health Care' (*haponline.org*, 9 April 2025) <https://www.haponline.org/Resource-Center?resourceid=1328> accessed 8 December 2025.

56 Maliha and others (n 54). See also Stacey B. Lee, 'Navigating AI Liability in Healthcare Technology Management' (*24x7mag.com*, 27 October 2025) <https://24x7mag.com/medical-equipment/software/ai/navigating-ai-liability-in-healthcare-technology-management/> accessed 8 December 2025.

57 Cestonaro and others (n 10).

incentive to work with the original developers when they are tuning AI models and carefully document any changes they make. Another institutional role is that of monitoring and incident reporting: hospitals should encourage a culture where clinicians can report AI misdiagnosis or "near misses" without fear of blame so that these can be investigated and fed back to developers and regulators. In the United Kingdom, there have even been proposals that a centralised database for AI incidents be implemented as part of the NHS, to support the post-market surveillance and transparency.[58] Hospitals are therefore the key to linking front-line user experience to external overseeing bodies.

AI developers and vendors (which range from startup companies to large medical device manufacturers and even big tech firms) arguably have the first responsibility in the causal chain – making systems that are safe and effective.[59] They are under regulatory burden (under FDA, MHRA or EU MDR or AI Act regulatory oversight) to build products in accordance with quality and safety standards and to test algorithms thoroughly (clinically and for technical robustness) prior to marketing. As discussed, they must monitor performance and field complaints or incident reports and make updates or recalls as needed. But beyond these legal directions, there is a starting understanding that there is an ethical stance of being transparent for AI developers about their models.[60] This includes providing adequate instructions for use, a description of the intended scope of the AI and known limitations. For example, an AI triage platform might include a warning that it is not validated for paediatric patients, or the radiology AI might tell a patient that certain rare tumour types are not included in its training. If developers over-sell their AI or allow it to be used inappropriately, they can be liable for damages, as well as for harming the patient.[61] Furthermore, as part of ongoing oversight, vendors should provide periodic performance reports to customers (e.g. release results of any re-training or known instances of algorithm drift).[62] Another critical vendor responsibility is to support human oversight: good design can ensure that the AI outputs are interpretable (as far as possible) and the users are able to request clarification.[63] In their safety-critical uses, such as in robotics, developers should build in fail-safes (such as an emergency stop button on a robotic surgeon or constraints on a system to recommend therapies in ways that are constrained by human-established ranges for doses). The law is gradually evolving to strengthen such duties – the EU AI

58 Regulatory Horizons Council (n 29) 48.

59 Emerge Digital, 'AI Accountability: Who's Responsible When AI Goes Wrong?' <https://emerge.digital/resources/ai-accountability-whos-responsible-when-ai-goes-wrong/> accessed 8 December 2025. Maya Sandalow, Katie Adams and Gabriel Loud, 'FDA Oversight: Understanding the Regulation of Health AI Tools' (*bipartisanpolicy.org*, 10 November 2025) <https://bipartisanpolicy.org/issue-brief/fda-oversight-understanding-the-regulation-of-health-ai-tools/> accessed 8 December 2025.

60 Hospital and Healthsystem Association of Pennsylvania (n 55).

61 Cestonaro and others (n 10).

62 Viraj Mehta and others, 'Evaluating Transparency in AI/ML Model Characteristics for FDA-reviewed Medical Devices' (2025) 8(1) npj Digital Medicine 673.

63 Hospital and Healthsystem Association of Pennsylvania (n 55).

Act requires high-risk AI providers to take risk management, data governance, transparency and human oversight measures throughout the lifecycle of the AI.[64] Non-compliance with these could result not only in regulatory sanctions, but also encourage claims for negligence when harm has been brought about by a lack of these measures. Finally, AI vendors are increasingly expected to work with end-users (clinicians and hospitals) even after they have been sold – e.g. through offering training programmes, sharing best practices and participating in continuous improvement with real-world feedback.[65] In summary, all the institutional actors have a role in the safe and accountable use of AI: clinicians must ensure wise use of AI, hospitals must prudently deploy and monitor AI and developers must make and support AI responsibly. It is only through multi-tiered accountability like this that the healthcare system can handle the complexity that AI brings.

VI. Towards Stronger Accountability and Reform

Whilst current legal frameworks in the European Union, United Kingdom and United States are adapting to AI in healthcare, there are gaps among them justifying reform. A foremost priority is to make sure patients who are injured due to AI-related errors are not left in a legal "liability limbo". The direction of the European Union provides one model: explicitly update strict liability legislation to cover AI and reduce the burden of proof for patients in complex cases involving AI.[66] Other jurisdictions can follow in its footsteps by clarifying that software and algorithms are products for the purposes of strict liability, not allowing software developers to avoid responsibility by arguing that AI is a "service". The United Kingdom, for instance, could amend its Consumer Protection Act to similar effect, and consider an AI injury compensation scheme to quickly deal with the patient harm without lengthy litigation. In the United States, where product liability is well-established, the issue is overcoming certain doctrines, such as learned intermediary, that may over-shield manufacturers. Courts or legislators could adjust this balance: there might be, for instance, some sort of carve-out such that, if an AI system caused harm through its own autonomous mistake, the manufacturer would not be able to simply point to the physician's involvement. Conversely, clinicians must have some clarity regarding their standard of care with AI. Professional bodies should articulate guidelines on "AI-aware" practice – e.g. when is it expected to get a second opinion on an AI's suggestion, or to inform patients of AI use. These guidelines can then be used to guide legal standards for malpractice cases. A few of the experts recommend creating safe harbours: to the extent that a clinician adheres to a validated AI recommendation consistent with clinical guidelines, perhaps they

64 Articles 9, 10, 13, 14 and 50 of the EU AI Act.

65 Rohan Misra, Pearse A. Keane and Henry David Jeffry Hogg, 'How Should We Train Clinicians for Artificial Intelligence in Healthcare?' (2024) 11(3) Future Healthcare Journal 100162.

66 Petruta Pirvan, 'AI as Product vs. AI as Service: Unpacking the Liability Divide in EU Safety Legislation' (*iapp.org*, 19 November 2025) <https://iapp.org/news/a/ai-as-product-vs-ai-as-service-unpacking-the-liability-divide-in-eu-safety-legislation> accessed 8 December 2025.

should have a defence against negligence (on the grounds that they followed a decision aid that had been approved by a regulatory body).[67] This in turn could provide incentives towards responsible AI implementation while ensuring that misuse can also be prevented.

On the regulatory front, a post-market regulatory oversight mechanism needs to be strengthened. One reform proposal is to create a national registry of AI in healthcare which records all approved AI systems, issues known and real-world performance data. This would encourage transparency and enable trends in safety to be identified (like drug regulators do with pharmacovigilance data). The United Kingdom's proposal to have a public database of performance for AI medical devices is illustrative.[68] In the United States, the FDA might mandate periodic reporting from the AI device makers on important performance parameters after the approval. In addition, making it a requirement that AI systems have an "audit trail", in which the system's inputs and outputs in each case are noted, could make it easier to analyse in the case of an adverse event, thus helping clinicians and lawyers understand what went wrong. Given how complex adaptive AI is, regulators could also be interested in third-party audits of high-risk AI algorithms. Independent auditors (perhaps certified under government programmes) could periodically subject an AI system to a review of its accuracy, bias and safety updates. This would provide an additional level of assurance beyond that of the manufacturer's attestation.

In relation to duty of care reforms, one of the proposals is to explicitly establish a duty for healthcare institutions to vet and supervise AI tools. For example, hospital accreditation standards could be changed to include requirements to form an AI oversight committee and specified processes for dealing with incidents involving AI. Failure to have such governance could be viewed as organisational negligence. Similarly, there is an argument for updating practices with regard to informed consent: patients could be informed when an AI is being made to play an important part in their care, and perhaps fostered to have a say (though this is linked to consent issues that are tackled in earlier chapters). Another forward-looking idea is imposing a requirement of explainability commensurate with risk: if an AI is being used in a critical diagnosis or treatment, the developer should be responsible for ensuring that the system in question is able to give a rationale that is understandable (or at least key factors that have been considered). Though explainability is not a traditional legal duty, including explainability could help alleviate the "black box" problem and enhance trust and accountability.

Finally, insurance and no-fault solutions should be paid attention. If AI becomes ubiquitous, the volume of litigation could increase; a no-fault compensation fund, paid by manufacturers of AI systems (in the same way vaccine-makers fund

67 Richter, Aliah, 'A Source of Deference or Interference?: An Investigation of the Impact of Medical Artificial Intelligence on the Standard of Care' (2024) 21(1) Ohio State Technology Law Journal 165–190.

68 Regulatory Horizons Council (n 29) 27, 55 and 56.

vaccine injury compensation in the United States) could treat this issue efficiently. This would involve a trade-off in liabilities for developers in return for guaranteed compensation to patients – a model that could provide an innovation spur by limiting catastrophic liability, while guaranteeing that injured patients would be looked after.[69] Legislators in the European Union have been hinting at such creative solutions, but concrete proposals are still yet to be made. Short of a fund, it is a pragmatic step to encourage or require liability insurance for AI developers as well as hospitals deploying AI. If all AI in healthcare is supported by an insurance policy or indemnity arrangement, then patients will have an avenue for recovery even if legal theories are uncertain.

VII. Conclusion

In conclusion, a work in progress in terms of getting the right balance of innovation and accountability in medical AI is in action across jurisdictions. The European Union's comprehensive regulatory strategy (the AI Act and liability directives) differs from the US combination of FDA guidance and evolving common law, and the United Kingdom is aiming at being flexible post-Brexit with guidance and standards. All three, however, understand that liability, safety and oversight in general need to evolve hand-in-hand. The comparative analysis reveals convergence on some principles – e.g. that manufacturers cannot be absolved of responsibility because a doctor was "in the loop", and that continuous learning AI requires continuous oversight. The practical reforms that are proposed – ranging from clarifying rules on liability to strengthening protections on post-market surveillance of AI technology and institutional roles – are intended to guarantee that patients will enjoy the successes of AI-driven healthcare without having to give up the protections and trust that decades of medical law and ethics have established. As AI technologies continue to advance, it is important for the legal and regulatory frameworks to also keep pace as a means of providing a dynamic scheme of oversight that includes protecting patients while driving responsible innovation in healthcare.

69 Mezrich (n 22).

Part III

Case Studies and Horizons

9 Frontier Applications

Generative AI and Extended Reality in Clinical Care

Abstract

This chapter explores the ways in which two frontier technologies – generative AI and XR – are revolutionising clinical care while at the same time challenging current legal, regulatory and ethical laws. Generative AI tools such as large language models used for documentation, triage and diagnostic support present complex issues of liability, uncertain regulatory classification, data protection, transparency and accountability. Similarly, the real-life applications of XR technologies, specifically VR and AR, in therapy, surgery and medical education are greatly increasing, which, among other issues, is raising medical device status, professional licensure, cross-border practice, privacy and security and product liability. In both fields, long-standing ethical principles, such as non-maleficence, autonomy, beneficence, justice and professional integrity, are challenged by immersive interfaces, opaque algorithms and distributed human-machine decision-making. The chapter argues that despite initial global regulator responses with updated instruments of AI governance or medical devices and telehealth reforms, there are large normative and oversight gaps. A socio-legal approach, with the integration of adaptive regulation, institutional mechanisms for governance and reinforced training of clinicians is essential. The chapter ends by finally asserting that it is only by virtue of solid legal accountability structures and ethically underpinned professional praxis that these frontier applications will be able to realise their clinical potential.

I. Introduction

Emerging technologies (like generative AI and extended reality, or XR) are at the cutting edge of innovation in the field of clinical care. These tools promise to revolutionise the way clinicians diagnose illnesses, provide therapy, train healthcare professionals, perform surgery and document clinical encounters. Yet despite and alongside their exciting potential, there are complex legal and ethical issues which require careful analysis. Regulators and ethicists are scrambling all around the world to keep up with the introduction of AI models and immersive XR devices in hospitals and clinics. Questions of patient safety, data privacy, accountability and professional standards are massive. This chapter provides a critical analysis of the clinical applications of generative AI and XR in turn, analysing how each

DOI: 10.4324/9781003785385-12

is being used in the delivery of care and identifying the key legal frameworks and ethical issues around the globe. Real-life examples will help to demonstrate the promise and pitfalls. Ultimately, a strict socio-legal approach is required so that these frontier technologies improve care without compromising fundamental rights and medical ethics.

II. Generative AI in Clinical Care

Generative AI refers to AI systems (such as large language models and image generators) that create new content – text, images or even treatment recommendations – as opposed to simply analysing data.[1] In medicine, generative AI has gone from the experimental laboratories to the clinical setting in a short time. For example, advanced language models can be used to write clinical notes from the conversation between a doctor and a patient, summarise medical research or even predict the possible diagnoses based on complex symptoms. A commonly publicised example in 2023 was the case describing a mother who opened up her child's mysterious findings to a generative AI (ChatGPT) which returned the diagnosis of tethered cord syndrome that had led to a diagnosis missed by multiple physicians – the diagnosis later confirmed by a neurosurgeon.[2] While not something we see on a daily basis, this is an example in which generative AI can aid even in an area such as diagnostic reasoning and uncovering rare conditions. Hospitals are also experimenting with generative AI in the form of "digital scribes" to automatically create clinical documentation and free up physician time from onerous paperwork, to deliberate chatbots that interact with patients for the purpose of triage or mental health counselling.[3] These applications point to a future where AI-generated content will take its place as a normal part of care delivery, from writing a referral letter to prescribing an individual therapy plan.

A. Legal and Regulatory Considerations

Generative AI integrating into healthcare poses new legal issues of regulation and liability. Some important challenges are ambiguity on liability for errors, regulatory classification of AI tools and data governance. Unlike traditional medical devices, many generative AI systems lack a specific certification to be used for medical applications and are more of a general-purpose AI. For example, a large language model, accessed as an application programming interface (API) or consumer interface, could affect a medical decision without having gone through health product

1 Ran He, Jie Cao and Tieniu Tan, 'Generative Artificial Intelligence: A Historical Perspective' (2025) 12(5) National Science Review nwaf050.

2 Kate Hull, 'ChatGPT Correctly Diagnosed a 4-year-old's Mysterious Disease after 17 Doctors Failed' (*businessinsider.com*, 13 September 2023) <https://www.businessinsider.com/chatgpt-diagnose-child-disease-tethered-cord-syndrome-doctors-2023-9> accessed 9 December 2025.

3 Adrien Laurent, 'AI in Hospitals: 2025 Adoption Trends & Statistics' (*intuitionlabs.ai*, 12 October 2025) <https://intuitionlabs.ai/articles/ai-adoption-us-hospitals-2025> accessed 10 December 2025.

regulatory approval.[4] In the United States, the FDA clearance process has been employed to clear many AI/ML-based software as medical devices, however primarily for narrow tasks such as imaging diagnostics.[5] By contrast, a general generative model (e.g. a chatbot giving medical advice) might be outside the boundaries of the existing frameworks used by the FDA unless the model is lead for a medical purpose. This regulatory gap puts the pressure on lawmakers: the EU AI Act 2024 is just one attempt to put such systems under regulation. The AI Act is the first comprehensive AI law in the world and classifies lots of healthcare AI applications as "high-risk" systems subject to strict requirements.[6] Significantly, the AI Act also includes obligations for providers of general-purpose AI that is used in high-risk contexts, which would mean companies behind large models could be required to ensure medical downstream "medical" uses are done with safety and transparency in mind. However, even this forward-looking law has been criticised as an inadequate measure on some fronts (for example, definitions and risk categories may not solve all ambiguity in a rapidly evolving field).[7] In some jurisdictions such as the United Kingdom, lawmakers are adapting the current MDR to AI – the MHRA affirmed in its publication that some of the AI-driven clinical decision software now qualifies as regulated medical devices, including enhanced compliance standards and liability considerations for developers.[8] Globally, we are seeing a patchwork with some countries relying on consumer protection and health-professional oversight overall in the absence of AI-specific laws while other countries (e.g. China) are starting to issue rules for healthcare generative AI use, including content control and data security. In all cases, there is still a lack of clarity regarding who is legally liable if this technology causes harm – is it the clinician user, the hospital deploying the system, or the AI's manufacturer? Ambiguous liability is a fundamental issue: if the responsibility is not clearly apportioned, patients and clinicians are both put at risk.[9] Existing malpractice law typically holds physicians to a standard of care that evolves with technology; therefore, if physicians are using AI, they must do so in a prudent way. We are likely to see case law and statutes that will clarify that the use of an AI recommendation will not free a clinician of obligation to exercise his or her own independent judgement. On the other hand, AI tool developers may be exposed to product liability claims if their software proves to be a "defective" product that led to injury – but this can be hard to prove in the

4 Gary E. Weissman, Toni Mankowitz and Genevieve P. Kanter, 'Unregulated Large Language Models Produce Medical Device-like Output' (2025) 8 npj Digital Medicine 148.

5 Mateo Aboy, Timo Minssen and Effy Vayena, 'Navigating the EU AI Act: Implications for Regulated Digital Medical Products' (2024) 7 npj Digital Medicine 237.

6 Article 6(2), Annex III and Recital 58 of the EU AI Act.

7 Yilin Ning and others, 'Generative Artificial Intelligence and Ethical Considerations in Health Care: A Scoping Review and Ethics Checklist' (2024) 6(11) Lancet Digit Health e848–e856.

8 MHRA, 'Digital Mental Health Technology – Regulation and Evaluation for Safe and Effective Products' (*gov.uk*, 3 February 2025, updated 3 July 2025) <https://assets.publishing.service.gov.uk/media/6866572fadfe29730ea3a9d5/MHRA_guidance_on_DMHT_-_Device_characterisation_regulatory_qualification_and_classification.pdf> accessed 10 December 2025.

9 Ning and others (n 7).

context of a learning algorithm. In sum, the world's regulators are trying to balance their role in fostering innovation while protecting their patients by providing proper legislation for generative AI use in the medical field.

B. Ethical Challenges

In addition to considering legal rules, there are ethical principles that offer an important lens to judge generative AI in the clinical care context. Numerous high-quality analyses have converged on various key ethical issues. First, *safety and non-maleficence* are paramount – generative AI can generate incorrect and even fabricated outputs (so-called "hallucinations"), which may pose a risk of harming the patient if blindly relied upon.[10] Ensuring that AI recommendations do not result in harmful decisions is an ethical responsibility and is also connected to the legal standard of care. Stringent validation and clinical oversight are required before we can trust in the content generated from AI models in making crucial decisions. Second, the issues of *bias and equity* require attention. Generative models trained on non-representative data can also perpetuate systemic biases, leading to their effect on the minority's condition, as suggested diagnosis or treatment actions can work less well for minority groups, thus reinforcing health disparities.[11] Ethically, developers and healthcare institutions have a responsibility to do their best to mitigate bias to advance fairness – for instance, by ensuring greater diversity in their training data and auditing the output of their AI systems for disparate impacts. Third, patients' *privacy and confidentiality* data is at stake. Generative AI is often based on huge datasets, which may contain sensitive health information. If patient records are being used to train models (even if de-identified), there is a risk (even if small) that the AI would accidentally regurgitate information that is identifiable and therefore breaks confidentiality. Strict compliance with data protection laws (such as GDPR in Europe and HIPAA in the United States) is required but not enough.[12] Indeed, scholars point out that HIPAA's Privacy Rule – which was enacted before the rise of AI – may not be able to stem new types of privacy violations perpetrated by advanced large language models.[13] Robust technical safeguards (like differential privacy and secure data enclaves) and new policies are necessary in order to protect patient data in the age of AI. A fourth concern is that of *transparency and explainability*. Generative AI models are often "black boxes" with opaque reasoning that is against ethics of transparency in medical decision-making.[14] Patients have a right to know the basis of clinical decisions; if there is

10 ibid.

11 Tina Tung, Shah Md Nehal Hasnaeen and Xiaopeng Zhao, 'Ethical and Practical Challenges of Generative AI in Healthcare and Proposed Solutions: A Survey' (2025) 17(7) Frontiers in Digital Health 1692517.

12 Ning and others (n 7).

13 Mason Marks and Claudia E. Haupt, 'AI Chatbots, Health Privacy, and Challenges to HIPAA Compliance' (2023) 330(4) JAMA 309–310.

14 Tung, Hasnaeen and Zhao (n 11).

an AI involved, it is difficult but important to explain how it got to the suggestion, as a matter of informed consent and trust. Some jurisdictions even have potential legal codifications for explainability requirements in high-risk domains of application for AI (transparency requirements are explicitly set forth in the EU AI Act[15]). Fifth, *accountability and trust* need to be preserved. Clinicians who incorporate AI into care must ensure that they are accountable to patients and there is a moral duty to explain "to whom and to what extent responsibility or legal liability" attaches for AI-driven results.[16] Ethically, a health provider should not cede the decision-making process to an algorithm without supervision. At the same time, if there is a known, effective AI tool that will improve outcomes, arguably there is an ethical beneficence duty to use it – presuming it is safe – to hopefully benefit patients. This presents a subtly complex situation: doctors have to recognise that they cannot ignore useful AI, nor trust it uncritically. Autonomy is relevant here: patients should not be deceived into believing all advice comes directly from a human clinician if in reality AI was used in drawing recommendations. Some ethicists have argued that the use of AI in patient interactions (e.g. AI chatbots for therapy) will need patient consent and continuous monitoring in order to respect the patient's dignity and autonomy.[17]

Notably, global institutions have begun issuing ethical guidelines to answer these issues. The WHO's recommendations for AI relating to health in 2021 identified some core principles – such as transparency, accountability, inclusiveness and safety – that should be the guiding principles for AI design and use.[18] These principles are consistent with the long-standing bioethics principles (beneficence, non-maleficence, autonomy, justice) and should be applied in the AI context. Professional bodies in the medical profession have similarly stressed the concept that AI has to augment, not replace, the judgement of humans and that doctors or clinicians need to be trained in ethical and governance procedures for AI.[19] Despite such efforts, ethical governance is usually not progressing at the same pace as technological deployment. A lot of healthcare AI systems are being rolled out without thorough ethical review and with little input from stakeholders. This gap highlights the importance of what one review referred to as "multi-layer, socio-technical approach" – this involves technical solutions and the concomitant development of new policies and education – ensuring that generative AI will be applied in a

15 See, for instance, Articles 13 and 50 of the EU AI Act.

16 Ning and others (n 7).

17 Namgyal J. Bhutia and others, 'Ethical Considerations in Artificial Intelligence Interventions for Mental Health and Well-Being: Ensuring Responsible Implementation and Impact' (2023) 13(7) Social Sciences 381.

18 WHO, 'Ethics and Governance of Artificial Intelligence for Health: WHO Guidance' (*WHO*, 2021) 23–30 <https://iris.who.int/server/api/core/bitstreams/f780d926-4ae3-42ce-a6d6-e898a5562621/content> accessed 10 December 2025.

19 World Medical Association, 'Statement on Artificial and Augmented Intelligence in Medical Care' (*wma.net*, October 2025) <https://www.wma.net/policies-post/wma-statement-on-artificial-and-augmented-intelligence-in-medical-care/> accessed 10 December 2025.

trustworthy, human-centred way in clinical care.[20] In summary, generative AI can undeniably help in clinical practice – making diagnostics more accurate, documentation more efficient and knowledge more accessible – but it also raises the risk of global ethical and legal challenges to which the healthcare community should improve its proactive responses. Responsible innovation guided by law and ethics will be of the utmost importance in realising the benefits of AI while ensuring the protection of the patient.

III. Extended Reality in Clinical Care

XR is an umbrella term that covers virtual reality (VR), augmented reality (AR) and mixed reality technologies.[21] XR immerses all users in computer-generated environments or overlays digital information onto the real environment.[22] In clinical medicine, XR technologies are opening new frontiers in the way care is delivered, and how their professionals are trained. Surgeons use AR headsets to visualise the internal anatomy superimposed in a patient to improve precision during an operation. For example, in a pioneering 2018 trial, surgeons at Imperial College London wore Microsoft HoloLens AR headsets to superimpose the images from patients' CT scans (including bones and blood vessels) onto the patients and "see through" tissues during reconstructive surgery.[23] This technology aided in finding and reconnecting blood vessels much faster, and that demonstrates the benefits of XR technology in regard to improving surgical outcomes. VR, on the other hand, has come along as a major therapeutic tool. In the domain of mental health, VR exposure therapy is being used to treat phobias and post-traumatic stress by exposing patients in a controlled and safe virtual environment to situations that trigger the conditions.[24] VR programs are also being used for pain management – immersing patients in relaxing virtual worlds in order to alleviate acute pain and anxiety.[25] Of significance, the potential of VR-based treatments to serve as legitimate medical interventions appears to have finally been woken up in the eyes of regulators: in 2021 the FDA approved the first VR therapeutic device (now marketed as RelieVRx, formerly EaseVRx) for chronic low back pain as a Class II medical

20 Tung, Hasnaeen and Zhao (n 11).

21 European Data Protection Supervisor, 'Extended Reality' (TechSonar report, 2022) <https://www.edps.europa.eu/data-protection/technology-monitoring/techsonar/extended-reality_en> accessed 10 December 2025.

22 ibid.

23 Ryan O'Hare, 'Augmented Reality Helps Surgeons 'see through' Tissue to Reconnect Blood Vessels' (*imperial.ac.uk*, 10 December 2025) <https://www.imperial.ac.uk/news/184520/augmented-reality-helps-surgeons-through-tissue> accessed 10 December 2025.

24 Jessica L. Maples-Keller and others, 'Virtual Reality–Enhanced Extinction of Phobias and Post-Traumatic Stress' (2017) 14 Neurotherapeutics 554.

25 Hunter G. Hoffman, David R. Patterson and Gretchen J. Carrougher, 'Use of Virtual Reality for Adjunctive Treatment of Adult Burn Pain during Physical Therapy: A Controlled Study' (2000) 16(3) The Clinical Journal of Pain 244–250.

device based on results from clinical trials showing significant reductions in pain.[26] This achievement is significant not only because it has shown that XR products can help meet the same level of safety and efficacy required of medical therapies, but has started to classify a new set of products, "digital therapeutics", delivered through VR. Apart from direct therapy, XR is changing the way we train medical practitioners and create simulations. VR can be used to recreate real-life clinical scenarios for students and professionals to practise procedures or decision-making without the risk of harm to a patient.[27] AR is applied in the field of medical education to visualise anatomy in 3D or to guide the trainees in complex tasks step-by-step.[28] Such applications have a tremendous potential in order to enhance the competencies and avoid errors. XR is even being studied in terms of clinical documentation and telepresence: for example, an AR headset could one day let a clinician look down at a patient's electronic health records and view them without using their hands while examining the patient, or let a remote specialist virtually "stand next to" a local surgeon and provide guidance (a kind of tele-surgery support). Clearly, the range of XR use-cases in healthcare is wide, from operating theatre to psychiatrist's office. This scope of application implies a comparably wide-ranging set of legal and ethical considerations.

A. Legal and Regulatory Considerations

As XR spreads to mainstream clinical practice, it is affected by existing health regulations – but it also pushes against some of them. A major question is at what point it is considered a medical device that requires regulatory approval for an XR system. The answer depends upon the intended purpose. If the VR or AR product is promoted for use in the treatment, diagnosis or management of a health condition, it will be considered a medical device (software-based), and is subject to safety and effectiveness requirements by regulators such as the FDA and EU authorities. This is highlighted in the example of the VR pain therapy device, in which the FDA's authorisation was actually preceded by stringent clinical data review, and the device must now comply with the controls of a medical device (including quality manufacturing and post-market surveillance).[29] In the European Union, software (including those for XR applications) for medical purposes is regulated under the MDR. Manufacturers have to pass a CE marking, by proving compliance

26 Todd Maddox and others, 'Virtual Reality-delivered Skills-based Therapy for Chronic Lower Back Pain: From Proof-of-concept to FDA Authorization to Clinical Implementation In-home and Beyond' (2025) 6 Frontiers in Virtual Reality 1613188.

27 Chukwuka Elendu and others, 'The Impact of Simulation-based Training in Medical Education: A Review' (2024) 103(27) Medicine e38813.

28 Priyom Bose, 'Augmented Reality in Anatomy Education and Training' (*News-Medical*, 13 May 2024) <https://www.news-medical.net/health/Augmented-Reality-in-Anatomy-Education-and-Training.aspx> accessed 11 December 2025.

29 Food and Drug Administration, 'Medical Devices; Physical Medicine Devices; Classification of the Virtual Reality Behavioral Therapy Device for Pain Relief' 88 FR 983 (6 January 2023).

with essential requirements which include a clinical evaluation of performance.[30] Regulatory classification is important because that will impact its degree of oversight: a simple meditation VR app may be unregulated wellness software, whereas an application that treats people with post-traumatic stress disorder is likely to be Class IIa or IIb medical devices (in Europe; or require de novo FDA classification in the United States).[31] Authorities are very active in the process of developing guidelines in this area. In the United Kingdom, as part of its demonstration of MHRA's 2025 guidance document, VR therapy tools for mental health are specifically included in the medical devices regime.[32] This means that the regulation of XR has become much more stringent, and developers of XR products have to adhere to a higher standard and can be held accountable if their product poses harm. With the use of XR hardware and software in the clinical setting, questions of product liability also arise. If an AR surgical guidance system failed or showed the wrong information causing an injury, the device maker could be liable under product safety laws. At the same time, however, there is a responsibility for those performing clinical duties to use XR tools as intended and to retain their personal skills – as a surgeon can be found liable for any mistakes made during surgery even if using an AR aid device, unless it is evident that the fault of the device was a primary cause.[33] The intersection between human and machine in XR-driven care will challenge the determination of fault legally in much of the same way as AI.

Data protection law is another very important area: XR devices tend to receive sensitive data. A VR therapy platform could record a patient's interactions, responses or even biometric data (e.g. eye movement, heart rate via sensors) that occur during therapy sessions. AR glasses used by a clinician could accidentally be videoing their patients or bystanders. All such data must also be processed according to the laws that govern privacy. Under GDPR in Europe, for example, processing data concerning people's health or biometric data leads to increased obligations (people's consent, strict security, minimum retention, etc).[34] In the United States, HIPAA would apply if XR tools interface with the protected health information within a covered entity.[35] One such challenge is that XR systems may collect novel streams of data (e.g. 3D activity logs, gaze tracking) which are not explicitly

30 Regulation (EU) 2017/745 (Medical Device Regulation), Articles 5, 10 and Annex I.

31 See, for example, Newel Health, 'ROHKEA® VR Therapy Achieves MDR Class IIa Certification, Marking Major Milestone in Digital Therapeutics for Chronic Pain' (*Digital Health Global*, 6 February 2025) <https://www.digitalhealthglobal.com/rohkea-vr-therapy-achieves-mdr-class-iia-certification-marking-major-milestone-in-digital-therapeutics-for-chronic-pain/> accessed 11 December 2025.

32 MHRA (n 8).

33 Brett Mason and others, 'AI in the Operating Room: Liability Issues for Device Makers' (*Troutman*, 16 April 2024) <https://www.troutman.com/insights/ai-in-the-operating-room-liability-issues-for-device-makers/> accessed 11 December 2025.

34 Kevin Henry, 'What Counts as Personal Data Under the GDPR? Real-World Scenarios and Examples' (*AccountableHQ blog*, 10 April 2025) <https://www.accountablehq.com/post/what-counts-as-personal-data-under-the-gdpr-real-world-scenarios-and-examples> accessed 11 December 2025.

35 HIPAA, 45 CFR §§160.102–103.

covered by existing health privacy frameworks, and will have to be interpreted carefully regarding what constitutes identifiable information. Security is a related legal issue: XR systems plugged into hospital networks have to be safeguarded from breach or hacking (a malicious hacker changing an AR display during surgery is a disturbing, if hypothetical, scenario). Regulators are likely to expect XR in healthcare to adhere to cybersecurity standards as part of devices being approved and then of hospitals being accredited.

Another emerging legal issue is that of professional licensure and cross-jurisdictional practice. XR enables telepresence and remote interactions – consider a psychologist performing a therapy session through VR for a patient in another country or a specialist "augmented" in an operating room in another unknown country through AR feed. Such scenarios lead to the blurring of jurisdictional lines. Licensure laws traditionally require that healthcare providers be licensed in the place of the patient.[36] Thus, an XR-powered cross-border consultation technically could be considered as unlicensed practice if the provider does not have a licence where the patient is located. Some jurisdictions are updating telehealth laws to make allowance for virtual care across borders (within limits or compacts),[37] but XR will stress-test these laws by making that virtual presence even more live. This is an area that is not legally settled and practitioners need to walk carefully in order to comply with licensing and telemedicine rules when using XR for remote care.

B. Ethical Challenges

XR in clinical care draws to the fore a different set of ethical considerations alongside (but different from) those of AI. A 2025 scoping review of XR in psychiatry distilled five fundamentally important ethical issues in XR clinical application.[38]

The first challenge is related to *patient safety* (beneficence and non-maleficence). XR needs to be utilised in ways that benefit and do not harm patients. This includes preventing them from being physically injured (e.g. a disoriented VR user tripping), causing cybersickness or any other adverse effects to result from exposure to VR and avoiding any negative psychological effects. The principle of non-maleficence requires that clinicians consider the risks of an XR intervention (for example, VR simulation may present the potential for triggering extreme

36 For instance, see AMA, 'AMA Issue Brief: Telehealth Licensure' (*AMA*, 2022, updated 8 May 2023) <https://www.ama-assn.org/system/files/issue-brief-telehealth-licensure.pdf> accessed 11 December 2025.

37 For instance, *Telehealth.HHS.gov* notes that multi-state compacts and limited licence reciprocity can preserve patient access to virtual care across state lines, while still respecting state oversight, see Health Resources and Services Administration, 'Licensing across State Lines' (*Telehealth.HHS.gov*, updated 30 April 2025) <https://telehealth.hhs.gov/licensure/licensing-across-state-lines> accessed 11 December 2025.

38 Marie-Hélène Goulet and others, 'What Are the Ethical Issues Surrounding Extended Reality in Mental Health? A Scoping Review of the Different Perspectives' (2025) 15(1) Behavioral Sciences (Basel, Switzerland) 1431.

anxiety or flashbacks in a trauma patient if not tightly controlled) against the benefits.[39] Ensuring safety may include having supervision during therapy sessions in XR, ensuring effectively designed content with clinical tests, and being ready to intervene should a patient become distressed. Beneficence, on the other hand, encourages us to actively practise XR when it can result in less pain or better outcomes – for example, using AR to make surgeries more accurate or VR to provide analgesic distraction from pain whilst wound care is carried out. These outcomes are not easy to balance, and it is an ethical tightrope that providers need to walk with each XR application.

The second challenge is that of *autonomy* and *informed consent*. XR's registering the ability to "alter reality" raises concerns about the patient's autonomy and understanding.[40] Patients and participants in XR experiences could have a reduced ability to differentiate virtual stimuli from real – especially in immersive VR – which could have impacts on their decision-making or sense of control. Ethically it is important to ensure robust informed consent prior to enrolling a patient in an XR-based intervention. This consent must describe what the XR experience will be like, possible psychological impacts and that what is seen or heard may be real to the user, but simulated. For example, a patient participating in VR exposure therapy for phobia must know completely that he/she will be challenged by virtual expressions of the fear and agree to such stress. During use, patients should be able to pause and/or withdraw from the XR experience in order to maintain their agency. Clinicians are even challenged with issues of autonomy: does the use of an AR decision support unduly guide the surgeon's action, thereby diminishing the independent judgement of the surgeon? On the whole, XR should be implemented in ways that respect and enhance patient autonomy – such as by empowering patients with a better understanding (visualising their condition in AR) – rather than diminishing it.

The third challenge is that of *privacy* and *confidentiality*. As noted, XR devices can be used to collect rich data, and could potentially intrude on spaces that previously were private.[41] A therapy session in VR is still a therapy session, which means that the conversation and behaviours are confidential medical information that needs to be protected. If an XR platform keeps records of the sessions and/or avatars' interactions, then who can access that information? Ethical practice requires utmost confidentiality.[42] There is also a concern that AR, when used in public (e.g. a doctor wearing smart glasses in a clinic), could inadvertently record

39 Guoyi Jia, 'The Hidden Worries of Immersive Therapy: Ethical Challenges and Considerations of Virtual Reality (VR) for Mental Health Treatment' (*Medium*, 12 October 2024) <https://medium.com/@guoyijiabetty/the-hidden-worries-of-immersive-therapy-ethical-challenges-and-considerations-of-virtual-reality-b8e62023588d> accessed 11 December 2025.

40 ibid.

41 Vítor Bernardo, 'Extended Reality' (*European Data Protection Supervisor*) <https://www.edps.europa.eu/data-protection/technology-monitoring/techsonar/extended-reality_en> accessed 11 December 2025.

42 Jia (n 39).

people or reveal sensitive information on the display visible to others. It is important to operate under privacy-by-design: any data should be encrypted, minimised and used solely in the benefit of the patient. In research settings, if XR is to be used in clinical trials, research participants should be informed as to what personal data is being collected (e.g. eye movement) and how it will be anonymised. The trust by patients in caregivers is extended to any tool the caregiver is using – so preserving confidentiality in XR is of paramount importance to keep trust.

The fourth challenge is *liability* and *professional integrity*. There is an ethical need to clarify responsibility when using XR in care.[43] If there is an adverse outcome to an XR-aided procedure or therapy, clinicians should not avoid blame by pointing to the technology. Integrity means acknowledging the limits of XR tools, and not overpromising the capabilities of these tools for the patients. For example, a surgeon should not promise that an AR headset will result in success – that would be misleading. Ethically, healthcare providers must also be within the bounds of their competence: adoption of XR methods requires that they be trained in order to use them appropriately, so that they will not expose their patients to unskilled experimentation.[44] On a systemic level, the introduction of XR should be combined with guidelines as well as training protocols to ensure that the practitioners work with these practice tools in an ethical and effective way. Healthcare institutions may devise policies on the use of XR (e.g. the grounding of certain VR therapies – at least by the presence of a technician; also checking the alignment of AR with patient anatomy beforehand in case of surgery). The distribution of responsibility where mixed human-technology workflows are involved is not only a legal issue but also an ethical issue related to fairness and responsibility between team members and tech providers.

The fifth challenge relates to *inclusiveness* and *equity*. As with many advanced technologies, XR could help to reduce healthcare disparities or contribute to them. On the ethical side, it is important that XR solutions are designed and implemented in an inclusive manner. This means making XR hardware and software available to people with disabilities (for example, subtitles or audio description in VR to people with hearing or vision impairments), making sure that content is culturally sensitive and doesn't marginalise groups. There is also the problem of access: it is possible to make XR equipment costly; if it is central to some therapies or training, will all clinics and patients have access to it? An ethical health system would try to prevent a scenario where only well-known hospitals in big cities have AR-guided surgery or only certain patients pay for an expensive kit of VR therapies that can be accessed at home. Efforts such as low-cost VR via the smartphone and open source AR software might help to democratise access. Additionally, having different stakeholders involved in the development of XR healthcare applications (including

43 World Medical Association, *Statement on Artificial and Augmented Intelligence in Medical Care* (October 2025) para 9 (Accountability) <https://www.wma.net/policies-post/wma-statement-on-artificial-and-augmented-intelligence-in-medical-care/> accessed 11 December 2025.

44 ibid para 44.

patients from different backgrounds) is important in order to identify biases or exclusions early. The principle of justice in healthcare ethics implores that the benefits from new technology are shared in a fair way and the existing inequities are not worsened.[45] Early evidence suggests this area is often overlooked – the scoping review found inclusiveness and equity were amongst the least discussed ethical aspects available in the XR literature.[46] As the use of XR scales up, equity needs to rise in importance in ethical considerations.

In facing these challenges, it should be noted that XR in healthcare is still a relatively new phenomenon and empirical ethics research is playing catch-up. There is a kind of "research void" when it comes to long-term implications of XR interventions, as well as the views of patients themselves with regard to these technologies.[47] This is such an uncertainty that it requires humility and caution when it comes to deployment. It may be appropriate, for example, to introduce small pilot programs and supervision of ethics when introducing a novel XR therapy, and to engage in the development of specific information consent protocols and safety checklists. Some institutions have developed multidisciplinary committees to examine digital health innovations (including using XR) for ethical compliance before authorising them for use in clinical settings.[48] Internationally, the absence of clear clinical and ethical guidelines for XR means that a lot of practitioners are guided by general medical ethics and individual judgement.[49] Initiatives are being made to have more tailored guidance – for example, the XR Safety Initiative and academic groups have produced some white papers about ethics in XR,[50] and the non-profit organisation IEEE have discussed ethics frameworks for XR and AI together.[51] These often have an emphasis on transparency, user safety and human oversight as central tenets. From a legal-ethical synergy perspective, one positive development is that when regulating the use of XR, regulators are, on occasion, at least referring to ethical considerations: the MHRA's guidance on digital mental health tools emphasised the importance of public trust, and provided guidelines to make certain that digital technologies are "safe and trustworthy" for patients.[52] This reflects an appreciation that regulation is not an administrative hurdle, but a way to ensure that ethical standards are in place in practise.

45 WHO (n 18) 29–30.

46 Goulet and others (n 38).

47 ibid.

48 Alan Cossitt, 'Why Health Care Organizations Need Technology Ethics Committees' (*Hastings Center Bioethics Forum*, 5 February 2020) <https://www.thehastingscenter.org/why-health-care-organizations-need-technology-ethics-committees/> accessed 11 December 2025.

49 Goulet and others (n 38).

50 Balaji Swaminathan, 'Beyond the Virtual Horizon: Safe Navigation of Extended Realities' (2024) 6 ISACA Journal 38–46.

51 Joaquim Jorge and Wolfgang Hürst, 'Extended Reality and Artificial Intelligence's Ethical Crossroads: From Sensory Manipulation to Creative Disruption' (2024) 57(9) Computer 14–20.

52 Esme Pearce, 'New Rules for Digital Mental Health Tech Companies' (*gosuperscript.com*, 11 March 2025) <https://gosuperscript.com/news-and-resources/new-rules-for-digital-mental-health-apps/> accessed 10 December 2025. Regarding the MHRA's guidance, see MHRA (n 8).

In summary, XR technologies provide transformative opportunities in clinical care – surgeons are able to operate with improved vision, patients are able to receive therapy in immersive worlds and medical trainees are able to gain experience risk-free. However, these benefits are accompanied by a number of ethical and legal responsibilities. Practitioners must take into account at all times the welfare of the patient, which must never be compromised for the sake of novelty. As the XR revolution in the field of healthcare continues to pick up pace, continued dialogue between technologists, clinicians, ethicists and legal experts will be required. Through anticipatory vision of issues that concern safety, consent, privacy, equity and accountability, XR can be integrated into medicine in ways that are compatible with the very high ethical ideals of healing professions.

IV. Conclusion

Generative AI and XR are on the cutting edge of technological innovation for clinical care. This chapter has examined how every technology is being used – from AI chatbots writing diagnoses to AR glasses that assist surgeons – to rip apart the various legal frameworks and ethical issues that are being faced as a result of these advancements in the world. A theme that lies integral to each is that law and ethics have to keep up with technology. Generative AI in healthcare is making us think differently about liability and regulatory schemas, and we're struggling with the implications of algorithmic opacity, bias and sanctity of patient data. XR has a potentially healing but also potentially harmful avenue of immersion that requires us to continue regular tenets of consent, safety and equity in unfamiliar lands of the virtual world. Across different jurisdictions, regulators are starting to respond (with the EU AI Act and approvals from different authorities in the United States and United Kingdom, etc.). However, there are still gaps and uncertainties left. It is down to the international community of health law and ethics to fill these gaps with clear guidelines, effective oversight and a commitment to things such as patient-centred care. Crucially, how these frontier technologies are embraced should not see a sacrifice of fundamental rights and incursion on the clinician-patient relationship. Rather, if mindful of ethical frameworks and the responsible governance of the law, generative AI and XR can be used to augment human expertise and compassion. They can automate the mundane, bring an image to the invisible and expand healing beyond traditional boundaries – all while the accountability, empathy and judgement that is unique to the human clinicians remains at the heart of medicine. In the process of moving forward, stakeholders must always ask the question: are these tools in the patient's best interest, are we ready to manage the risks they present? By rigorously analysing and responding to the legal and ethical dimensions to the extent that we have begun to do so here, we can answer in the affirmative and ensure that these frontier applications deliver their promise in improving clinical care globally.

10 Future Directions and Closing Synthesis

Abstract

This chapter synthesises the legal, regulatory and ethical issues covered throughout the book and outlines the future directions in the governance of AI in healthcare. It argues that regulatory systems need to adapt towards oversight systems that are adaptive, iterative and able to track the rapidly developing technology like adaptive algorithms and generative AI: static systems on authoring pre-market approvals are increasingly inadequate. Strengthening the autonomy of clinicians and human control becomes an underlying nexus to ensure that AI does not substitute but augments the professional judgement and maintains trust of the patient. The chapter also argues that innovating and ensuring patient safety are not in tension but rather mutually reinforcing objectives – after proper governance of AI development, structured incentives should be put in place to incentivise the generation of explicit evidence, robust post-market monitoring and systematic efforts to tackle bias in order to ensure clinical fairness. Education and institutional culture change are recognised as key with clinicians needing AI literacy and healthcare organisations needing governance structures able to deal with the ongoing monitoring and ethical deployment of AI. Finally, the chapter outlines a research agenda for the future which focuses on clinical validation, explainability, liability reform and interdisciplinary policy design. It concludes that the adoption of responsible AI necessitates the embedding of these technologies into well-built accountability structures and ethical professional practices which can facilitate the use of AI to improve, instead of destabilising, the provision of safe and equitable healthcare.

I. Regulatory Evolution and Global Alignment

Over the preceding chapters, a pattern became clear: although the promises of AI regarding transformative improvements in healthcare are great, existing legal frameworks are being stretched to the limit. No single approach to regulation has a monopoly either on safety or innovation. The European Union has a precautionary regime that does less harm but could take time to promote beneficial tools, while the United States has a flexible one which has a quick pace of innovation but pays the price in supervision. The experiments of the United Kingdom are in-between. Moving forward, regulators will need to be dynamic and may need to learn from

DOI: 10.4324/9781003785385-13

each other's strengths. Regulatory adequacy in the age of AI will require continuous updates of regulations with respect to rules and guidance as technologies evolve. Not significantly, even the US FDA admits its traditional device regulations were not designed for adaptive machine learning systems.[1] Agencies are now working on creating new frameworks – for example, FDA's PCCPs to manage learning algorithms – to ensure that progressively advanced AI tools are used under the veil of constant monitoring and safety.[2] The EU AI Act has done the same with high-risk AI, requiring lifecycle risk management, which represents a consensus that static once-off approvals are no longer adequate.[3] In a nutshell, future regulation needs to be iterative: authorities need to use adaptive regulation (e.g. conditional approvals coupled with mandatory updates, "sandbox" environments for real-world testing), for beneficial AI to reach the patients without circumvention of safety checks.

International harmonisation is another priority of the future. Divergent rules at national level are likely to open up loopholes or create uncertainty, particularly in the age of AI products travelling beyond borders. Already, forums of convergence are growing. Scholars and global bodies have asked for the WHO and others to help bring about common standards.[4] The 2021 report about AI by the WHO called for AI for health to be guided by shared principles (human dignity, equity, transparency, accountability) and observed the worrying "lack of harmonisation" between countries.[5] Regulatory authorities are finding it difficult to keep up with the fast-evolving tools such as generative AI that are capable of producing unexpected outcomes.[6] Accordingly, the WHO calls for adaptive and multi-stakeholder governance and even hints at the inclusion of AI norms in the international health regulations.[7] A possible future direction may be a series of baseline global requirements – similar to the way GDPR established global standards for data – for safe and ethical AI in healthcare.[8] In the meantime, coordination in the form of voluntary guidelines and mutual recognition of approvals can help overcome some gaps. Regulators should have an ongoing conversation among them and share best practices with one another so that the best safeguards in one jurisdiction can inform others. Ultimately, regulatory evolution will be relatively ongoing: law will have to continue learning and iterating alongside the AI systems that it regulates.

1 FDA, 'Artificial Intelligence in Software as a Medical Device' (*fda.gov*, 23 March 2025) <https://www.fda.gov/medical-devices/software-medical-device-samd/artificial-intelligence-software-medical-device> accessed 12 December 2025.

2 ibid.

3 Article 9 of the EU AI Act.

4 Rabaï Bouderhem, 'Shaping the Future of AI in Healthcare through Ethics and Governance' (2024) 11 Humanities and Social Sciences Communications 416.

5 WHO, 'Ethics and Governance of Artificial Intelligence for Health: WHO Guidance' (*WHO*, 2021) 23–30 and 109 <https://iris.who.int/server/api/core/bitstreams/f780d926-4ae3-42ce-a6d6-e898a5562621/content> accessed 10 December 2025.

6 Bouderhem (n 4).

7 ibid.

8 ibid.

II. Clinician Autonomy and Ethical Oversight

A recurring theme is the need for the importance of clinician autonomy and professional judgement to be at centre stage even as AI becomes more powerful. Clinical AI should only be a tool for decision-making, not a replacement for it. Previous chapters illustrated that problems such as black box algorithms and automation bias could potentially overtake physicians' roles if left uncontrolled. To overcome this, future governance should aim to further entrench the principle of human oversight. A lot of regulations already require a "human in the loop" for high-risk AI. This trend will continue – and probably strengthen – to ensure that the responsibility for care decisions rests with the doctors. Human oversight is not only a legal requirement but also an ethical obligation: it maintains the accountability of the physician, as well as the patient's trust, in an AI-assisted healthcare system. The EU AI Act, for example, contains an explicit provision that people using medical AI should be given proper information as well as that AI machines should be designed to allow control and intervention by humans.[9] Likewise, US policy and professional guidelines (e.g. from the AMA) stress that clinicians should understand the output of an AI, and not blindly defer to it.[10] Going forward, we can expect more explicit duties placed on healthcare providers to use their independent judgement when using AI – analogous to the "learned intermediary" doctrine in drug prescribing. In fact, as discussed above, a recommendation by an AI will not shield a clinician from liability if it was not reasonable to rely on it. Future case law and policies will probably clarify this point, emphasising that the standard of care will change as technologies change: physicians should use AI as appropriate but should also know its limitations. To make this easier, there is a need for regulators and institutions to invest in transparency and explainability tools. Requiring that AI systems come with interpretable explanations or at least detailedinformational documentation will help clinicians to understand how a result was reached. Indeed, transparency obligations (technical documentation, disclosure of an AI's intended use and performance) are already being inserted into the law. In the future, it may often become the norm to see routine practices such as AI fact sheets or model "nutrition labels" made available to clinical users, describing an algorithm's training data, accuracy and caveats that we know about. Such measures are what allow clinicians to incorporate AI safely into their workflow without giving up their autonomy or the underlying fiduciary duty to patients.

9 Article 14 of the EU AI Act.

10 Kate Feske-Kirby, Kaveh Shojania and Patricia McGaffigan, *Artificial Intelligence in Health Care: Implications for Patient and Workforce Safety* (*Institute for Healthcare Improvement*, 2024) 14 <https://www.ihi.org/sites/default/files/2024-05/Artificial-Intelligence-in-Health-Care-Implications-for-Safety.pdf> accessed 12 December 2025. See also John T. Carlo, *Explainability of Artificial/Augmented Intelligence and Machine Learning Algorithms* (*AMA*, 2025) <https://councilreports.ama-assn.org/councilreports/downloadreport?uri=/councilreports/CSAPH_8_A_25_AI_Explainability_Finalized_1812.pdf> accessed 12 December 2025.

Preserving patient autonomy is also very important. Informed consent processes will need to be updated to ensure that patients are made aware that AI is part of their care and know what AI is being used for in their care. Chapter 6 contended that the classic doctrine of consent is required to be expanded: patients should be informed not only about treatment options, but if and how an algorithm contributed to the development of treatment options. This forward-looking idea is likely to be adopted in policy. For example, some jurisdictions are looking at leveraging patient-facing disclosures as measures for substantial AI use for diagnosis or treatment.[11] At the very least, transparency to patients is in line with the ethical imperative of respect and truth-telling. In practice, what can be expected is that clinicians will include in their consent discussions something along these lines: "We have an AI tool that helps review your scans, it has recommended X, and here is what that means". And such openness may in fact lead to building trust, as patients will appreciate the fact that there are safeguards in place (including human review). In sum, the future of AI in healthcare is human-centred: there are regulations and professional norms which should continue to put the responsibility on final decisions in the hands of qualified clinicians and ensure they use the technology as an actor who serves to support – but not replace – the clinical encounter.

III. Fostering Innovation While Ensuring Safety

The major challenge in the future is how to promote good innovation for AI without sacrificing safety or inequity. The lessons learned in Chapters 2–9 advise for a balanced way. On the one hand, extremely rigid controls may hamper beneficial developments – for example, life-saving diagnostic algorithms held back by red tape. On the other hand, permissive approaches that allow unproven tools onto the market introduce patients to harm and pose barriers of trust for AI. Achieving this balance requires what we can and should call "responsible innovation" policies. Regulators are even now looking at ways to be able to fast track promising AI systems, while still maintaining important enforcement of safeguards. For instance, the US FDA's approval of more AI devices has been accompanied by an increasing degree of scrutiny for evidence: there is awareness that many of the approved tools had limited validation.[12] For high-risk AI, future policy will more likely increase the evidentiary bar. Commentators hold that AI algorithms should undergo clinical trial-like testing, similar to drugs, to really prove better patient outcomes from

11 For instance, see California Assembly Bill 3030 (Cal. Health & Safety Code § 1339.75, eff. Jan. 1, 2025) and Utah's 2023 law (Utah Code §13-72-103).

12 Ram Sivakumar, Brian Lue and Shinjini Kundu, 'FDA Approval of Artificial Intelligence and Machine Learning Devices in Radiology: A Systematic Review' (2025) 8(11) JAMA Network Open e2542338 (highlighting the rapid increase to 950+ AI devices by 2024 and significant gaps in premarket testing); Shadi Ebrahimian and others, 'FDA-Regulated AI Algorithms: Trends, Strengths, and Gaps of Validation Studies' (2022) 29(4) Academic Radiology 559 (finding that only 16% of evaluated FDA-cleared imaging AI devices reported multi-centre validation).

different groups.[13] It is expected to see more requirements for prospective trials or real-world performance studies, both prior to and after deployment. Post-market surveillance will also be a greater focus: there will be requirements from authorities to continuously monitor the error rates of AI, report on adverse incidents and periodically re-certify learning models. In the European Union, the continuing compliance burdens of the AI Act and revised Product Liability rules (shifting burden of proof for defects) are the forerunners of this more stringent safety culture.[14] In the United States, activities such as the Section 1557 non-discrimination rule will force bias audits of clinical algorithms in use, linking safety and efficacy with fairness results as well.[15] These moves are symbolic of a greater principle for the future that any innovation in AI needs to go hand-in-hand with accountability.

On the innovation front, the regulators can construct enabling pathways to ensure safety. For example, through adaptive trial design and conditional approvals, AI tools could have access to the marketplace earlier with strict guardrails (limited use settings, needing data collection, etc.). Regulatory sandboxes – time-limited, directly monitored piloting environments – are another avenue being popularly piloted in jurisdictions to allow innovators to experiment in an oversight environment. These approaches need further research and refinement. The desire is a "best of both worlds" scenario, where patients can benefit sooner from the advances in AI, and anything that might go wrong is caught and dealt with in a controlled way. One tangible approach is the creation of an AI registry in which new AI algorithms are deployed in healthcare and different individual performance measures thereof are registered together with updates.[16] This would facilitate transparency, enable regulators and researchers to identify trends and help identify systemic problems and quick spread of safety notices or improvements. Another proposal is no-fault compensation funds for injuries that AI caused in healthcare.[17] Such schemes (potentially funded by industry) could speed up bringing relief to patients while the liability law catches up, and so keep public confidence in innovation.

13 Ryan Han and others, 'Randomised Controlled Trials Evaluating Artificial Intelligence in Clinical Practice: A Scoping Review' (2024) 6(5) The Lancet Digital Health e367–e373 (documenting the need for more clinical trial evidence for AI tools and that 92% of AI randomised controlled trials, or RCTs, to date were single-country, often lacking population diversity).

14 Article 8 of the EU AI Act; Article 10 of the revised Product Liability Directive (Directive (EU) 2024/2853 of the European Parliament and of the Council of 23 October 2024 on liability for defective products and repealing Council Directive 85/374/EEC).

15 Office for Civil Rights, HHS, 'Nondiscrimination in Health Programs & Activities – Proposed Rule' 87 Fed. Reg. 47824, 47897. See also William G. La Cava, I. Glenn Cohen and Jaya Aysola, 'The Future of Algorithmic Nondiscrimination Compliance in the Affordable Care Act' (2025) npj Digital Medicine.

16 Michael J. Pencina, Jonathan McCall and Nicoleta J. Economou-Zavlanos, 'A Federated Registration System for Artificial Intelligence in Health' (2024) 332(10) JAMA 789–790.

17 Søren Holm, Catherine Stanton and Benjamin Bartlett, 'A New Argument for No-Fault Compensation in Health Care: The Introduction of Artificial Intelligence Systems' (2021) 29(3) Health Care Analysis 171–188.

A critical element in balancing innovation with safety is dealing with algorithmic bias and health equity, which are detailed in Chapter 7. If innovations in AI only favour certain groups, at the expense of others, then "innovation" is illusory. Future research should be done on ways to develop algorithms that generalise fairly across populations – which means things like ways to debias training data and better test on minority subgroups. These expectations are likely to be institutionalised by regulators. It is expected that necessary fairness certifications or assessments of bias impact have to be made before AI tools can be put in use on a wide scale. And, ensuring safety, therefore, also means ensuring the AI does not safely work only for a privileged few. This ties back to innovation – a system that is not safe or equitable to broader sections of society is not a true clinical advance. Innovation and safety may be two of the mandates and not conflicting aspects for AI governance. By creating a regulatory regime that is innovation-friendly but safety-obsessed – a system that benefits people through transparency and punishes for negligence, as well as one that collects data on outcomes constantly – we can harness the power of AI while avoiding begging backlash or harm.

IV. Education, Training and Culture Change

Adapting to AI in healthcare is not just something for lawmakers and engineers to do, but something that needs to be done by the people who work on the frontlines of healthcare: clinicians, patients and institutional leaders. A forward-looking strategy therefore has to make an investment in education and training to enable a network of workforce people who are AI-aware and resilient. Prior chapters highlighted the fact that many clinicians are still wary of AI or unfamiliar with how it works (e.g. surveys highlight that a majority of doctors still see more challenges than benefits in current AI tools[18]). It is important to bridge this gap. Medical schools and continuing professional development applications should include fundamental concepts of data science, capabilities and limitations of AI. In the near future, it will become routine that clinicians will be trained in how to interpret the outputs of AI systems, how to incorporate these results into diagnostic reasoning and how to converse with patients about AI systems. Importantly, training should also focus on what failure modes to watch for – e.g. recognising when an AI might be out of its depth, bias, etc. Professional bodies have started to issue some guidance on these issues, and the movement will increase. For example, the Topol Review in the United Kingdom placed great emphasis on realising the successful uptake of AI depends on developing a digitally literate healthcare workforce and resources for clinicians to upskill in emerging technologies.[19] More such initiatives around

18 AMA, 'Physician Sentiments around the Use of AI in Health Care: Motivations, Opportunities, Risks, and Use Cases' (*AMA*, February 2025) <https://www.ama-assn.org/system/files/physician-ai-sentiment-report.pdf> accessed 12 December 2025.

19 Cora Lydon, 'HEE Reviews Progress of Topol Review Recommendations' (*digitalhealth.net*, 28 February 2023) <https://www.digitalhealth.net/2023/02/hee-reviews-progress-of-topol-review-recommendations/> accessed 12 December 2025.

the world can be expected. Hospitals might consider mandatory AI competency modules or simulation exercises where doctors get to practise using AI tools in an entirely safe environment. The ethos should be that mastering AI is part of the professional competence in 21st-century medicine, just as evidence-based medicine and informatics became integral in decades past.

Technical knowledge aside, fostering the right culture is of prime importance. Healthcare institutions will have to develop an environment in which ethical considerations and critical appraisal of AI become second nature. This means enabling multidisciplinary oversight: ethicists, IT specialists and personnel working there on the frontlines should all have a voice when it comes to deciding or deploying an AI system. A culture of safety promotes reports of AI errors or near misses without criticism, so that the organisation can learn and improve (more like the model of reporting patient safety incidents already in place). It also means leadership setting the tone that compliance and ethics are as important as efficiency. For example, if an AI model demonstrates signs of bias or begins to show indicators of decline in job performance, a culture of patient welfare will hit the "pause" button and fix the problem rather than driving towards achieving their business goals. Clinician autonomy, as discussed, is part of this culture: doctors and nurses should not simply feel that they are permitted to question or to override the AI recommendations if they conflict with their clinical judgement or with patient values; they should be required to do so. In the longer term, one of the ways to foster trust in AI – both between clinicians and patients – will be by demonstrating that institutions see the use of AI as something to be controlled and audited, not a flawless oracle.

In order to foster this cultural change, education of the patient and the public must not be ignored. Health systems and regulators might consider creating some public-facing materials to explain AI in layman's language, address people's fears and spotlight any oversight measures in place. An informed patient population is able to participate in shared decision-making that incorporates information on AI. This is going to become more relevant when health AI consumer-facing items (such as symptom checker chats or wearables) become common. If patients know that, for example, an algorithm is assisting with their care and that they have rights to information and recourse, then their level of trust in the system's overall responsibility increases.

V. Research Agenda and Conclusion

As this synthesis is being concluded, it's clear that there are some knowledge gaps left to be considered, which provide a good agenda for further research and policy development. Clinical validation research is a high priority: the medical community needs more prospective studies testing AI tools in a variety of real-world clinical settings. Only through such evidence will it be possible to develop better thresholds of regulations that will determine which AI applications actually lead to better outcomes. Likewise, more research should be done on making AI systems more explainable while not compromising performance – a technical and human-factors challenge that sits at the nexus of computer science, ethics and cognitive psychology. On the legal side, more research needs to be done into how to adapt the traditional doctrines (such as malpractice, product liability or informed consent) to AI, or if entirely new legal constructs (e.g. an "AI fiduciary" duty of manufacturers or updated licensing requirements for AI-integrated clinical practice) are warranted. Policymakers will benefit from interdisciplinary research to pilot novel mechanisms for governance (such as auditing methodologies, strategies for bias mitigation or evaluation of accountability) and gain insight into their effectiveness in healthcare contexts.

In closing, the incorporation of AI in healthcare is a journey – one that needs to be vigilant, adaptive and steadily looking at core medical ethics. The chapters in this book have covered the landscape from regulatory frameworks and ethics principles to data governance, patient rights, bias, liability and frontier technologies. The important lessons can be summed up quite simply: put patients first, and use technology in service of that end. If we strengthen the normative bases – safety, efficacy, equity, autonomy, accountability – by means of smart regulation and deliberate use, then AI will be a very important ally in the process of healing. This final chapter has set out some ideas about how we could do it: through regulatory evolution, accomplished by balancing innovation and protection, through empowering clinicians and patients and through organisational governance that puts some teeth in the use of ethical AI. The way forward requires collaboration to be achieved between regulators, healthcare institutions, technology developers and society at large. By resolving the challenges and defending the idea of responsible AI, it is expected that AI technologies can be applied in healthcare in a better and equitable way for all individuals.

Index

Note: Page numbers in **bold** reference tables.

21st Century Cures Act (2016) (US) 21, 30
accountability 5, 48–51, 74; developer accountability 111; generative AI 137; for outcomes 109; reforms 128–130
accountability gaps 49, 108–110
adaptive learning systems, oversight of 122–125
adaptivity of regulation 33–36
affirmative fairness measures 57
Affordable Care Act (US) 54, 105
age-based inequalities 101
AI Act (EU) 8–9, 13, 16, 21, 23, 30, 33–34, 36–37, 46, 120; accountability 48; automation biases 53; autonomy of clinicians 148–149; bias mitigation 103–104; Code of Practice 124; continuous learning AI systems 123; data governance 64–67; fairness 54; generative AI 135; human oversight 51–53; privacy 67; regulatory evolution 146–147; transparency 47
AI algorithms 4
AI Ethics Initiative, United Kingdom 107
AI fairness 110; *see also* fairness
AI governance 57; *see also* ethics
AI liability 114–115; *see also* liability for AI-driven harm
AI Liability Directive, European Union 18–19, 40, 49, 104
AI oversight committees 49
AI-aware practice 128
algorithm drift 120–121
algorithmic explainability requirements 47
algorithmic impact analysis 54
algorithms 12; decision support algorithms 20; learning versus fixed algorithms 13–14
AMA *see* American Medical Association
ambiguous liability 135
American Medical Association (AMA) 23, 125
anonymisation 63
application programming interface (API) 134
AR *see* augmented reality
Artificial Intelligence and Machine Learning Software as a Medical Device Action Plan, United States 17
auditing 102–103, 110; high-risk AI algorithms 129
augmented reality (AR) 139–140, 143
automation biases 53
autonomous actions 85
autonomous authorization 87
autonomous persons 84–85
autonomy: of clinicians 148–149; extended reality (XR) 142; informed consent 83–86, 96; model 80, 82–83; of patients 149; of surgical robots 27–28

beneficence model 80, 82
bias audits 102, 110
bias mitigation: European Union 103–104; United Kingdom 106–108; United States 104–106
biases 4–5, 21, 55, 64–65; automation biases 53; clinical AI 99–100; generative AI 136; United States 55–56
black boxes 5, 12, 15, 39, 108, 118, 136
Black patients: biases 100; subgroup disparities 100–101

CAG *see* confidentiality advisory group
California Department of Social Services (CDSS) 30, 38, 91–92; informed consent 96–97; new moral requirement 92–94
Care Quality Commission, United Kingdom 106

CDS *see* clinical decision support
CDSS *see* California Department of Social Services
ChatGPT 125
civil rights enforcement, United States 104–106
classification of AI systems 30–33
clinical AI 98–99, 112–113, 148–149; accountability gaps 108–110; biases 99–100; fairness 102–103; subgroup disparities 100–101; towards fair and accountable AI 110–111
clinical care: data governance 62–65; extended reality (XR) 138–145; generative AI 134–138
clinical decision support (CDS) 11, 19–21; comparative regulatory approaches 21–23; governance and guidelines 23–24; institutional responsibilities 125–128
clinical model, informed consent 89n45, 90–91
clinical validation research 152–153
clinician autonomy 148–149
Clinician's Checklist 76–77
clinicians, liability for AI-driven harm 117–118
Code of Practice 124
Common Rule (US) 73–74
compensation 6, 128–129
compliance 39; European Union 150
confidentiality: extended reality (XR) 142–143; generative AI 136
confidentiality advisory group (CAG) 68
conformity assessment 48, 103
consent 73–74; *see also* informed consent
Consumer Protection Act 1987, United Kingdom 26, 40–41, 115–116, 128
continuous learning AI systems, oversight of 122–125
culture change 151–152

da Vinci Surgical System 24–25
data governance 54, 62–65, 73–74; biases 64; in clinical care 62–65; European Union 65–67; Privacy Impact Matrix 75–77; United Kingdom 67–70; United States 70–73
data minimisation 74
data protection law, extended reality (XR) 140–141
data protection legislation 4
De Novo classification 17, 31–32
decision support algorithms 20
deep learning 12, 14
defects, proving 118
de-identification 63
Department of Health and Human Services (HHS) (US) 71, 105–106
design bias 99
developer accountability 111
diagnostics 14; liability 17–19; real-world adoption and evidence 14–15; regulatory classification 15–17; standards of care 17–19
digital pathology slides 14
digital therapeutics 139
disclosure 46, 91; new moral requirement 92–93
disparities in AI performance 100–101
distributed responsibility 118
documentation requirements 46
duty of care 5, 129
duty of warning for risks 116
duty to not use 117

electronic personhood 26
embodied AI 25
emerging doctrine and proposals 118–119
Enlightenment **81**
enterprise liability 118–119
Epic Sepsis Model 32
Equality Act 2010, United Kingdom 107
equity, extended reality (XR) 143
Equity and Human Rights Commission (EHRC) 106
ethical governance, generative AI 137
ethics 6–7, 45–46, 57–58; accountability 48–51; extended reality (XR) 141–145; fairness 53–57; generative AI 136–138; human oversight 51–53; transparency 46–48
European Union: accountability 48; AI Act *see* AI Act; AI Liability Directive 18–19, 40, 49, 104; bias mitigation 103–104; burden of proof 111; classification of AI systems 31; clinical decision support 21–23; compliance 150; continuous learning AI systems 123; diagnostics 15–16; embodied AI 25; General Data Protection Regulation (GDPR) 4, 21, 62–63, 65–67, 74; governance of clinical decision support 23; institutional responsibilities 127; liability for AI-driven harm 39–40, 108, 115–117; Medical Devices Regulation (MDR) 15–16, 22, 30–31, 33, 103–105,

119; Product Liability Directive 18, 26, 39, 50, 115; proving defects and causation 117–118; regulatory evolution 146–147; Revised Product Liability Directive 115; software 140; transparency requirements 36–37
Evidence Standards Framework, United Kingdom 23
explainable AI 12
extended reality (XR) 138–139, 145; ethical challenges 141–145; legal and regulatory considerations 139–141

fail-safes 127
fairness 53–57, 106, 109–111; clinical AI 102–103
false alarms 7
FDA *see* Food and Drug Administration
FDA PMA approval 41
Federal Food, Drug, and Cosmetic Act (US) 41
Federal Trade Commission (FTC) 72, 75
financial barriers to care 90
fixed algorithms, versus learning 13–14
Food and Drug Administration (FDA) (US) 6, 9, 72–73; 21st Century Cures Act (2016) 21–22, 30; adaptivity of regulation 34–35; *Artificial Intelligence and Machine Learning Software as a Medical Device Action Plan* 17; bias mitigation 105–106; classification of AI systems 31–32; diagnostics 17; human oversight 53; liability for AI-driven harm 41–42; medical software 13; Predetermined Change Control Plan (PCCPs) 13, 123; surgical robots 26–27; transparency 46–47
forward-looking strategy 151
FTC *see* Federal Trade Commission

General Data Protection Regulation (GDPR) (EU) 4, 21, 62–63, 74; anonymisation 63; data governance 65–67; privacy 66–67; re-identification risk 63
General Medical Council, United States 126
generalisability 15
generative AI 13, 134, 145; in clinical care 134–138; ethical challenges 136–138; legal and regulatory considerations 134–136; United States 135
ghost surgery 95
global alignment 146–147
Good Machine Learning Practice (GMLP) 69, 72
Good Medical Practice, United Kingdom 126
guidelines for clinical decision support 23–24

hallucinations 136
Health Insurance Portability and Accountability Act (HIPPA) 4, 62–63, 70–74; Privacy Rule 136
health literacy of vulnerable people 89–90
high-risk AI algorithms 149–150
HIPPA *see* Health Insurance Portability and Accountability Act
hospital accreditation standards 129
hospitals, responsibilities 126–127
"human in the loop" 27–28
human oversight 51–52, 124; institutional responsibilities 128

ICO *see* Information Commissioner's Office
inclusive design 112
inclusiveness, extended reality (XR) 143
independent algorithmic auditing 102
information duties 46
informational safety update reports 33
informed consent 78–80, 96–97; for AI-driven healthcare 88–96; autonomy 83–86, 96; extended reality (XR) 142; historical review of 80–82; nature 86–88; theoretical review of 83–88
injury compensation 128
innovation, fostering while ensuring safety 149–151
institutional responsibilities 125–128
insurance 130
international harmonisation 147
interpretability 47
intersectional biases 101

justice 5; extended reality (XR) 144
justifications, informed consent 93–96

knowledgeable consent *see* informed consent

label biases 99
large language models, safety of 124
laws, as guardrails 6–7
learned intermediaries 116, 125

learning versus fixed algorithms 13–14
liability for AI-driven harm 39, 49, 114–115; diagnostics 17–19; emerging doctrine and proposals 118–119; European Union 39–40; extended reality (XR) 143; medical malpractice 117–118; product liability 115–117; proving defects and causation 117–118; United Kingdom 40–41, 50; United States 41–43, 116; *see also* medical negligence
Lindbergh Operation 24

machine learning 12, 89
malpractice suits, surgical robots 25
mammography 14
MDR *see* Medical Devices Regulation
Medical Devices (Post-Market Surveillance Requirements) (Amendment) (Great Britain) Regulations 2024, United Kingdom 16
Medical Devices Regulation (MDR) (EU) 15–16, 30, 33; bias mitigation 103–104; classification of AI systems 31
medical imaging 14–15
medical malpractice 117–118
medical negligence 115–117; United Kingdom 40–41
medical software 13
Medicines and Healthcare products Regulatory Agency (MHRA) (UK) 22–23, 30, 36–37, 69–70, 106–107, 124, 135, 140, 144
Medicines and Medical Devices Act, United Kingdom 124
MHRA *see* Medicines and Healthcare products Regulatory Agency
Middle Ages **81**
misdiagnosed patients 5; accountability gaps 108–110
model documentation frameworks 102
model of communication between Ancient Greece and 19th Century **81**
model of liability 49; *see also* liability for AI-driven harm
Modern British and American medicine **81**

National Health Service (NHS) (UK): Code of Conduct for AI 16, 37, 52, 107; confidentiality 68–69; data governance 23, 47, 54, 62; fit for purpose 102; triage 19
National Institute for Health and Care Excellence (NICE), United Kingdom 23
natural language processing 12–13
nature, informed consent 86–88
new moral requirement, informed consent 92–93
NHS *see* National Health Service
NHS Act, United Kingdom 68
NHS AI Lab 107
NICE *see* National Institute for Health and Care Excellence
no-fault compensation funds 150
no-fault solutions 129
non-autonomous persons 85
non-discrimination, United States 150
non-malcficcncc 141
nutrition labels 148

Office of Civil Rights (OCR) (US) 71–72
OpenAI 125
oversight 8, 122–125

paternalism 80
pathology 14
patient autonomy 149
patient safety, extended reality (XR) 141
PCCPs *see* Predetermined Change Control Plan
performance monitoring of AI systems 119–122
periodic safety update reports (PSURs) 36
personal health information (PHI) 62–63, 74
PHI *see* personal health information
PMS *see* post-market surveillance
PMSRs *see* post-market surveillance reports
post-market oversight 33–36
post-market regulatory oversight mechanism 129
post-market surveillance (PMS) 35–36, 121
post-market surveillance reports (PMSRs) 36
Predetermined Change Control Plan (PCCPs) 13, 34–35, 123
pre-emption 42
premarket requirements for AI systems 30
privacy 73–74; extended reality (XR) 142–143; General Data Protection Regulation (GDPR) (EU) 66–67; generative AI 136; Health Insurance Portability and Accountability Act (HIPPA) 70–71; Privacy Impact Matrix 75–77

Privacy Impact Matrix 75–77
Privacy Rule, Health Insurance Portability and Accountability Act (HIPPA) 136
product liability 115–117; United States 41–43, 128
Product Liability Directive, European Union 18, 26, 39, 50, 115
professional integrity, extended reality (XR) 143
professional standards 125
Project Glass Box 37
promise of AI in healthcare 4–6
proving defects and causation 117–118
PSURs *see* periodic safety update reports

radiology 14–15, 17
reasonable patient standard 94–95
reasonable physician standards 93–94, 96; United States 87–88
regulation: classification of AI systems 30–33; evolution of 146–147; of generative AI 134–136; post-market oversight 33–36; of surgical robots 25–27; transparency requirements 36–39
regulatory classification, diagnostics 15–17
regulatory sandboxes 150
re-identification risk 63–64
relevant information, informed consent 90
research model, informed consent 89n45
Revised Product Liability Directive 115
Riegel vs. Medtronic 41
right to explanation 109
risk classification 48
robots *see also* surgical robots

safety: of AI systems 119–122; of generative AI 136; of surgical robots 25; while fostering innovation 149–151
Salgo v. Leland Stanford Jr., University Board of Trustees 82
Schloendorff v. The Society of New York Hospital 80–81
self-regulation 125
self-updating AI 13
sepsis detection, Epic Sepsis Model 32
shared fault 117
Software and AI as a Medical Device Change Programme (UK) 69
standards and certification of fairness 110–111
standards of care, diagnostics 17–19
strict liability 118
subgroup disparities in AI performance 100–101
surgical robots 24–25; autonomy 27–28; regulation of 25–27; safety of 25

target bias 99
Taylor v. Intuitive Surgical, Inc. 19, 25–26, 42
TPO *see* treatment, payment, or healthcare operations
training 151–152
training data 8, 17, 21, 54, 64, 69, 92, 99, 112, 136, 151
transparency 46–48; algorithmic explainability requirements 47
transparency requirements: for regulation 36–39; United Kingdom 37; United States 38
treatment, payment, or healthcare operations (TPO) 63
treatment failure, risk of 94
triage 8, 19–20, 127
trust 7; generative AI 137
trustworthy AI 8–9, 56

UK GDPR 67–70
under-diagnosis 4
underrepresentation in training data 4
United Kingdom: bias mitigation 106–108; clinical decision support 22–23; Consumer Protection Act 1987 26, 40–41, 115–116, 128; data governance 67–70, 75; diagnostics 16–17; Equality Act 2010 108; Evidence Standards Framework 23; fairness 55; General Medical Council 126; human oversight 53; Information Commissioner's Office (ICO) 68; liability for AI-driven harm 40–41, 50, 115–116; *Medical Devices (Post-Market Surveillance Requirements) (Amendment) (Great Britain) Regulations 2024* 16; Medical Devices Regulations 16–17; medical negligence 40–41; Medicines and Healthcare products Regulatory Agency (MHRA) 22–23, 30, 36–37, 69–70, 106–107, 124, 135, 140, 144; Medicines and Medical Devices Act 124; NHS Act 68; oversight 9; post-market regulation 35–36; post-market surveillance 120; proving defects and causation 117–118; regulatory evolution 147; safety of AI systems 124; transparency 37, 47; triage 19–20
United States: 21st Century Cures Act (2016) 21, 30; accountability 49;

adaptivity of regulation 34–35; Affordable Care Act 54, 105; bias mitigation 104–106; biases 55–56; civil rights enforcement 104–106; classification of AI systems 31–32; clinical decision support 21–23; Common Rule 73–74; data governance 70–73; Department of Health and Human Services (HHS) 71, 105–106; diagnostics 17; extended reality (XR) 140; fairness 55; Federal Food, Drug and Cosmetic Act 41; Food and Drug Administration *see* Food and Drug Administration; generative AI 135; Health Insurance Portability and Accountability Act (HIPPA) 4, 62–63, 70–74; human oversight 53; informed consent 87–88; institutional responsibilities 125–128; liability for AI-driven harm 41–42; non-discrimination 150; Office of Civil Rights (OCR) 71–72; product liability 116–117, 128; reasonable physician standard 87–88; safety of AI systems 122; surgical robots 26–27; *Taylor v. Intuitive Surgical, Inc.* 19, 25–26, 42; transparency 38, 46–47; Watson for Oncology 20

virtual reality (VR) 138–143
VR pain therapy device 139

Watson for Oncology 20

XR *see* extended reality
XR Safety Initiative 144

Made in the USA
Monee, IL
12 November 2026

debe3a77-8ee6-4b75-93f2-f59e8308f44aR01